THE BIG ONE!

HOW TO ANTICIPATE AND SURVIVE THE COMING ECONOMIC MEGA-CRASH

DR. RAY YOUNG

Quantum Discovery
A LITERARY AGENCY

The Big One!
Copyright © 2023 by Dr. Ray Young

All Scripture references are taken from the New
King James Version (NKJV) of the Bible.

ISBN
978-1-961601-04-8 (Paperback)
978-1-961601-05-5 (eBook)
978-1-961601-03-1 (Hardcover)

THE

BIG
ONE!

Table of Contents

Dedication

There is an old saying that says, *"Behind every successful man is a good woman, pushing!"* This book would never have come into existence without the faithful prodding of my loving wife, Beverly. I was busily engaged in writing one of the episodes of our series on the End Times called *Unrolling the Scroll* when Bev came to me and said that she was getting very strongly from the Holy Spirit that I was to suspend work on that project and put all the materials in my *"How to Survive the Coming Crash"* PowerPoint series into book form. I had begun working on this project back in 1998, when the Lord spoke to me about an impending economic disaster which would sweep over America and the world. Then a few years later I had the opportunity to develop the materials further into a series of six PowerPoint sermons. After that presentation, however, the materials went into a dormant state and stayed that way while I went through the devastating circumstances of a heart attack, inoperable, malignant cancer, being fired by the church I was pastoring because they thought I would die and being betrayed by my Assistant Pastor and the District Superintendent.

In all of this, only one person stayed faithful to me – my lovely and beloved wife. It was she who nursed me through the crisis when I was so weak I couldn't even stand up. It was she who drove me daily to the hospital for radiation treatments. It was she who helped get everything ready to move when I was so fragile and so weak that I could only pack about one box a day. Every step of the way she has been there, supporting, upholding, and, yes, when I finally got strong enough, pushing me to do what I knew deep in my heart of hearts I was supposed to do.

To you, dear Beverly, this book is dedicated. Once the project was started, it came together with startling rapidity. And now this book is being distributed all across the United States and even into other countries. It is only fitting that your name should travel with this book, for without your encouragement and exhortation it would never have come into existence. I love you, my darling and I thank God for you. Proverbs Chapter 31 says it best: *"Charm is deceitful and beauty is fleeting, but a woman who fears the Lord is greatly to be praised."* My darling, according to the commandment of Scripture, I praise you and I praise God for you.

Preface

Nobody likes bad news. The old adage about killing the messenger because you don't like the message is as true today as it ever was. And so to begin a book by stating on the cover that you must prepare for an inevitable economic disaster seems both sensationalistic and irrational. Yet in the forty plus years that I have been researching this matter, I have become more and more convinced that absolutely nothing can prevent what is about to happen to America, the church and the world. I do not ask you to accept this statement at face value but rather to be like the Bereans in the Book of Acts who listened carefully and rationally to what Paul had to say and then searched the Scriptures themselves to see if those things were true. Many years ago the Lord gave me an interesting little motto. It goes something like this: *"I have the <u>revelation</u> by <u>inspiration</u>, but the <u>confirmation</u> by <u>investigation</u>."* I urge you to do the same. Follow with me as we walk through both the Holy Scriptures and clearly documented economic facts in order to discover one of the most amazing and frightening warnings hidden in the pages of the Bible. And then together, we will draw a series of logical and prayerful conclusions about what this implies for America today, the church in its current moral condition and the world at large, all centering around how *The Ultimate Crash* is going to trigger *The Final Great Awakening*, which will in turn bring about *The Tribulation, The Great Tribulation* and finally, last but certainly not least, *The Rapture.* For a decade and a half, the Lord has been pouring into me a vast array of revelation, knowledge and insight into matters political, economic and spiritual and it is now time for me to in turn pour this knowledge into you, my dear reader and friend. Above all else, as we journey through the amazing and frightening world of tomorrow, remember that Jesus promised that He would never leave us or forsake us but would be with us to the End of the Age. That end is upon us and He has shown me the sequence of events which must take place beginning in the very near future. There will be a lot to chew on and pray about in this book. It is not a *"How to be Healthy, Wealthy and Wise in 7 Easy Steps"* booklet. Rather, it is a prayerful, thoughtful, detailed explanation of what is about to happen and what you must do in order to be prepared to survive until His Sign lights up the sky from the east to the west. Please do not be deceived into thinking that the church will escape difficulty and hardship unscathed. That is a Pollyanna delusion which I once held myself. But extensive research into the Word of God, analyzing the Revelation of Jesus Christ and all supportive Scripture and repeated exposure to our brothers and sisters in the

Third World have convinced me that we are simply kidding ourselves in America about avoiding the period of time known as the *Tribulation*. In fact, according to the Revelation timeline laid down by Jesus Himself, we will have to endure both the Tribulation and something referred to in both the Olivet Discourse found in Matthew Chapter 24 and 25 and the Revelation of Jesus Christ as the *Great Tribulation*, a separate and distinct series of events clearly documented in both books. Don't believe me? That's okay. All I ask is that you set aside your prejudices and predispositions and walk with me through the facts as presented in this book. Then at the end of the journey we will see if you still hold fast to your original thoughts on the matter. Some of this material is deep and technical. It will take some reading and re-reading. But I have written this book not as some scholarly work intended to sit on some dusty shelf somewhere but rather as a book that the average believer could take in hand and slowly but surely digest and come to understand. Be patient with both me and yourself and you will be amazed at the knowledge and understanding that you will garner as you read, study and meditate upon the truths found in this book. They will change your life forever and enable you to walk in such a manner as to be prepared to endure, for Christ Himself said in Matthew Chapter 24 that he who endures to the end shall be saved. I say to you, as I always say to everyone in all of my writing, *"May God richly bless you as you walk in faith and obedience to Him!"* Amen and Amen!

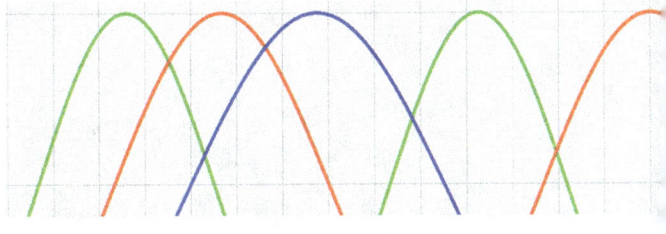

CHAPTER 1

What's A Biorhythm?

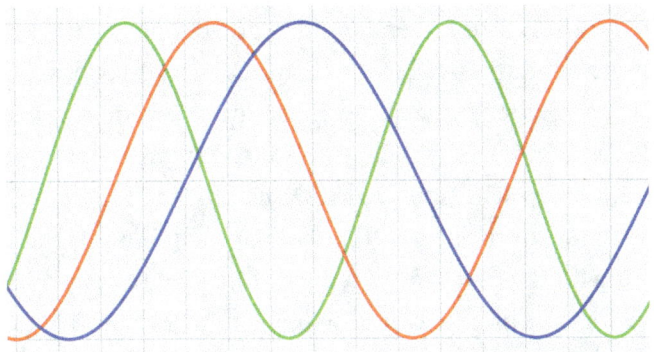

"*The theory of biorhythms claims one's lifecycle is affected by **rhythmic cycles** and makes approximate predictions of cycles of **physical**, **mental** and **emotional** characteristics. A rhythm or a cycle is a characteristic that is **periodically repeated in a predictable and measurable way**. These inherent rhythms are said to control or initiate various biological processes and are classically composed of three cyclic rhythms that are said to govern human behavior. In its simplest general form, the theory states that **from birth to death every human is governed by internal biophysical cycles**: the **physical**, the **emotional**, and the **intellectual**.*"

-- *UNKNOWN*

Wow. Nice definition. But what does all that gobbledygook mean, anyway? Let's bring this nice, formal definition down to where people live and take a look at some practical examples along the way. In its simplest terms, a rhythm is a **constant, predictable beat** that allows a musician to weave his song around it. I can clearly remember in high school when I was in marching band. It was hilarious to everyone except the band director when we first started practicing at the beginning of the school year. Some of us who had been brought up with music already had an ear for the tune and a toe for the beat. Others who were doing this sort of thing for the first time or who, unfortunately, simply had no concept of beat would struggle hopelessly to try and match the cadence we were marching to. I still remember a lovely young lady named Ginny. She had a beautiful voice and was quite a musician but her big toe was a living testimony to the fact that some folk just ain't got rhythm! Her boyfriend Charles first pointed it out to us while she was singing a solo. *"Look at her big toe"*, he said with a smirk, *"It has no idea what the rest of her is doing!"* Sure enough, her toe was moving spasmodically up and down with no real connection to the beat of the song she was singing. We never let her forget that fact either.

Without rhythmic, repetitive cycles in our lives we would be paralyzed just trying to accomplish even the most basic tasks. We develop standard repeatable patterns for just about everything we do in life. There are good reasons for that. Imagine, for example, how much time you would waste on simple motor functions if you had to think about the standard patterns you use during the first hour that you are awake in the morning. Bev and I always sleep on the same sides of the bed. That's a repeating pattern. Because of damage that I received to my throat and saliva glands from radiation therapy when I was battling cancer I keep a bottle of water on my nightstand. That's a repeating pattern. When I wake up I have to rotate and flex my feet and ankles to overcome the effects of something called peripheral neuropathy, another nasty side effect of the chemo that I was given when I had cancer. I then massage the soles of my feet. Yet another repeatable pattern. Then I put my slippers on and find my way to the bathroom. From that point on, you don't want to know. I have the first hour or so of every morning totally mapped out. Because of that fact, I can perform other higher functions like write, pray, talk on the phone, watch ESPN and eat breakfast, all without struggling to try and create new patterns. Without those manufactured patterns, most of us would never get anything done at all. We'd be paralyzed just trying to micro-manage the minutiae of every moment.

Biorhythms are similar to that but different in a very powerful and often disturbing way. Everything that I described in the last paragraph was something that **I** decided to do that way. The ball was in my court and I made the call. Every time you encounter a new situation or fact in your life your mind searches its database to see if there is an existing pattern or subroutine that it can call on to handle it. If nothing applies, a creative individual will either **adapt an existing pattern** to the new situation or **create something from scratch**, which then gets filed in the library of available solutions for future reference. But biorhythms are not something that you decide on.

They are something that are really **imposed on you from the outside** (economic) or **inside** (circadian/biological). Biorhythms always involve forces beyond our rational, cognitive minds; something so deep and so primitive that it impacts our lives without us even being aware of it most of the time. Even when we are aware of them they still dictate a significant portion of our lives to us with or without a note from mom to the teacher.

With that in mind, we have to ask ourselves a somewhat disturbing question: just exactly how much of our lives are really under our conscious, cognitive control and how much of them are already laid out for us, predetermined and unalterable? There are several answers to this question. The first and most obvious answer is that it depends on the individual. Some folks are methodical, plodding, uninventive and just plain *"stuck in a rut"*. They've run the wagon over this road so many times that it has worn a groove in the road, creating a *"rut"*, a standard behavior pattern that they will use, rain or shine, for the rest of their lives. And nothing and I mean **nothing** will make them change their minds. As a pastor I have often heard it said that the seven last words of any church before it starts to die are *"We've never done it that way before"*. What people don't realize is that today's **tradition** was once yesterday's **brainstorm**. And once people realized it worked well in that situation they continued to use it year after year even if the circumstances which had necessitated the bright idea have changed and the bright idea is no longer quite so brilliant. Last year, for the first time, Pastor Joe's little church decided to release balloons on Easter, signifying the resurrection, with little prayer phrases or the names of the members of the church inside the balloons. Next year, it will be automatic. *"Why pastor"*, the chairperson of the committee will say, *"We've always done it that way!"* To which Pastor Joe will sigh and roll his eyes to the heavens, wondering how so many good people could develop total amnesia in so short a period of time.

But even the best, creative and most innovative of us are still governed by these various biorhythms far more than we realize. During the winter months, some people literally become ill with a *"disease"* called *SAD* (Seasonal Affective Disorder), a biological response to not having enough sunlight. The treatment? More light. Even more fundamental are things like the monthly cycle which ladies have to endure during their child-bearing years and the related emotional conditions which their husbands have to endure before that monthly cycle has started. Cycles are woven into the very fabric of life. Our moon passes through a thirty day cycle. Any ER nurse can tell you that violent behavior and strange events coincide with the full moon, hence the term *"lunacy"*. Our planet rotates every twenty-four hours, producing a standard cycle of eight hours of sleep, generally during the night. Folks who transfer from day shift to graveyard shift can readily attest to the fact that it is no small thing to try and go to bed at three o'clock in the afternoon. Our planet also rotates around the sun every 365 or so days a year. That produces other cycles. Clearly, as we look around ourselves, we are surrounded by cycles of every conceivable kind, most of which we have absolutely no control over.

So the question is not whether these biorhythms exist or not. The question is more of a philosophical nature. **Exactly how important a role do these multiple biorhythms play in our lives?** Are we free moral agents, swimming bravely against the current or are we doomed to forever repeat the sins of our fathers or our own sins, failing again and again because of factors totally beyond our control? If you travel across the world, you will find two prevailing patterns of thought on this matter. Let's take a good hard look at these two world views.

WESTERN THOUGHT: THE ARROW OF TIME

To our mindset in the Western World, we see time as an arrow shot from a bow. The arrow had a starting point and it is always moving toward a desired target or goal. It is this kind of thinking which frankly produces progress. Historically speaking, any culture which makes a decision that it is going to look at the passage of time in this manner will exhibit growth and achieve things. The Arrow of Time always assumes that it is going somewhere to do something and that most of the time that something has meaning and purpose. You couldn't hold a business meeting, set agendas, build houses, cook meals, attend classes or even get up if you didn't have a reasonable expectation that what you were doing would eventually be completed and accomplish a task. This kind of task-driven, results-oriented philosophy has been emulated successfully all across the world, giving us the level of civilization we currently enjoy. But as successful as it has been, it is not without its own pitfalls and problems. If we begin a task expecting a successful completion and a satisfying result and it doesn't happen, we become frustrated and angry. We in the Western World expect to do something for a period of time and then be done with it. If we are forced to do the same thing over and over again without achieving a result, discouragement sets in and then apathy and finally, defeat.

If we observe nature in action, can we support this Arrow of Time philosophy? Of course! Many things in our lives have an observable beginning and ending. At the risk of being ridiculous, here are some examples:

- ✓ The words that I am typing on the page have a beginning and an end.
- ✓ The sentence that contains those words has a beginning and an end.

- ✓ The paragraph that contains that sentence has a beginning and an end.
- ✓ The chapter that contains that paragraph has a beginning and an end.
- ✓ The book containing that chapter has a beginning and an end.
- ✓ Every second has a beginning and an end.
- ✓ Every minute has a beginning and an end.
- ✓ Every hour, every day, every week, every month, every year and every decade all have a beginning and an end.

So much for the small end of things. But what about larger things?

- ✓ Every life has a beginning and an end.
- ✓ Every civilization has a beginning and an end.
- ✓ Every species has a beginning and an end (disturbing thought!).
- ✓ Every planet has a beginning and an end.
- ✓ Every star has a beginning and an end.
- ✓ Every universe has a beginning and an end (as far as we know).

Hmm…so everything including the observable universe seems to have a beginning and an end. What does the Bible have to say about the Arrow of Time? Let's take a look at the last book in the Bible, the Revelation of Jesus Christ and see if Scripture supports the concept:

> " [7] *Behold, He is coming with clouds, and every eye will see Him, even they who pierced Him. And all the tribes of the earth will mourn*

because of Him. Even so, Amen. [8] *'I am the* ***Alpha*** *and the* ***Omega***, *the* ***Beginning*** *and the* ***End***,*' says the Lord, 'who is and who was and who is to come, the Almighty.' "*

-- REVELATION 1:7-8

Wow. That's pretty conclusive, isn't it? If Jesus Himself is the **Alpha** (first letter in the Greek alphabet) and the **Omega** (last letter in the Greek alphabet), that pretty well covers it all. And, just to emphasize the fact that there is an Alpha point and an Omega point, He adds that He also is the **Beginning** and the **End** and in a passage a little later, adds that He is also the **First** and the **Last**. There can be no doubt about it; the Bible supports the concept of the Arrow of Time.

If the Arrow of Time were the only way of looking at things, I could quit writing here and now, but as we have already discussed, there's more than one way to look at reality, which brings us to our next major viewpoint, **The Wheel of Karma.**

EASTERN THOUGHT: THE WHEEL OF KARMA

While the philosophy of Linear Time came to dominate the Western World, the Eastern World was going in an entirely different direction. Taking the same set of observable circumstances, eastern religion and philosophy came to a totally different set of conclusions: that everything in life tended to be **repetitive** and **cyclical** in nature. Although there are many symbols in Eastern thought that express this idea, including the Yin and Yang of Buddhism, no symbol captures the concept of cyclical thought better than the **Hindu Wheel of Karma**.

As someone who has been raised in a Christian, Western environment, I personally find the Wheel of Karma to be somewhat offensive. Now, if you believe in Karma or are a Hindu, please accept my immediate apology. But also give me a few moments to explain why I recoil from this philosophy even though there is just as much truth to it as there is in the Arrow of Time. The Wheel of Karma is the philosophy of Cyclical Time taken to its logical extreme. India, of all the countries in the world, probably has as much promise and poverty coexisting at the same time as any nation on the planet. I firmly believe that if the people of India had the yoke of the Wheel of Karma taken off of their shoulders they could rise up in a matter of a few generations and come to dominate the world in any number of areas. One of the reasons that America excelled and came to dominate the world economically, politically and militarily was that America, unlike Europe where most of our ancestors came from originally, was a land of opportunity. Here, it did not matter who or what your father had been or done. It did not matter if he was an Irish peasant digging potatoes for a living or a gilded gentleman living in a mansion and casually enjoying the luxuries which his father or mother had bequeathed to him. In America, intelligence, creativity and hard work defined your success or failure. This is why people have poured into this country all through our history, even to this day. Despite growing problems with culture, race, religious and monetary issues, America is still by far the best country in the world to move to if you are interested in starting your life over from scratch. Although we are no longer the limitless plain with a mule and forty acres for each settler, nonetheless America is still better by far than almost any other country in the world. Freedom in the hands of people who are willing to work together to achieve something is one of the most powerful forces for good in the world. God provided an amazing, unique opportunity to the Founding Fathers to create One Nation under God with Liberty and Justice for All. No other nation had this opportunity to be a blank slate or *tabula raza* in the hands of people who chafed under brutal totalitarianism, aristocratically arrogant monarchies or morally corrupt theocracies. For the first time since the founding of the nation of Israel in the days of Joshua, a nation was being carved out from scratch with land, the basis of all prosperity, being placed into the hands of every family and every individual.

It is precisely this inalienable right granted by God Almighty that every man should have the opportunity to create his own future and make his own decisions that Karma takes away from those who are Hindus. According to Hinduism, there really is no such thing as an Alpha and an Omega point in life. You are born into a caste system based on your Karma from your **previous** lifetime no matter if you are an despised untouchable or a supposedly superior Brahmin. Regardless of what your station in life is you are there **because you deserve to be there** based on your conduct in your previous life. If you are poor it is because you deserve to be poor. If you are a leper it is because you deserve to be a leper. If you are a child, orphaned when your untouchable parents were killed in an accident and you are slowly dying of starvation, begging for even a scrap of bread and scavenging through trash heaps for rotten food it is because you deserve it. What a hellish doctrine! And since you deserve what you do or do not have, where you live and what your situation is no matter how horrible, then there is no sense to ever try to change anything. Your best option consists of merely suffering in silence, in order to create *"good"* Karma so that your next lifetime will be just a little bit better. And so it goes, according to the Wheel of Karma, endlessly recycling your soul and spirit from one body to another until perhaps, after ten thousand or more lifetimes, you finally move far enough up the ladder that you can obtain Nirvana. What is Nirvana? It is a condition in which you simply **cease to exist** and merge back into God. If ever there was a doctrine of demons, the doctrine of reincarnation is it. No hope, no future, no realistic possibility of ever obtaining what Christianity gives full assurance of through the shed blood of Jesus Christ, all in the span of a single lifetime. Why then is India not fully Christian? Because we have not walked in the power of the Holy Spirit; in signs, wonders and miracles and in true Christian love and character. If the church would only show the people of India the true power and love of God, the Indian subcontinent would change in just one generation, transform itself and then transform the world. Interesting enough, when I first wrote those words back in 2006, India was less than 3% Christian. But then, only three years later in 2009 as I was revising and updating this book, a massive revival broke out on the Indian subcontinent, complete with mass conversions, healings, signs, wonders, miracles and yes, intense persecution as well. Many estimates at that time placed the Christian population of India at nearly 25 percent, an astronomical increase in only three short years! Ironically, official statistics do not support that statement, but for a very good reason. The vast increase in Christians has occurred among the untouchable class, the lowest level in the Hindu caste system. As untouchables, individuals are also eligible for newly created assistance programs, but only if they officially list themselves as Hindu or Muslim. Christian untouchables are relentlessly discriminated against. As we walk through this book together you will find that many of the things I predicted or prophesied only a few years ago either have come to pass or are coming to pass as we speak. I can take no credit for these things. All I can gratefully do is to give the credit where all the credit belongs, in the hands of an Almighty God who does **nothing** without first revealing it to His servants the prophets!

Despite all of that, there is an element of truth to the Wheel of Karma. It is correct to say that things do repeat themselves on a regular, cyclical basis. But it is not the kind of cycle which **traps** the individual in an eternal loop without an exit point. It is rather a predictable, anticipatable event which the wise man can **see coming** and **take action to avoid**. If you are a race car driver driving the Brickyard in Indianapolis and you know that the last turn is a bit on the steep side you can adjust accordingly. And you can adjust each and every time that you come around that turn because you know the pattern and the cycle that exists there. This is the power of the Wheel. It was never designed or intended by God to trap or enslave those who encounter the normal biorhythms of this universe. It is rather designed as an early warning signal, a flashing light that says, *"Warning! Danger ahead! Take care!"* There is an old saying, full of wisdom, which simply states, *"Those who fail to learn from history are doomed to repeat it"*. How very true this is. Each generation comes into this world with both opportunities and pitfalls. The enemy stands ready to use his same old bag of tricks on a whole new bunch of rubes and suckers. But we have something, a wonderful weapon, which we never seem to use and that is the weapon of wisdom, based on experience and founded in the historical record and also given sovereignly by God through the Holy Spirit. If only we would take the time to examine the cycle, we would see where we are in the loop and what it is that we have to do to avoid the next bump in the road.

Again, we must ask ourselves, *"Is this doctrine Biblical?"* This time, we must visit the wisest man who ever lived, King Solomon. Listen to what this son of David says in his book called Ecclesiastes:

> *"[4] One generation passes away, and another generation comes; but the earth abides forever. [5] The sun also rises, and the sun goes down, and **hastens to the place where it arose**. [6] The wind goes toward the south, and turns around to the north; the wind whirls about continually, and **comes again on its circuit**. [7] All the rivers run into the sea, yet the sea is not full; to the place*

from which the rivers come, there they return again. [8] *All things are full of labor; man cannot express it. The eye is not satisfied with seeing, nor the ear filled with hearing.* [9] ***That which has been is what will be, that which is done is what will be done, and there is nothing new under the sun.*** [10] ***Is there anything of which it may be said, 'See, this is new?' It has already been in ancient times before us.*** [11] *There is no remembrance of former things, nor will there be any remembrance of things that are to come by those who will come after."*

-- *ECCLESIASTES 1:4-11*

Clearly, there can be no doubt. The Bible also supports the Cyclical view of time. But how can both the Linear and Cyclical views of time be right at the same time? Is the Bible in error? Hardly! Instead, it hints at a marvelous mystery woven into its fabric. Many of the deep things of God are not readily visible. He hides them to see who will have the diligence to search them out. And sad to say, very few of us do. Most Christians have only the most superficial understanding of this marvelous covenant which we have been given. Most do not understand or appreciate the power that has been placed into our hands. And very few indeed are willing to devote the time and effort required to walk in either the power or the deep things of God. All of them require a price, some more steep than others.

So, what then is the truth? Is time Linear or Cyclical? The answer is that it is **neither** but rather **both**. What? Is an explanation required? Absolutely, or this first chapter wouldn't be necessary. To understand the true nature of time does not mean that you can control it. We **exist** in **four dimensions** but have **mobility** in only **three**. In a very similar fashion, we are a **triune being**, made by a **Triune God**. Our basic makeup is that of **spirit**, **soul** and **flesh**. And even the soul itself is a combination of three things; **mind**, **will** and **emotion**. Understanding that dichotomy is not part of this book. Suffice it to say that you come to earth as a spirit, enter into a body and develop a soul. When you die, your spirit and soul leave this earth, casting the old, worn out flesh aside for the guarantee that you will inherit a new body, indestructible and eternal. That is true for believers and unbelievers alike. Most people don't know that. For those who love the Lord, that immortal body will live forever in the New Jerusalem, saturated with His love and glory. For those who don't, that same immortal body will die forever, constantly enduring the agonies of death without ever being able to experience a termination point in the Lake of Fire. This horrible, eternal fate is what Revelation calls the **Second Death**. Our first death is **temporal**, **temporary.** We get sick or old and we die. We are in a car crash and we die. That death has a point where it begins and where it ends. Not so with the Second Death. Oh, yes, it has a beginning point all right but it has no ending point, stretching forever into eternity. The New Jerusalem and eternal glory or the Lake of Fire and eternal terror and pain. Take your pick. Either way, the process will be on-going and eternal.

Not only is our being triune, but **the universe in which we have mobility is also triune**. What do I mean by that? Consider. A **straight line** consists of only **one** dimension, **length**. A **square** requires **two** dimensions, **length** and **height**. A **cube** requires **three** dimensions, **length, height** and **depth**. We have mobility, the ability to move and interact, in those three dimensions. I can move forward or backwards. I can move left or right. And within reason I can jump up and down. I have mobility in all three physical dimensions. But if you will remember, I said that we exist in four dimensions, not three. What is the fourth? **Time**. It is in time that we have no mobility. We are caught in the river of time like a leaf, swirling around on the surface of the water but constantly moving forward with no control of our own. We cannot arbitrarily move forward or backward out of sequence with the time stream. Despite all the wonderful science fiction stories about time travel, it is simply not possible for us in our mortal bodies to move in either direction. Since our bodies are trapped in the time stream, if we were to suddenly move forward in time twenty years our bodies would accordingly age twenty years. Eventually we would come to a place where we would no longer exist. The same is true if we were able to move backwards in time. We would come to a place where our physical bodies had not yet come into existence. In terms of our **spirit**, we are **eternal**. In terms of our **flesh**, we are clearly **temporal** and **temporary**.

The only way to circumvent this nasty little problem would be to surround the individual with a bubble of temporality, a little slice of *"now"* in which we would have to safely stay put, not straying into the *"yesterday"* or *"tomorrow"* we were visiting. Science fiction? For the moment, yes. For the future, definitely not. There will come a time in the future of mankind where those who have been transformed into Sons of the Living God will possess indestructible, immortal bodies not subject to the laws of space and time as we know them. Jesus has such a body right now. It is the only one of its kind in the universe. He is a *"first fruit"* or prototype of what we will become. And that, dear friends, is very exciting. After His resurrection, He made certain very interesting incursions into the time stream, interacting with mankind at critical junctures in the past in order to shape our future into the present that He needed it to be. Head hurt yet? Don't worry. Suffice it to say that all through the Old Testament there are what the theologians call *"theophanies"* or guest appearances by the Son of God in His resurrection body. The Fourth Man in the Fiery Furnace and Melchizedek are two examples of such interventions but there are a number of others that we don't have time to talk about.

For the moment, we cannot move through time. But we can analyze it, determine what kinds of biorhythmic cycles exist in it and anticipate and plan for their occurrences when they do come. It is no different than going to bed at a reasonable hour (which we rarely do in our house) so that you can get up bright and early the next morning to go to work. It just takes a little more planning and insight to understand these larger cycles.

All of that is true, but I said earlier that time is neither Linear nor Cyclical, but rather a combination of both. How is that possible? Consider the following example. Let's say that I was holding a crayon in my hand with my arm extended over my head. That would be **one point in time**. I would then start to slowly move my arm at its full extension around and around in front of me. It would create a **circle** or a **two-dimensional entity**. If I just kept doing that the crayon circle would get thicker and thicker as more and more lines were laid down. But what if as I moved my arm with the crayon in my hand in a circle, I started to **walk forward**? What kind of geometric form would I create? Now stop and think about this for a second. In fact, go ahead and grab a pencil or pen and actually do it yourself. Have you figured it out yet? No? Let me help you a bit. You would create a **Spiral**, a **circle extended over width**. A coil or spring is an example of a spiral. It goes not only around and around in a cyclical pattern but also goes forward from a fixed starting point to a fixed termination point. In other words, if you combine **Linear** geometry with **Cyclical** geometry you always come up with a **Spiral**. And that, dear friends, is the **true nature of time**. Not merely going from one point to another. Not merely repeating the same dreary loop over and over again. But a divine combination of the two. Progress from a determinable point of origin to an equally determinable point of termination. A start and an end. An Alpha and an Omega. A first and a last. A beginning and an end. Yet, within that movement through time there are always predictable, determinable cyclical patterns of behavior that can be analyzed and anticipated in order to best respond to them. What shall we call this view of time? How about…

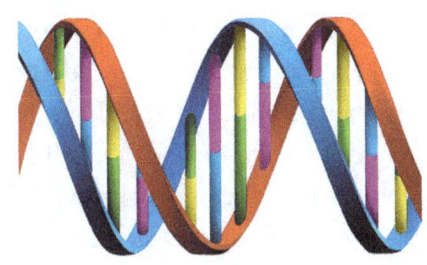

BIBLICAL THOUGHT: THE DOUBLE HELIX OF LIFE

When God created mankind, He wove together a marvelous biochemical computational system capable of analyzing data, responding to new situations and, incredibly enough, capable of creating new computational systems by combining the best of the two previous systems. I am referring, of course, to the marvelous way in which almost all creatures on this planet create new life. There is always an egg from the mother containing all of the DNA programming that took her from being a single-celled individual traveling down her mother's fallopian tube and crash landing on the wall of her uterus to eventually grow into the being that she is now. There is always a sperm containing all of the DNA programming from the father. And when these two meet, a marvelous and frankly both mystical and scientific event occurs, a new combined program results and a totally unique life form is created. But it is the way in which that information is encoded that I want to look at more closely. For a long time, we really didn't understand how the DNA molecule was woven together. But as science has advanced the frontier of knowledge we have come to realize that it is constructed as a **double helix**, or two interwoven helixes (helices for the more sophisticated of you out there!). What's a helix? Well, take a good look at the picture on the previous page. There you see two helices wound together around one another in a double helix. Why a helix? That is a good question and one that I'm not totally sure that I have the answer to. But I'd be willing to bet that it has something to do with creating a mechanism in which **two different sets of encoding are bound together in the most durable fashion geometrically possible.** That's exactly what DNA needs. You have one set of encoding or programming coming from the father and another set of encoding or programming coming from the mother. It's almost as if the structure binds the two dissimilar chains of information together in a bond that cannot be broken. As a pastor I can see all kinds of analogies pouring out of that picture, many relating to marriage, some to Christ and the Church and some pointing to the perfect **three-fold cord** referred to in Ecclesiastes which I always take to represent a husband, his wife and the Lord Jesus Christ. Any time material is interwoven in this fashion it drastically increases the strength of the cord that is formed. And that's really what we are looking at; a biological cord joining two previous lives into one new life with a dramatically increased strength of unity.

In fact, if you search the Scriptures you will find that many things in the Bible come in matched pairs, such as faith and works, holiness and grace, liberty and responsibility and the like. Always, true Christianity involves taking the two opposites, both of which are equally true, and intertwining them together to achieve a harmonious balance between the two. Faith without works is dead, says James the brother of Jesus. Yet works without faith cannot save either, says the Apostle Paul. Both are equally true, yet if one tries to exist without the other, eventually the individual will veer off to one side or the other and become unbalanced and unstable. Consider the individual who says they have faith, yet has nothing in their life that indicates that faith is there. Can that kind of empty faith save them? James reminds us that even the demons know that God exists and that He is one and they tremble in fear. On the other side of the pole are those individuals who have been in church all their lives and are constantly doing something in their church. God bless them for their activity, but their motives are also important; in fact, **why** they do what they do is often more important than **what** they actually do. Many people spend their whole life trying to build up enough good works to make Heaven. That will never happen, no matter how hard they try. The Bible says that none are righteous, no not one, and that all have sinned and fallen short of the glory of God. That's why we need a Savior. If we could save ourselves there would be no need for someone else to save us. Here's the catch: no amount of good works will save you, only faith and faith alone. Yet **true** faith will **always** produce as many good works as the person who has no faith yet works constantly trying to gain approval from God for their deeds. Do I have you scratching your head? Let me explain. I do not work for God because I **have** to work for Him in order to make Heaven. I am saved by grace through faith and not of works lest any man should boast. But it is precisely because I **am** saved that I love Him so and **want** to work mightily for Him all the time. So my living faith produces an ongoing stream of good works not in substitution **for** faith but **because** of faith. Another person sitting beside me may have never really trusted Jesus to save them and are convinced by bad doctrine or incorrect reasoning that the more things they do for God the better the chance that they will make heaven. Unfortunately there is never a point of *"enough"* because it is always based on **man's** righteousness, not **God's. Self-righteousness** is the one thing that Jesus constantly fought against and constantly condemned. The only true righteousness comes from God and is given as a free gift to all who ask in faith, believing. It is this relationship with God by faith as the basis and foundation of Christianity that marks it as being totally different at its core from all other religions.

Christianity is based on the righteousness of **Christ**. All other religions are based on the righteousness of the **individual.** Salvation is what God does for man through Christ. In all other religions, salvation is what a man achieves on his own. Only the Gospel of Jesus Christ produces this **paired bonding of faith and works that produces balanced and enduring results.**

Now, take these concepts that we have been discussing and transfer them over to the understanding of time. Again, we have two polar opposites, **Linear Time** and **Cyclical Time.** On the surface it seems that the two are completely incompatible and cannot exist in the presence of one another, just like matter and anti-matter. Yet, when we look closely at the two we find that they cannot exist **apart** from one another and must have one another in order for things to run properly and in balance. And just as with the DNA double helix, we combine two different things to come up with something which doesn't compromise the content of the original two programs but rather creates a marvelous new single entity out of the two. Think with me for just a second about all the things that we have been talking about in this chapter. We need **Linear Time** in order to be able to move from one point to another, achieving goals and accomplishing projects. Without it there could be absolutely no **change** and change is indispensable to the process of **growth.** And without growth there is no way that **life can exist in the universe.** All life is constantly in the process of growing and changing. I have heard it said that your body replaces 100 percent of its cells once every seven years. If that is true then the person you are at a cellular level now is not the same person you were seven years ago. It is common medical knowledge that your body grows and expands until about the age of twenty-five or so. At that point it begins to lose its viability and starts to age. From that point on until your death you are fighting a losing battle, slowly but surely giving ground against that most evil of all enemies, death. I am 74 as of the current editing of this labor of love and I can painfully attest to what I have just described. No matter how hard I work, I find myself slowly but surely losing ground with less strength, less stamina, less vitality. Constantly on my mind are thoughts about how to regain and recapture what I once had but have now lost.

What theologians call **the Law of Sin and Death** is also what scientists call **the Law of Entropy**. The Law of Entropy simply says that left to themselves, things break down, fall apart and die. That applies to everything from radioactive decay to the expanding universe theory. It is believed that our universe is constantly expanding. Some scientists believe that it will someday stop expanding and will begin to collapse in on itself, finally recompressing into a microdot of incredibly dense material, only to explode all over again. Other scientists believe in something they call *"The Big Rip"*, a condition in which the entire universe will expand so far and so fast that it will literally tear apart at a molecular level and cease to exist. Interestingly enough, this latter theory just happens to match what the Bible says will happen at the end of the Millennial Reign just prior to the Great White Throne Bema Seat Judgment (Revelation 20:11). The universe in which we dwell right now is seriously damaged, and is being held together by the power of the risen Christ, Who created all of this that we see and live in. But once this universe is worn out it will be discarded and replaced with a brand new one, bright and shiny but without the double helix of time loaded into it. Why? Because everything that needed to be accomplished was accomplished in the universe in which we all live right now.

Just as we need **Linear Time** in this universe in which we live, we also need **Cyclical Time** as well. Why? Because the existence of Cyclical Time inside the mechanism enables us to **create and detect repetitive patterns within Linear Time.** These eliminate the need to micro-manage the fundamentals of our lives, just as I described with my morning routine. Otherwise, without the ability to create cyclical patterns of our own or be governed by larger cyclical patterns like the myriad biorhythms that constantly surround us, we would be paralyzed into total inaction just breathing, walking or doing even the most fundamental of actions.

What is the result of merging Linear Time and Cyclical Time? The **Biblical Pattern of the Double Helix of Life,** a brilliant merging of two **different kinds of time** into something totally new for the purpose of **repeating a series of patterns until a desired goal is finally achieved.** If at first, you don't succeed…you get the picture. It was a triune Being originally called the **Lord,** the **Word** and the **Spirit** who mutually agreed to create this kind of time so that a fourth entity, called the **Bride**, could be woven into the matrix of Divinity in Eternity. Had this new kind of time not been introduced, no change would have been possible and several critical goals could not have been met. First of all, the **Lord** desired to also become a **Father.** The **Word** also desired to become a **Son** and a **Groom**. In order to do that a kind of time had to be introduced and woven into a fabric called space/time so that these changes could take place. All of this triggered the creation of an intelligent race of beings on an obscure planet on the edge of the Milky Way Galaxy. This new species would be a unique blending of **flesh** and **spirit**, something never done before up until that point (I can't say that point in time because time didn't exist as we know it back then!). Out of this previously unheard of blending of flesh and spirit would eventually come a group of people who would willingly respond to the still small voice of the Holy Spirit and would draw near to God to be cleansed and purified until they could merge into a totally new being called **the Bride.** With the creation of this entity, it allowed the Word to become a **Groom**, giving Him a Mate for all eternity. In order to do this He found it necessary to enter into human form and take on a flesh suit like all mankind, thus becoming **the only begotten or naturally born Son of God.** In doing so and becoming a Son, it allowed the **Lord** to become a **Father,** for no man is a father until he has a child. I start out as a child.

I become a man. I marry and become a husband. But it is not until I **produce a child** that I am considered a **father**.

What made all of this possible? **The Double Helix of Time**, weaving direction and purpose together with repetitive patterns to simplify and shorten the process. Oh yes, dear friends, it **did** shorten the process, immeasurably so. As a programmer I learned a very important lesson early in my programming career. **Never reinvent the wheel.** Don't write and rewrite code over and over again when a **standard, repetitive subroutine or module can be written that can be used over and over again.** Hence the cyclical nature of the double helix. Woven together for strength. Carrying the virtues of both parents without any of the evils. **Creating something new so that something wonderful could be created using it.**

You may ask yourself, *"I thought this book was all about some upcoming economic crash. How come this first chapter is all about science and theology and metaphysics?"* Well, let me put it to you this way: **You will never be able to play the game successfully unless you understand the rules.** And a book about the Biblical biorhythms that govern the economic cycles we will be examining will never make sense to you until you understand what a biorhythm is, how it is constructed and why it is necessary. I know that you just wanted to know what time it is and we kind of told you first how the watch is put together but we will get to that subject in the very next chapter. I just couldn't help wanting to share with you just a little about how the watch is made so that you can **learn to tell the time properly.** If you know the times and the seasons you will not be caught unawares when the events that this book predicts come to pass. Instead, you and your family will be prepared to escape the Wrath that is to come and you will be able to survive, endure and be victorious. And that, my dear reader, is what this book is all about!

CHAPTER 2

The Perfect Economy

DIFFERENT WAYS TO SOLVE THE SAME PROBLEM

The history of our planet has been filled with hundreds if not thousands of various ideas and schemes created for **government** and **economy**. All of these models are designed to address the three most fundamental needs of humanity: **food, clothing** and **shelter**. Once those basic needs are addressed, then supplemental needs begin to enter into the picture. Things like **peace, prosperity** and **health** become major issues. Once those issues are addressed then things like **education, culture, religion** and **entertainment** take front stage. As a pastor I would like to see religion take a more prominent role and a higher priority in people's lives, but given that we are creatures of the flesh first and foremost on this planet, it's not likely to happen on its own any time soon. As I have interacted with people in other countries I find that things are the same all over the world. Although living conditions are clearly not the same the basic needs and wants of mankind are universal. There can be no doubt about it; from our genetic makeup to our emotional needs, mankind is clearly one species. We all grow hungry when we are not fed, we all grow cold when we are not clothed, we all feel pain when we are injured, we all weep when we are grieved in our hearts and we all rejoice when victory over adversity is achieved.

The means of supplying each of these needs are as varied as the kinds of humanity that occupy this increasingly crowded globe. Religious systems include the **Big Four: Christianity**, **Islam**, **Hinduism** and **Buddhism** and then splinter into a million pieces, including Judaism, Shintoism, Ancestor Worship and a vast variety of other sects, cults and groups. Although Judaism is foundational to two of the Big Four, Christianity and Islam, I can't include it in the Big Four because the world-wide number of adherents simply isn't there.

In the political realm we have tried everything from soup to nuts (and a great many nuts, if the historical record can be believed!), including, but not limited to: **Monarchies, Theocracies, Democracies, Totalitarian Regimes, Anarchies, Republics** and a wide variety of combinations of the above. Although I have had the privilege of being raised in a democracy, my study of history has proven conclusively to me that people can live quite comfortably in any form of government so long as their basic creature comforts are taken care of on a consistent basis. In Imperial Rome all that was required to keep the psychopathic, murderous, incompetent Caesars in power was to provide the masses with **bread** and **games.** In our culture today it would equate to Mixed Martial Arts or the World Wrestling Federation and McDonald's. Freedom of action and speech, which we value so highly, are considered to be extraneous options in many cultures. Some cultures, such as those found in China and Russia, have really never known a time of freedom from oppression. After the breakup of the USSR in 1991 Russians tried to embrace the concepts of democracy and freedom. Many of them failed miserably at the effort and today are moving back toward a culture based on the kind of control once exercised by the Czars and men like Joseph Stalin. In fact if you examine the kind of government that will be exercised during the Millennial Reign you will find that it has nothing to do with Representative Democracy, the form of government which we are accustomed to here in the United States. Instead, it will be a government which will be a combination of a **Monarchy,** a **Theocracy** and an **Oligarchy.** What on earth is that? Well, we are accustomed to saying that **Jesus will rule and reign on the throne of His father David.** The fact that we have mentioned a throne clearly indicates that a Monarchy will be involved. Monarchies involve the presence of a King or Queen. In this case, we already proclaim Him as **King of Kings** and **Lord of Lords.** In addition, since He is also **God in the flesh and the Only Naturally Born Son of God** it makes this period of time a **Theocracy** or the rule of man by God. But it is the other, unique feature of government during this thousand year period that makes it most interesting. The Bible clearly says that **we will be Priests and Kings unto the Lord our God** and that **we will rule and reign with him.** Now, an **Oligarchy** is the rule of a **privileged few** over the **unprivileged many.** Jesus specifically said that those of us who were good and faithful servants, having been faithful in small matters, would be put in charge of **ten cities.** That will make us **administrators or governors acting on His behalf and in His place on a local and regional level.** To further complicate the matter, at that point in time **we will be immortal, with resurrection bodies, incapable of dying. Our subjects**, the people that we will rule over, **will be mortal**, the shattered remnants of mankind who were not raptured and may or may not know Christ but are nonetheless human but with radically extended lives, probably back to the near-thousand-year mark which we once enjoyed during the period after the expulsion from the Garden but before the devastation of the Flood. From these battered, bloodied survivors will spring up a restored version of humanity, once again populating the globe. And it will be that restored humanity which, when Satan is let loose from the Abyss after a thousand years and can once again begin whispering in their ears, tempting them, will begin to bitterly resent we Immortals who rule over them. At some point, that resentment will trigger a global assault on Jerusalem, the world capital, we Immortals and our King and Savior, Jesus. Their armies will amass around the valley of Megiddo, either unaware or uncaring about what already happened there once, preparing a final assault on the city when suddenly fire from Heaven will come down on all of them and destroy them. Sound like science fiction or something I made up out of my own head? I challenge you to read Revelation Chapter 20, Verses 1-10 and ask yourself what implications can be drawn from that passage. You will find yourself right where I am right now.

After the Millennial Reign is over and this physical universe in which we live has been destroyed there will be a transitional period between universes known as the **Great White Throne** or **Bema Seat Judgment.** After that, we will see the creation of a **New Heavens** and a **New Earth.** While it is not totally clear what form of government will be in place during this final, eternal period, it is clear that **the Father** will be in total control with the Son submitted to Him. Beyond that, we will just have to wait and see. It is probable that no other kind of government will be necessary since we will be totally interfaced into the Trinity as the Fourth Member of the Godhead, commonly referred to as **the Bride.** We will know God as well as He now knows us. We will know one another as well as He knows us. We will be interfaced into a kind of Divine Star Trek Borg Collective, yet without sacrificing any of our individuality. It will be a state of being which we can only speculate on right now, because it is beyond our ability to understand. Once we are fully immortal and fully divine, like Christ in every respect, we will have the **Mind of Christ** fully activated in us and our intellects will skyrocket beyond any measurable scale. Based on my studies and a whole lot of prayer, it looks like we will be linked into a kind of super-massive **neural network**, using the power of the Holy Spirit as the interfacing device and all directly interfaced into the Father Himself. It boggles my imagination to think about this and most Christians think that I am espousing some kind of heretical doctrine when I simply take what Scripture says and retranslate it into plain English. Rest assured, sitting on clouds and strumming harps is **not** what God the Father has in store for us.

ECONOMIC INSTABILITY

But this chapter doesn't really concern itself with the form of government that will be perfect in the Millennium Reign but rather a form of **economy** that can be **nearly perfect here on Earth.** No matter what kind of political institution you put in place, **it is only as stable as the economy on which it rests.** If you destabilize the **economic** situation you also destabilize the **political** situation. As I write these words in 2022, it is obvious that America is beginning to experience what I wrote about all the way back in 2006. During the Obama administration, all manner of crisis legislation was pushed through Congress without paying any attention to the details. But as they say, the Devil is in the details and so our economy struggled, a patient on life support, not really breathing on its own. When President Trump took office, many people shuddered thinking about what would happen to our country.

Was Trump unstable? Probably. Did he ever listen to the counsel of those around him? Hardly ever. Was he hard to work for? Just ask former Indiana Governor Mike Pence. Trump successfully managed to alienate his own Vice President and turn Pence against him. Trump was and continues to be a bizarre mixture of the right man doing the right thing but seemingly always doing it in the wrong way. Under his administration the American economy experienced a time of recovery and a robustness that it hadn't had in decades. But every move that Trump made outraged the radical left and caused a continuing state of conflict, accusation and bitter resentment. Trump never learned to turn his cell phone off and leave Twitter and other social media outlets alone. If he had been the shining but silent executive figure, letting Pence do the talking for him, things would have gone a lot smoother for everyone, including those who supported him as I and my wife did.

The Biden administration inherited an economy which, despite Covid, was running at near peak efficiency. But the radical left, so immersed in Socialist doctrine that they couldn't see beyond their darling theories, was determined to undo everything that Trump had done. Sad to say, they were largely successful and in doing so have significantly destabilized the American economy once again. Instead of prices staying low, they are now rapidly escalating. As of November, 2022, grocery prices had jumped the most since 1979 over the past year. The 13.5% cost increase for all food at home through the 12-month period ending in August was led by eggs, the prices of which soared 40%. According to a web report by NBC, many food categories had double-digit 12-month increases, led by eggs, which surged by 40%; margarine, up by 38%; and flour, which jumped by 23%. In a food price index report issued at that time, the Agriculture Department said factors across the economy, including supply chain issues and higher energy, transportation and labor costs, have contributed to increases in prices across food categories. But underneath all of those so-called factors lies that fact that massive Democrat policy changes and mandates destroyed everything which Trump had worked so hard to rebuild and get running again. There can be no doubt of several things. Can Trump run a business successfully? Absolutely! Was he able to translate those financial principles into policy decisions that worked for our country? Absolutely! Was he also the most irritating, aggravating, contentious, most politically incompetent individual to ever serve in the office? Absolutely! But they also said the same things about Lincoln. What do we say about that man now? Only time will tell what Trump's place in history will be. As of 2022, there is strong speculation that he will run for President again. My only hope and prayer is that if he does he will learn from his mistakes in his first term in office and find better ways of accomplishing his goals. In the meantime, the current Democrat administration continues to do one thing after another to destabilize our economy. They have a "long game" whose goals and methods are highly disturbing to me.

What they really intend to accomplish will destroy American democracy as we know it, will deliberately plunge our country and most of the rest of the world into the worst economic depression to ever occur in the history of our species and establish an Oligarchy like the one I described earlier with a privileged few ruling over the oppressed many. The middle class as we know it will be completely destroyed. They really don't care what happens to the rest of us. They only care what happens to them. As long as they retain power, that is all that matters. Has that generated unrest? Absolutely! Any time I think about our current political situation, who is in charge, how they got there and the results of their policies and doctrines, I am enraged. If I weren't a Christian and a Minister of the Gospel to boot, I might be looking for my rifle on the back of my pickup truck and practicing to improve my aim. A vast number of people in this country, aided and abetted by the current economic chaos and the fact that a continued deterioration of our economy seems inevitable, are already up in arms. I will say this before moving on to my next point. If American does not have a massive revival, an outpouring of the Holy Spirit that changes the hearts and minds of most Americans, we will have a revolution just like the one that saw the birth of our country. Revival or revolution. Peace or violence. Restoration of the principles that founded our country and made us great once or the destruction of everything around us. If you think that the violence in the inner cities of America like the rioting that destroyed a good part of Minneapolis was bad, just wait. Without revival, hatred, resentment and violence will tear a hole in the heart of our country that may or may not be fixable. The worse our economy gets, the closer we also get to unrestrained chaos, death and destruction.

During the 1980's the Communists used this same technique to introduce Communism into South and Central America time and time again. They would pick out a country in which the level of poverty was extreme (not hard to do in South America!) and which also had an oppressive, authoritarian form of government which was also significantly insensitive to the needs of the people. They would then use **terrorism** to destabilize the economic picture. Remember, as long as there are bread and games, people will put up with nearly anything. Don't believe me? Then take a little trip on the internet and begin to study the methodical erosion of personal freedom in this country over the last two hundred years, coupled with the equally massive erosion of state's rights and then compare what the original framers of the Declaration of Independence said compared to what we have today. In fact several years ago a group of researchers took the Bill of Rights and went out on the street, asking people to give their opinion of the various components of the Bill of Rights without actually knowing that it **was** the Bill of Rights. Much to their amazement the vast majority of the American public interviewed rejected those materials, considering them to be far too radical to be used in American democracy! In fact, many of the people polled asked if this was some sort of Communist Manifesto! Given the current political trends in our country, it won't be too long before we have become a completely Socialist country with near Totalitarian control by the government over our individual lives. It is not without significance that immediately after the sub-prime lending market meltdown and the consequent massive, almost **one trillion dollar bailout** of 2009, one of the major news magazines in the US featured a front cover trumpeting the almost victorious phrase, *"We are all Socialists now!"* I shook my head sadly when I read those words. Without fail when anyone, be it private individual or corporate monolith, accepts government money it always comes with **government control.** During the three year period after I first wrote this book, I watched the rapid erosion of the free enterprise system in America. Who would have believed back then that Fannie Mae and Freddie Mac would both be nationalized within the span of a single month? Or that Detroit would come begging, hat in hand, asking for government bailouts and willing to accept the leash that would be placed around their necks as a result? Now we are looking at the nationalization of the entire lending industry including most of the banking giants. The destabilization of our own economy has led to a hue and cry for order and security as imposed by government.

As long as economy is stable, government is stable. But the problem with economy is that it **isn't** stable all of the time. And any time the economy takes a nosedive the grumbling in the ranks begins immediately. But what if there was a **perfect economy**, one that would **never** experience a crash? And what if that economy was so incredibly efficient that it produced a population in which **only 5 percent were poor, 90 percent were middle class, and only 5 percent were rich?** It is virtually impossible to overthrow a government based on such an economy. Here's how it works: As long as **all** of us are poor, sleep on the floor and eat only one small meal a day, it's all right. Why? Because we are all suffering **equally.** No one is better off than any other and so no one feel cheated or disenfranchised because everyone is in the same boat. But let's say that one farmer is walking in the woods one day near his little plot of ground and he discovers oil, just like old Jed Clampett of the TV sitcom *The Beverly Hillbillies.* Suddenly the oil companies are knocking on his door offering him large amounts of money for the use of his ground. Suddenly, he is eating **three** meals a day instead of just one. And just as suddenly there is resentment among many of those around him. Before you know it he isn't walking any more. Now, he is riding around **on a bicycle!** And then, sinful man that he is, he actually goes out and **buys a car!!!** Now, everyone in the neighborhood is looking at his massive prosperity and comparing themselves to him, not to each other. Now they realize just how disenfranchised they really are, simply because they have a **new basis of comparison.**

Sound far-fetched? Not really. In fact, I ran into this very situation with just a few minor modifications in regard to a ministry that we worked with in India some years ago. God began to bless them and prosper them. Then resentment began to arise against them on the part of other ministers in the area. When we spoke with one another about the matter they shared an Indian parable with me. It seems that a visitor came to India from another country. As he was walking along the shoreline, he came across an Indian fisherman who was catching crabs and throwing them in a basket. Although there were many crabs in the basket and they were all very much alive the fisherman didn't have the lid to the basket closed. And yet even with the top of the basket within easy reach of the crabs none of them were climbing out. The passerby expressed his astonishment at the fact that none of the crabs were crawling out. *"Oh"*, said the fisherman, *"That's no great surprise. You see, these are Indian crabs!"* The visitor was confused and confessed that he didn't understand what that had to do with anything. *"It's simple"*, replied the fisherman, *"When any one crab tries to crawl back out of the basket, the other crabs become jealous and pull him back down with them!"* This simple Indian tale represents the very heart of economic and political stability and instability. As long as all the crabs were in the basket and on their way to being eaten, being eaten seemed to be a reasonable fate, **since that fate was shared by all.** But the minute one of the crabs began to crawl out of that fate, the others became enraged. Instead of rejoicing in their brother crab's break for freedom they actually resented it and attempted to hinder it. The only way for **one** crab to escape was for **all of them** to escape and to escape **at the same time.**

In the same fashion, the only way to produce a **politically stable environment** is to undergird it with an **economically stable environment in which the vast majority of the people all enjoy the same <u>relative</u> level of prosperity and success.** If we were to put it into a chart, it would look something like this:

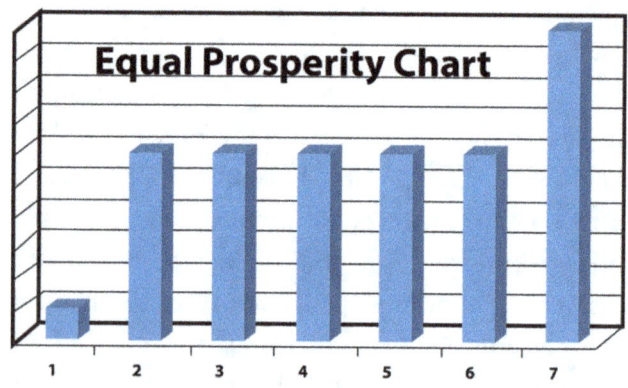

Please note that from a geometric standpoint, if this chart were a single piece of material, it would be very stable with a wide and **uniformly even base**. It would be very hard to overturn it because of the wide, uniformly stable foundation. The same thing holds true from an economic basis. **When the wealth of a society is uniformly distributed among a majority of the people, that society will also be uniformly stable.**

Unfortunately, that is not the way it is in most of the world. In Haiti, for example, **5 families control 95 percent of the wealth.** There is virtually no middle class and the remainder of the people, probably 90 percent, live in abject poverty. Let's take that economic model and see what it looks like as a chart.

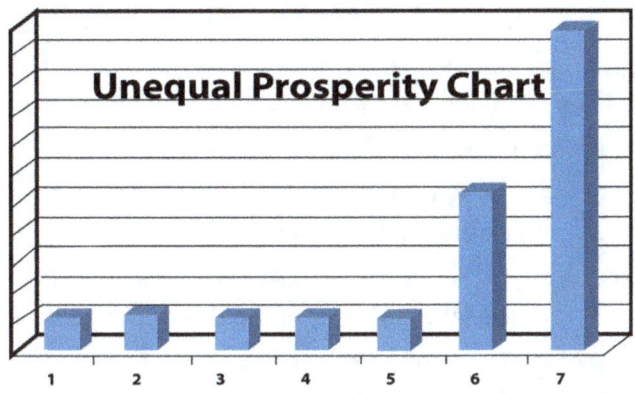

The structural instability of this model is immediately apparent. Virtually everyone is living in a state of having **barely anything.** Yet they must constantly look at a very small group of people who have **almost everything.** Resentment, bitterness, anger, revolt and revolution are the logical consequences of such massive inequality. And it isn't just Haiti that struggles with such **inequity** and **iniquity**. (As an aside, I find it fascinating that those two words are spelled so much alike. Perhaps because they have so much in common with each other.) No, it's not just Haiti. It's the entire Third World. Small wonder, then, that it is so difficult to maintain political stability in countries where the resources are so badly and unevenly distributed. It is a sin against God and man. This automatically puts **those who have too much** in the potential role as **abusers of what they have** and **those who have too little** in the potential role of **being abused.** Many years ago I had the opportunity to go to Haiti for three days for what would have been a ground-breaking contract.

Fifteen years before TBN came into Haiti we had a signed agreement with the government of Haiti to bring Christian TV into the country. Since more than half of the country's 6.5 million inhabitants live in Port Au Prince, the nation's capital, we planned on locating several key mini-dishes on the side of the horseshoe of mountains overlooking the flat sandy bay where the city is located. We had the money. We had the land. We had government approval. Yet the deal died. Why? Because of two greedy, carnal *"Christian"* businessmen, one in Louisville and one in Evansville, who both wanted 51 percent and controlling interest in the corporation. One businessman controlled the money, the technology and the know-how (of which I was a part). The other businessman controlled the contract with the government and the land where our dishes would have been located. **One lousy percent kept 6.5 million people from having Christian TV!** I was so torn up by the situation that it made me sick for months afterwards. Think of all the souls that were lost to the bowels of Hell over one lousy percent! And one of those *"Christian"* businessmen was an Abuser First Class. I remember that he showed up one day at the orphanage where we were staying (He stayed at the ritziest hotel in town, in air-conditioned comfort, while we slept at the orphanage in sweltering, breezeless heat. Notice how the inequality of the situation still generates feelings of anger and frustration in me to this day?), bringing with him a large container of hard candy. Perching himself majestically on the top of the steps leading up to the orphanage, he simply reposed as if he were some sort of imperial king awaiting his adoring subjects. Then, without a word being spoken, children of all ages began to pour into the orphanage, assembling themselves on the steps, all with eager eyes poised toward His Imperial Majesty, **the King of Candy**. And then, to my horror, he simply began to pitch candy out into the crowd. Now in America in a place of abundance, when candy is tossed out to the crowd during a Thanksgiving Day parade there may be a brief scuffle for the candy but it only lasts for a moment. The children along the parade route know good and well that another group will be coming down the street in just a moment and should they fail miserably and get no candy at all mom and dad will cover for them and take them to Dairy Queen where they can overload on sugar for the rest of the day. Not so with these children. As far as they knew, when **this** candy was gone, they might never see another piece of candy **for the rest of their lives.** And so there was no gentle scuffling around for candy. It was a knock-down, drag-out **fight** for candy. Larger children had no compunctions about taking the candy right out of the hands of the smaller children. Many children were knocked down. It's a small miracle that none of them were hurt. I turned and looked at this man in absolute disbelief. How could he so recklessly put these precious children at such risk? **Yet there was no recognition of the danger in his eyes at all!** He was so accustomed to using his money to put him in controlling, abusing situations that it came naturally with no sense of shame or concern for the people that he was abusing. That is the danger of a monarchy. Power corrupts. Absolute power corrupts absolutely. Unless, of course, **He** who wields that power is also **absolutely incorruptible.** That's why the only monarchy that will ever work in the history of the world will be the **Millennial Reign of King Jesus.**

Let's take this analogy a step further, shall we? The people of America have a difficult time understanding why we are hated by so much of the rest of the world. Now would be a good time to apply the lessons and principles you have just learned. Let's see… America is the most **uniformly wealthy nation in the history of the world with the exception of Israel under Solomon.** It is not without significance that whenever a nation chooses *Yahweh*, or *YHWH*, if you prefer, that nation becomes **blessed, prosperous and dominant in the world.** It is also significant that any nation or empire that has chosen to **persecute the Jews and reject God has been destroyed in just a few generations.** America has become the most affluent, prosperous, powerful nation in the world **not** just because of the great natural resources found on our shores, **nor** just because we are united and definitely **not** just because of the economic opportunities afforded by a seemingly endless frontier but rather because **this nation chose at its inception to make the Lord God of Israel its God.** All of the other things that I have talked about earlier in this book happened **because God intervened in our history time and time again.**

There could just as easily have been as many as **nine** separate nations on this continent and not one. There could have been two English-speaking nations, the *United States of America* and the *Confederate States of America*, located on the Eastern Seaboard, separated by the Civil War permanently. There could have been the French-speaking *Republic of Louisiana*, cutting the continent in half, controlling one side of the Mississippi River, all the way from the Canadian border to the Gulf of Mexico. There could have been and actually was a separate *Republic of Texas* speaking southern drawl, something distantly related to English. There could have been a Spanish-speaking nation of *Calamexico* controlling all of Mexico and the entire West Coast, all the way to Canada. And there could have been a Caribbean nation called *Hispaniola*, embracing Florida, Cuba and the Caribbean islands, speaking a combination of French, Spanish and Creole. The

Pacific Northwest could also have been an English-speaking nation of its own called the *Palisades*. Last but not least, what we today call the state of Alaska would still belong to *Russia* (and they still want it back, by the way!), and *Hawaii* would belong to the Japanese. I am told that they really do own it, with something like 90 percent of the land ownership on the islands now in Japanese hands. One final note on Russian influence on the North American continent. Some time ago I came across some remarkable research and documentation about Russia's actual involvement. It seems that they had several outposts/communities in what is now Alaska and the head of those activities actively lobbied the Czar of the time to expand their outreach down the West Coast all the way to Mexico. Fortunately for us, the Czar lacked the vision to see the incredible economic opportunity that this would have availed them of. Clearly, without God's intervention, none of what we have today would have come to pass.

Like England before us, as we embraced the Gospel of Jesus Christ, He began to fulfill the promises found in Deuteronomy 28:1-14. Like England before us, we became the dominant nation in the world as a result of it. And, like England before us, we have become **abusers of our privilege as the wealthiest nation in the history of the world.** Now, I'm not saying that there might not have been empires that collectively had more wealth. But there has never been a nation in which that wealth and the opportunity to create wealth were more **uniformly distributed among the vast majority of the populace.**

That also has created the most **uniformly stable political system in the history of the world.** It has also created the most uniformly stable and fair legal system in the history of the world. American jurisprudence, having been based on the English model, which was in turn based on the Biblical model of Deuteronomy and Leviticus, became the standard globally, often imitated but never really duplicated. But no sooner had we truly begun to realize the wonderful promises of God found in Scripture than we began to abuse them. We began to assume that we were prosperous by the strength of our own hands, we were always right, we were experts at everything and we knew everything. I have seen this trait in rich people time and time again. They think that because they have become successful at **something** that this makes them an expert at how to do **everything.** As a result, we began to tell the rest of the world how to run its business. Then we began to **make** the rest of the world run their business as if it **were** our business. As a result the image of the **Ugly American** became famous across the globe, reaching its height in the 1950's, after World War II and before the Korean *"Conflict".* (Heaven's sake, it really wouldn't do to say that we didn't win a war. Let's just call it a conflict, shall we?) Even though we have been extraordinarily generous with other countries, particularly those whom we have conquered and even though many of our actions have been based in genuine Christian concern for the needs of those less fortunate, it has been inevitable that we would become abusers of our privileged position and that the rest of the world would see itself as abused, manipulated and controlled by us in an unfair manner. Truthfully, the conduct of our country regarding the CIA and other covert operations has been in many ways reprehensible. Put yourself in the position of the Third World for just a second if you can. Imagine that you are the people of a Third World country, living at a level of squalor and poverty that is beyond comprehension. And then imagine that America is the rich *"Christian"* businessman, pitching hard candy at you with no real concern for your well-being. Can you see how it would be impossible for there not to be a level of frustration, jealousy and anger that you couldn't control? Even the poorest of us in America are staggeringly wealthy compared to the vast majority of the people in the rest of the world. There are times when I complain to God about our finances. Then I go and look at the pictures I have of 50 precious children sprawled all over the ground asleep, their pillow the crook of their arm, their blanket the sole garment that they own and their mattress the hard, often wet ground of the compound. And then I remember that these are the **lucky** ones, for they have a roof over their heads even though it leaks like a sieve when it rains. At least they get a real meal once a day **most** of the time. Where they came from on the streets of India with no parents or relatives to care for them, dumpster-diving is a way of life and rotten, spoiled food with maggots in it and flies swarming around it is their customary cuisine. **We have so much and take it for granted. They have so little and cherish it all.** I know I have spent a great deal of time on this subject but unless you understand what the economic disparity between us and them has created you will never understand world politics or the events leading up to the Tribulation and the Great Tribulation. And, like the Apostle Paul, I do not want you to be ignorant, brethren. Knowledge is power. And understanding the signs of the times may be the key to your very survival.

GOD'S ECONOMIC MODEL

This is the condition of the world. But it need not be this way. It was never meant to be this way. God selected a nation who was chosen to demonstrate **His economic model to the rest of the world.** Had Israel actually implemented the genius-level economic plan given to them in the wilderness, Israel would have become the most prosperous nation in the world with an economy that would have never failed, never crashed and would have continually redistributed wealth among all its inhabitants using the universally acceptable standards of opportunity, intelligence and hard work. Israel would have expanded from its original tribal allotments to claim the property originally promised to it, stretching from the Mediterranean Sea all the way to the Euphrates River and then north, swallowing up Iraq, Syria, Lebanon, Jordan and part of the Sinai Peninsula, effectively ending the Palestinian problem as well as the Muslim problem. With the descendants of Ishmael enjoying equal economic opportunity with the descendants of Isaac, there would be no hatred in the Middle East and the powder keg which will eventually fuel Armageddon would never have been ignited. Under the reign of Solomon these territorial boundaries were actually realized for a brief period of time but the foolishness of his ill-advised son Rehoboam the Retard destroyed what had taken three generations to build in just three short days.

Unfortunately for all of us, the peace and prosperity which would have originated from the implementation of God's perfect economic plan never happened, exactly as the Lord foretold and we are stuck with the mess we have today. How fortunate for us that the Bible promises that **all** things, even our mistakes, work together for the good of them that love the Lord and are called according to His purposes. But it is highly instructive to take a close look at the model that **He** invented and **we** never implemented. Since the Lord already knew that all things perform in repeating patterns or biorhythms across linear time, having created it that way to begin with, it only makes sense that there would be **economic** loops, just as there are biological, emotional and circadian loops. Where in the Bible are these loops found? They are found specifically in the Pentateuch or first five books of the Bible that are attributed to Moses. All the social interaction and religious rules and regulations for Israel are outlined there and it only stands to reason that the economic models should be found there as well. Before we begin looking at the first of these cyclical patterns, I want to share with you a graph that I created to illustrate visually the relationship between the 50-year Year of Jubilee Cycle and the 7-Year Debt Cancellation Cycles. I searched the internet in vain to find even one single graph illustrating this monumentally important economic model, so with the limited graphic skills I have, I created one of my own. We'll display the graph to start and then explain the two sets of economic principles embedded in the Year of Jubilee model:

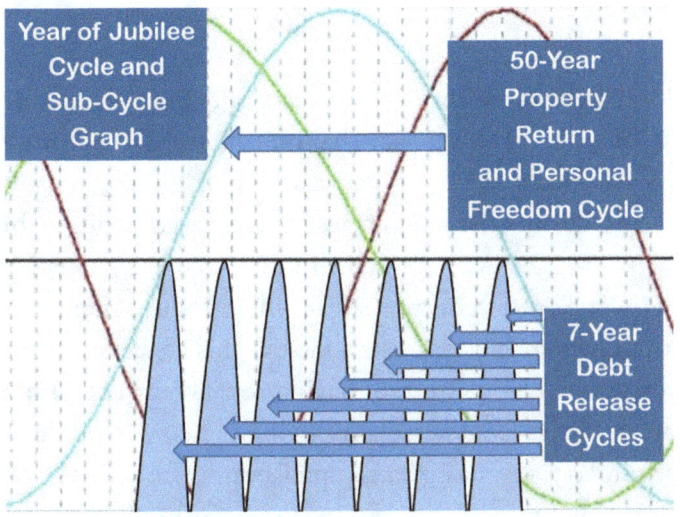

Principle # 1 – The Seven Year Cycle of Debt Release

" [1] *At the end of every* **seven years** *you shall* **grant a release of debts**. [2] *And this is the form of the release: Every creditor who has lent anything to his neighbor shall release it; he shall not require it of his neighbor or his brother, because* **it is called the LORD's release**. [3] *Of a foreigner you may require it; but you shall give up your claim to what is owed by your brother,* [4] **except when there may be no poor among you; for the LORD will greatly bless you**

> **in the land which the LORD your God is giving you to possess as an inheritance** — [5] only if you carefully obey the voice of the LORD your God, to observe with care all these commandments which I command you today."

– DEUTERONOMY 15:1-5

These five simple verses introduce an economic principle so revolutionary that **no** country in the history of the world has **ever** implemented it, fearing that it would destroy the economy of the country that did so. In actuality it would have **delivered** that economy, coupled with one other concept that we will introduce later on in this chapter. But let's take a look at this concept for just a second. The concept of having **seven-year economic mini-cycles** is interesting enough and many of our laws in America regarding bankruptcy borrow from this seven year time frame as do certain laws regarding the statute of limitations involving prosecution for certain kinds of crimes and litigation. But to **totally remove debt every seven years? Unthinkable!** Yet the Lord specifically promises that if this seven-year debt forgiveness cycle is obeyed that there will be no poor in the land, thus eliminating **poverty**, a constant curse, from the economy. He also promises that He will **greatly bless** the individuals in the land, provided, of course, that they carefully obey Him and observe His commandments. How could such a seemingly insane action actually cause the elimination of poverty and enhance prosperity? Actually it is not only the action of forgiving debt every seven years that causes these changes to take place, it is the **value system and moral code** that are enforced because of the rule that bring about the desired result. Let's think through what would actually happen if America implemented this rule tomorrow morning.

Day has dawned and **all debt has been cancelled across the entire United States.** The initial impact would be devastating to existing lending institutions. Banks with multitudes of thirty-year mortgages would be brought to their knees. Those banks without a solid asset-liability ratio would be forced into insolvency and probable bankruptcy within the day. High risk loans, particularly to Third World countries, would be in default immediately. Frankly, **it would trigger a total economic collapse world-wide** and bring about the Final Great Crash prematurely. It would be like taking an addict off of crack cocaine cold turkey and just throwing him into a corner to sweat it out. Although the economic system that would arise out of the ashes of the current one would be stable and self-rejuvenating, the human misery and suffering that would be triggered would not be worth it, so let's scale the plan back a little. Let's say that instead of canceling all debt immediately, we will grant **a seven year transitional period** to allow both lenders and borrowers to restructure and reconfigure the current mess they're in and try to find a way out of it. Time to restart, then, with a fresh set of assumptions.

And so, beginning tomorrow, **no new loans will be made of more than seven years in duration**. This is going to mark a massive paradigm change for the entire lending community. No lender is going to issue a loan exceeding seven years because any **outstanding balance at the end of that seven-year period would automatically be forfeited by the lender**. How will this change lending practices in the housing industry?

THE ZERO PERCENT DECEPTION

It used to be that when you wanted to buy a home you had to have 25 percent or more of the total price of the house in hand before you went to the bank to borrow money. Because I am 74 as of the time that this is being written, I have had the privilege of watching things change slowly but surely over the last half-century and hardly any of those changes have been for the good. Gradually, over a period of time, the down payment required by lenders has decreased and decreased until for some time now, lenders have been advertising zero percent down payment mortgages. That seems on the surface to be a wonderful thing, allowing more and more people to own homes without having to accumulate a significant down payment. And the lenders have been quick to advertise it as just such; a wonderful, visionary thing that they are doing to help the potential homeowner. **Nothing could be further from the truth.** Over the years, I have dealt with banks and bankers as both a homeowner and as a business owner. In all that time I have only discovered one banker who did **anything** for their customers that did not inherently benefit the bank first and foremost. Let me give you an example of what this zero percent down lending philosophy has created in America. Some years ago, I knew a wonderful, Spirit-filled Christian couple named Al and Betty (fictitious names). They owned a Christian bookstore in the town where I lived. Al worked for a large public utility and Betty ran the bookstore. Together they had planned their dream home and had designed all the details. Even though they didn't have the money, a local lender had the *"vision"* to offer them 100 percent financing, zero down. They dutifully began to search for a piece of property that seemed right to both of them. They found it. And then they *"purchased"* the land and constructed their dream home, combining the entire project into a single loan at the bank. Sounds perfectly normal in today's lending environment, doesn't it? They moved in and everyone lived happily ever after, right? Wrong! A few years later, I happened to come by the bookstore to say hi to Betty, who had become a good friend. I found her in the back office, clutching her chest and unable to breathe properly. At first we suspected a heart attack had happened but as she calmed down it became apparent that she had suffered a panic attack. Why? Because the financial pressures of the store plus the **enormous house payment** that they were making were pushing she and Al closer and closer to bankruptcy. I began to ask some practical questions about their financing and their home. Yes, the home was beautiful. Yes, it was everything that they had ever wanted. But no, **it was not something that they could really afford**. They had been lured by lenders and merchants alike into **living beyond their means.** In doing so, they had simply been following the lead established by their own U.S. government, which has been living in a **deficit spending environment** ever since the 1930s. As much as we might want to, we cannot live beyond our means for very long. Sooner or later it catches up to us. Not only was the house payment far beyond their realistic means to pay it, but in the process of examining their financial situation we also made several other disturbing discoveries. In the dollar values of that time, their home was worth one hundred thousand dollars on the open market. Today, it would be worth at least three hundred and fifty thousand dollars, given the location and features of the house. I asked her about the term of her mortgage. It was, like so many others, a standard 30 year mortgage. We then took their **monthly mortgage payment and multiplied it by 360 months or 30 years.** I gently tore the calculator tape off and showed it to Betty. They had constructed a home worth one hundred thousand dollars in the market place at the time it was built. But over the thirty years of the mortgage they were going to pay **three hundred thousand dollars for that one hundred thousand dollar home!** The bank was going to walk off with a nifty **two hundred thousand dollar profit** based solely on usurious interest paid to them by Al and Betty. That's a 200 percent profit margin. That is nothing short of highway robbery. It's also **a clear violation of the Scriptures as well.**

THE DEADLY RULE OF 78'S

Back then, this was the exception. Today, it is the expected and advertised norm. Why? Because the banks know that they can make a killing off of the fact that Americans simply will not **defer their need for**

immediate gratification. This would be bad enough but there's something equally insidious at work at the same time. It's called the **Rule of 78's.** Simply put, it allows banks and other lenders to collect the vast majority of the interest due during the term of a loan up front and then, only when most of the interest has been collected, to collect the principle borrowed. How does that work? In the great online encyclopedia *Wikipedia*, the definition for the Rule of 78's goes like this:

> *"Also known as the sum-of-the-digits method, the* ***Rule of 78's*** *is a term used in lending that refers to a method of yearly interest calculation. The name comes from the total number of months' interest that is being calculated in a year (the first month is 1 month's interest, whereas the second month contains 2 months' interest, etc.). This is an accurate interest model only based on the assumption that the lessee pays only the amount due each month.* ***If the lessee pays off the loan early, this method maximizes the amount paid by*** <u>***applying funds to interest before principal.***</u>*"*

I hope you didn't skip over that last sentence. Read it again. Then read it again and again until you realize what was just said. Bluntly put, it **penalizes** the diligent debtor who pays the loan off early by making sure that **every penny of interest is collected before the principle is paid off.** It ought to be a criminal offense to do so. Unfortunately, it is not, and is probably even viewed by many bankers as a recommended procedure. *Wikipedia* then goes on to explain how the calculations are made.

"A simple fraction (as with 12/78) consists of a numerator (the top number, 12 in the example) and a denominator (the bottom number, 78 in the example). The denominator of a Rule of 78's loan is the sum of the digits, the sum of the number of monthly payments in the loan. **For a 12 month loan, the sum of numbers from 1 to 12 is 78 (1 + 2 + 3 +... +12 = 78).** *For a 24 month loan, the denominator is 300. The sum of the numbers from 1 to n is given by the equation n (n+1) / 2. If n were 24, the sum of the numbers from 1 to 24 is 24 (24+1) / 2 = 12 x 25 = 300, which is the loan's denominator, D."*

"For a 12 month loan, 12/78's of the finance charge is assessed as the first month's portion of the finance charge, 11/78's of the finance charge is assessed as the second month's portion of the finance charge and so on until the 12th month at which time 1/78's of the finance charge is assessed as that month's portion of the finance charge. *Following the same pattern, 24/300's of the finance charge is assessed as the first month's portion of a 24 month precomputed loan."*

Now, let's put some plain English on this and decode what was just said. Let's look at the speed with which the borrower actually pays back the **principle** of the loan over the **term** of the loan. Let's assume that the amount borrowed was one hundred thousand dollars and that the interest rate was 6 percent. Let's also assume that the term of the loan was thirty years or 360 months. I found a loan calculator online and ran the numbers to see what the results would be. Even if you don't understand the math these online loan calculators are invaluable. They can be smart for you. The one I used for this example is located at www.bankrate.com.

THE INSIDIOUS LENDING TRAP

When all the smoke had cleared and the gears were done spinning, I found myself staring at a monthly payment of **$599.55**. That seems reasonable enough until we look at how that $599.55 is broken down. The first time I would sit down and write my monthly mortgage check for that amount, only **$99.55** of that amount would be applied to the **principle** of the loan, and **$500.00** would be applied to the **interest!** The following month wouldn't be much better with a split of **$100.05** and **$499.50**, respectively. Ouch! The split between principle and interest doesn't even out until **eighteen years have elapsed in the term of the loan.** It now becomes obvious what is going on: **the bank is bleeding you to get all of the interest out of you as quickly as it can.** Why? Several reasons come to mind. The first is that **you might default at some time on the loan.** That way, the bank minimizes its risk in lending money to you. The second is more insidious. It seems that the number seven shows up all the time in human affairs. You've heard of the old movie starring Marilyn Monroe called *"The Seven Year Itch"*? It deals with the fact that many relationships only last seven years before thoughts of adultery began to drift through the minds of the couple involved. It also so happens that the normal *"homeowner"* only lives in their home for an average of **seven years!** That means that the typical thirty year mortgage **only lasts for seven years before it is refinanced and placed into the hands of a new *"homeowner"*.** With numbers like this, the whole concept of actually owning a home by purchasing it through a mortgage becomes ludicrous. All any of us are doing is simply paying the bank almost **pure interest** for the privilege of living in the home of our choice. To truly own anything means that there is no debt or liability on that object. That means that the vast percentage of Americans who delude themselves into thinking that they *"own"* their own homes are really no better off than their renting neighbors. We *"buy"* a home in order to have some reasonable control over what we can and cannot do with the place we live in. We also *"buy"* a home so that we can *"build equity"*. But explain to me, please, how in the world anyone can build equity when you are paying interest instead of principle at a ratio that can be as bad as 5 to 1 or even worse?

There is another reality hidden in this whole new mechanism. It used to be that lenders were concerned with the viability of the loan itself. A bank that had a high percentage of defaulted loans was looked down upon by the lending industry. Banks prided themselves in being conservative, reliable and dependable. They were, after all, the financial cornerstone of the community in which they were located. But with the purchase of most local banks by regional banks, who were in turn purchased by national banks, who were in turn purchased by multinational banks the banking industry effectively lost its local conscience. **Profit** replaced **integrity** as the driving force in the industry. And then the mega-bank conglomerates made a disturbing discovery: it was no longer in their best interest to make absolutely sure that all loans were paid off and never defaulted. In fact, given the fact that there was a long-standing housing shortage and the fact that fickle American consumers traded homes every seven years, it dawned on the industry that the only thing that mattered was **keeping the**

homeowner in a continuous, repeating, seven-year loop which restarted the entire interest calculation process over and over again. If a homeowner enticed by unrealistic lending terms was drawn into a mortgage and then defaulted a few years later, all the better, since it **restarted the interest payment process with a new homeowner.** The home would quickly sell because the housing market was always in a shortage condition. The bank ran almost no risk of swallowing the home. A little fix-up here and there and the home was back on the market, ready to begin the process of virtually **pure interest** and **pure profit** all over again.

It would not be until the collapse of the sub-prime market that justice and chaos would both catch up to the greedy lending industry. Donald Trump, famous for his book *"The Art of the Deal"* leveraged himself so deeply in debt that the only things that saved him from total bankruptcy on several occasions were that (1) he was so deep into the pockets of the banks he dealt with that if he had gone down he would have taken them with him and (2) the fact that he was kept afloat by the constant, irrational **appreciation in property values**, even when **no real value was being added to the property.** Despite the earlier popping of the Dot-Com bubble in the 1990s, it never dawned on the lending industry that the housing market might be headed in the same direction. Again, I made the original statements found in this book in 2006 when everything seemed to be hunky-dory. The subsequent collapse of the industry in 2009 and the near-collapse of the world financial community as a result made me want to say, ***"I told you so!!!"***

The longer the period of time a loan is taken for, the worse the abuse of the borrower by the lender. So what does the Lord do in response to this kind of hypocritical, manipulative situation? He takes the gun out of the hands of the shooter. He reduces the maximum term of any loan to seven years. This dramatically **decreases the amount that can be borrowed.** It also dramatically **decreases the amount of interest that will be paid.** And it also **forces potential borrowers to live within their means and deploy long-term frugality and savings plans.** I am told that the average Japanese worker saves **20 percent** of their gross income! How do they do it? Simple! **They live within their means.** Saving money for future purchases is their main priority. They modify their life styles accordingly. It used to be that the United States operated in the same fashion. If something broke, you didn't throw it away. You fixed it. And if you wanted to buy something, you began to save your money until you could afford to purchase it. Cash on the barrelhead. No debt. No interest.

THE END OF UNRESTRAINED CREDIT AND USURIOUS INTEREST

Once the shock of this new financial model had passed, people would begin to notice certain significant changes in their lifestyles. Our culture of unrestricted credit would simply fold up and disappear.

Terms and conditions for lending would become much more restrictive. People would begin to rethink their lifestyles and spending habits. A more conservative mindset would begin to take over America. This mindset would ripple from our **personal** spending habits into our **national** spending habits. If we as individuals were forced to live within our means and save a meaningful percentage of our income eventually our government would begin to adopt the same philosophy. Deficit spending would become a thing of the past. The budget would really be just that, a budget, restricting what could be spent in any calendar year on any project. America would begin to set monies aside to help begin to pay back our national debt, a seemingly impossible task given the obscene amount which we owe. At the end of World War II we were the greatest **creditor** nation in the history of the world. We had the greatest uniform prosperity in the history of the world. We could and did lend astronomical amounts of money to nations all over the world. Today in just over seventy years we have become the greatest **debtor** nation in the history of the world. Once we bought up huge tracts of ground all over the world and bought controlling interest in foreign corporations, so much so that our involvement and manipulation was bitterly resented. But today, the tables have been turned. Today it is the Germans, the Japanese and in recent years the Chinese, most of whom were the very countries that we defeated in the Second World War and who we helped to rebuild who are today methodically buying up property and companies all over the US and the world. We are no longer in control of our own fate. We are owned and operated by overseas interests. And it is getting worse every single year. How did the Germans and the Japanese do it? By researching the concepts found in the Bible regarding debt, interest, spending and saving and **applying the principles of the Gospel without actually applying the Gospel itself.** Unfortunately for rebellious believers and fortunately for obedient unbelievers the principles found in the Word of God will work for anyone who applies them whether they believe the Gospel or not. America is filled with Christians who are in total financial, emotional and spiritual ruin because even though they say they believe they stubbornly refuse to implement in their lives the principles which God has outlined in His Word. Since God watches over His Word to perform it, when others operate within the boundaries of His Word He honors it every single time. The rain falls on the just and the unjust alike. Only those with the wisdom to bring umbrellas stay dry.

Having begun this seven year transitional period, lenders and borrowers with loans that will not terminate within this remaining grace period now act to restructure those loans so that they terminate on December 31st of the seventh year. Why? Because at the end of that period of time **all debt will be cancelled.** In canceling the debt of **all individuals every seven years**, it creates a safety valve on the economic pressure of debt that lifts and releases the pent up steam in the kettle every seven years without fail. We already know the enormous power this paradigm will carry in redefining the atmosphere of the lending industry. But it also carries a delivering power for those who, despite their best efforts, have fallen into serious debt and are unable to deliver themselves. Who might be in such a group? Well, me, for one. Let me tell you my story. When I was younger, stronger and stupider I decided that I could rule the world so I started my own computer company. Although I was never really all that successful the company was slightly better than break-even for ten of the twelve years it was in existence. It paid my employees (as many as nine), it paid our vendors and it occasionally paid me a modest salary which allowed us to live at least part of the American dream. But then I went through a series of disasters that threw me into the ditch. In the last two years of the company, it added on forty thousand dollars worth of debt. How did that happen? Suffice it to say that the market went one way when I thought it would go another way and we got killed trying to sell equipment from a much larger and more expensive retail location instead of selling programming services from a small, low-overhead office. The massive debt and the pressure that came with it helped to destroy my marriage and eventually plunged me into total bankruptcy, both corporate and personal. I was mentally, emotionally and spiritually drained and unable to continue any further. The bankruptcy purged me of most of my debts. Unfortunately there were several debts that I couldn't discharge because of the laws governing the process. And because I was not able to discharge them seven years later I was forced back into personal reorganizational bankruptcy because of them. This time, however, I was able to come out of the reorganizational bankruptcy after about four or five years, several years early. I've never gone back and actually figured out how much time I had left. I was just so glad to be rid of it that I just shouted *"Halleluiah!!!"* for about three hours and then went on my way. Had the Biblical model been in place during my first run at bankruptcy there would have been no second trip into the ditch. Not only would it have eliminated that second trip but since **all** debt is cancelled every seven years there would have been no **stigma on my financial record** because of it. Every seven years every individual and company would be given a fresh start. If you were solvent, Amen and God bless you! But if you were in debt for whatever reason all of your debt would be cancelled and the terrible burden you had been carrying would be washed away. In my case it was business-related but there are many other people in the US who have been buried alive with **medical expenses**. Their so-called medical insurance programs have been so jury-rigged as to leave them with little or no coverage. Medicare leads the way in this crazy quilt of rules and regulations. There is a gap in Medicare Part D drug prescription coverage which happens to most people on it every single year. You get to a certain point in your coverage and suddenly it ceases completely until you spend a certain amount on your own. For those on fixed incomes who are dependent on various medications to keep them functioning, these gaps can be life-threatening. I talked with a Medicare representative several years ago regarding my own coverage, and discovered this deliberate gap. She told me that many people call her up weeping in nausea and pain because they can't afford their medicine. An equal number of people have to choose between buying food, buying medicine or paying the rent so they can have a place to live. This is not right. A seven year debt cancellation process would mean that no one would have to live with two hundred and fifty thousand dollars or more of medical debt on their backs. Impossible? You haven't read the statistics. In addition, given that **all debt** would be cancelled, it would also mean the end of all **IRS back tax debt.** Every seven years you would have the satisfaction of telling the IRS to go mind their own business! I've had my battles with the IRS as well and I know of too many godly people that the IRS has buried with penalties and interest. It is not uncommon for a tax debt of two thousand dollars or so to balloon up to twenty thousand dollars or more in a matter of a few years because of the never-ending penalties and interest that the IRS piles on without fail.

Add to this the cancellation of all business debt and suddenly you have also changed the way in which America does business. Then-businessman Donald Trump would either have to totally redefine the way he does business or simply go out of business altogether. Why? Because Trump constantly lived with a high level of corporate debt. He is highly leveraged and not to his advantage. There have been several times in his career when his creditors wanted to shut him down but he was into them too deeply for loans. Had he gone down they would have lost everything. And so in desperation his creditors shored him up and continued to fund him in the hope that he would finally right himself and become profitable again. Fortunately for them he did just that. In the event of a major crash, you would have had to put a safety net underneath the windows of Trump Towers or wherever he had been staying at that point in time.

The severe limit on the **term** of debt would also limit the **amount** of debt. This would also militate against large, multinational corporations with huge assets but also huge amounts of debt. It would tend to strengthen the small, independent entrepreneur with limited amounts of debt and limited assets. It would restore America and the world to an economy in which every man worked for himself or at the least it would restore a working model of local and regional employment where employer and employee are forced to live with one another in the same community, forcing a sense of corporate responsibility and community awareness. This increased sense of responsibility and awareness would be enforced by the Lord Himself as He supplemented the prosperity already being generated by the new economic model in place.

> " [6] *For the LORD your God **will bless you just as He promised you**; you shall **lend to many nations**, but you **shall not borrow**; you shall **reign over many nations**, but they shall **not reign over you.** [7] "If there is among you a poor man of your brethren, within any*

*of the gates in your land which the LORD your God is giving you, **you shall not harden your heart nor shut your hand from your poor brother**,* [8] *but you shall **open your hand wide to him** and **willingly lend him sufficient for his need, whatever he needs**.* [9] *Beware lest there be a wicked thought in your heart, saying, 'The seventh year, the year of release, is at hand,' and your eye be evil against your poor brother and **you give him nothing**, and he cry out to the LORD against you, and **it become sin among you**."*

— DEUTERONOMY 15:6-9

THE INCREDIBLE SHRINKING CREDIT LINE

A fascinating side effect of the seven-year cancellation of debt is that the amount available for lending would shrink annually as the Year of Cancellation drew closer. For example, let's say a property was worth seventy thousand dollars. Let's further assume that in this particular case the lender was going to lend to the borrower at no interest. And finally let's also assume that the borrower could only pay back ten thousand dollars a year. We are approaching this example in a simplistic manner in order to keep the math easy to understand. If it was January 1 of the new seven-year cycle, one day after the Day of Debt Relief, a lender would probably be willing to lend the full seventy thousand dollars that the property was worth, knowing that the borrower would be able to pay back the full amount before the next Day of Debt Relief came due. But what if that same borrower came to the lender at the beginning of the second year in the cycle? If all the factors were the same the lender would have no choice but to demand one of two things out of the borrower. Either the borrower would have to agree to a higher annual payment or would have to provide $10,000 in down payment as a matter of good faith. Each year that passed in the cycle would either decrease the amount that could be borrowed, increase the annual payment or increase the amount of down payment that the borrower would have to provide up front.

The Lord, knowing human nature as He does, anticipated this incrementally increasing tight-fistedness on the part of the lender. He warned that there would be a penalty for those lenders who hardened their hearts to needy borrowers. While the economic reset would be based on a seven-year cycle the occurrence of crisis and disaster could not be expected to respect that same cycle. God also promised to bless those lenders who, despite the nearing of the Year of Debt Cancellation, would nonetheless act according to His Word instead of their bottom line. In essence, God was saying to all lenders, *"Don't worry about crisis-based lending. I will cover your bottom line if you honor My Word. If you take care of **My** business, I will take care of **yours**."*

As a result of a general increase in prosperity and general decrease in debt more funds would become available for charitable giving, both on a personal and a corporate level. As a result of the increase in cash available for discretionary spending and charitable giving, personal lending on a short-term basis would increase along with a corresponding decrease in the number of personal loans which the lenders would require to eventually be paid back. One of the things I have noticed down through the years as a pastor is that the very first thing that is affected by an economic downturn is not discretionary spending but rather charitable giving. The sad truth is that most folks will stop helping others long before they stop treating themselves. The even sadder truth is that this pattern extends directly into the church. Instead of giving themselves out of the financial ditch that they are in most Christians tighten up their belt even more, thus choking off the very flow that could have rescued them.

Principle # 2 – The Fifty Year Cycle of Income Restoration

If all God had provided to us was the seven year cycle of debt release it would have been incredibly useful and would have forestalled economic disaster for a long time but it would not have prevented it. Why? Because the seven year cycle is actually a sub-cycle of a larger cycle, the fifty year cycle of income restoration. The core Scripture for this larger economic loop is found in Leviticus Chapter 25:

> " [8] *And you shall count seven sabbaths of years for yourself,* **seven times seven years**; *and the time of the seven sabbaths of years shall be to you forty-nine years.* [9] *Then you shall cause the trumpet of the Jubilee to sound on the* **tenth day of the seventh month**; *on the* **Day of Atonement** *you shall make the trumpet to sound throughout all your land.* [10] *And you shall* **consecrate the fiftieth year, and proclaim liberty throughout all the land to all its inhabitants**. *It shall be a Jubilee for you; and* **each of you shall return to his possession, and each of you shall return to his family**."
>
> – *LEVITICUS 25:8-10*

God has this thing for sevens, doesn't He? It's actually kind of a neat thing when you think about it, almost like some complicated rhythm in a musical piece with a little *"hiccup"* at the very end before we begin the score again. Count seven beats, dump the debt, count seven beats, dump the debt…repeat seven times. Then pause a single beat…restore the income and repeat the measure. As a former programmer, what I see when I look at this Scripture is pure programming logic with what are called *"iterations"* or subroutines inside a larger main routine or program. I constantly marvel at the genius of God. We rave about people when they are very smart yet when God does something that is absolutely out of this world we simply shrug our shoulders and take it for granted.

There's another little fun factoid hidden in this Scripture. The Jewish calendar is very different from ours so their first month is not the equivalent of our January. The first month of their civil year is called **Tishri** and starts sometime in our September. Their sacred calendar's first month is called **Nisan** and starts in our March. But I find it fascinating that their financial *"Declaration of Independence"* occurs in the 7th **month** on the 10th day while the celebration of our national Declaration of Independence is also held in **our** 7th **month**, the month of **July**, on the fourth day. Equally fascinating is that **Purim**, the Jewish holiday celebrating the Jew's victory through Queen Esther over the wicked Haman just happens to be a time when all Jews observe a time of **feasting** and **joy** and the **sending of presents to one another.** This holiday just happens to fall in the **twelfth** month, the month of **Adar**, on the fourteenth and fifteenth days. And in America, we celebrate the birth of Christ in our **twelfth** month, the month of **December**, on the twenty-fifth day. During this time we too celebrate and send presents to one another. And finally, it just so happens that the Jews observed **three major holidays during the year when the men of Israel had to present themselves before the Lord**. In America we pastors joke that most men only show themselves in church **three times a year,** at **Thanksgiving,** at **Christmas** and at **Easter.** Later on in this book I will discuss the amazing parallels between Israel and America. Just add this little set of notations to the rest of the amazing facts when you get there.

Some of you may have noticed what appears to be a discrepancy between what the Scripture quote on page 82 says and what I said about it. My heading talks about **income restoration,** while the Scripture talks about *"returning to his possession".* Actually, when you boil all economics down to their most fundamental elements, it's the same thing. Let me explain why.

IT'S ALL ABOUT THE LAND

All throughout history, the source of all wealth has always been **the ownership and utilization of land.** Let me give you some concrete examples. Oh, wait,

I just did! Let's take **concrete**, for instance. Concrete is typically made of Portland cement, some sort of aggregate (generally gravel and sand), water and something called admixtures. Portland cement is made by heating limestone with clay and then grinding this product with gypsum. Where do all these things come from? **The land.** All of the basic elements that make up concrete have to be mined from the land and then combined into the proper mixture. My grandfather worked for a cement manufacturing company in a little town called Stockertown, Pennsylvania for many years. I can still remember how everything at the plant was covered with a thin powdery gray covering of dust from the process of making the product. Let's follow that process to see how crucial ownership of land is to everything financial.

1. Mine limestone from the land.
2. Mine clay from the land.
3. Heat both items together in oven sitting on the land.
4. Mine gypsum from the land.
5. Grind limestone/clay compound with gypsum in device sitting on the land.
6. Various devices used in the process are made from steel which is made from iron which is mined from the land.
7. Mix that compound with aggregate (gravel and sand) dredged from a river bed which runs on top of the land.
8. Add water from pipes or hoses made from various materials which come from the land.

9. Mix together and put in a hole which you have just dug in the land.
10. Build building on concrete foundation sitting on the land.
11. Etc., etc., etc., in a never-ending fashion.

Stop and think about it for just a second. What do you have in your life that doesn't come directly or indirectly from the land? **All wealth is derived from the utilization of land and the resources which it contains or supports.** Even the more esoteric ways of earning money such as stock trading and software development still require buildings, phone lines or cell phones, tables, chairs, carpets, steel, wood, concrete and a never-ending list of items which have to be mined and manufactured from resources found in or on the land. Somebody has to own that land. Can you become wealthy and not own land? Absolutely. Can you make a living and not own land? Absolutely. But you can't go very far down the supply chain before you encounter land ownership entering into the picture.

In ancient Israel, everyone owned land, even the priests and Levites. After countless centuries of being nomads, living off the land but not having ownership of it and 430 years as slaves in Egypt where private land ownership was lost during the Great Famine, it had to have been painfully obvious to Moses and every other thinking person in the thirteen tribes that if God was going to bring them into the Promised Land it would also have to entail **private ownership of the land for**

everyone involved. In fact, there is a lot of Scripture in the Old Testament devoted to outlining exactly where each of the tribes was to be located. That piece of ground was to be their land. Within that tribal inheritance, each clan had inheritances of their own and within the clan individual families owned property. For those priests and Levites who owned land within a city the ownership was limited to a house. But for the many priests and Levites who served in the temple at Jerusalem on a monthly rotating basis land ownership involved owning farmland which they faithfully used to grow their own crops and raise their own livestock. Remember how earlier in this chapter I mentioned that **economies are stable as long as everyone is relatively equal?** That is exactly what God engineered for Israel when they came into the Promised Land. Granted, each tribe was responsible for conquering the territory assigned to it but hey, nothing's perfect, right? But once the enemy tribes had been driven out of the land every single family received their own piece of ground which was supposed to be theirs in perpetuity. And it was at this point in the process that the genius of the Almighty was once again manifested in plain and clear terms. Land ownership was nothing new in the history of the world. Nomadic tribes viewed the land as a shared resource between them and the wildlife which they hunted, just like the American Indians. But when men began to settle in one spot and stay there land ownership became an issue. Ever since then **disenfranchisement from the land would eventually produce poverty** and the **accumulation of land and its resources would**

produce wealth. The rich would get richer and the poor would get poorer, all through the ownership of the land.

During Israel's stay in the wilderness, land ownership was once again non-existent although it would have been meaningless regarding who wanted to own a stretch of barren, inhospitable, arid desert. By the time that the Children of Israel had crossed over the Jordan River, however, future property assignments had been mapped out. All of this was really nothing new and nothing revolutionary. But what followed next was. After assigning who was to get what, the Lord added several revolutionary new concepts to the Hebrew notions of land ownership.

A NEW WAY OF LOOKING AT LAND OWNERSHIP

First of all, land ownership was to be a **joint venture between God and man with God holding the final mortgage on all properties.** Israel was to view herself as leasing the land in perpetuity from Yahweh. He actually owned the land but placed it in a condition of **perpetual trust** into the hands of the various tribes and individual families. Because **He** owned the land it was not possible for a tribe, family or individual to **sell what they did not own.** Instead of owning the family farm they were merely leasing it from God. And since they could not sell the property they could only **sub-lease it to someone else.** It is at this point that the Biblical view of land ownership skews dramatically from all previous traditional views of property and property ownership. Just as with the concept of canceling all debt every seven years, this concept was at total variance with prevailing world philosophies on this matter. In addition to retaining ownership of all land God further placed a stipulation on all properties that had been subleased. Regardless of the terms of the sublease **all properties had to be returned to their original owners every fifty years.** In Israel when you *"sold"* your property you were merely *"selling"* the leasehold rights to the property until such time as the next Year of Jubilee came around. At that point in time **all properties all over Israel were to be returned to their original family ownership.** Again, a single idea is all that God needs to totally transform a situation. The implications of this concept were even more staggering economically than the seven-year debt cancellation clause was. Let's look more closely at those implications and the terms under which property could be *"sold"*.

Let's say, for example, that Johnnie Johannsen migrated from Sweden to the United States in 1853. After landing in New York Johnnie moved west and north until he found himself in what we know today as Minnesota. Ambitious and hardworking, he started out with forty acres and a mule. Soon a little Swedish gal named Inga caught his eye. Before long they were married and not long after that a few new little blonde-haired Johannsens were running around in the back yard. At that point Johnnie saw the need to expand. His neighbors were moving out and heading for California and Johnnie was able to purchase their forty acres and two mules for a very reasonable price. After several years Johnnie was able to add an additional eighty acres to his homestead. Before he died he had accumulated five hundred acres and multiple barns, tractors, crops and little blonde-haired Johannsens, all saying things like *"Ya!"* and *"You betcha, sure!"* Johnnie had done quite well for himself. The farm was taken over by Johnnie Junior or *"Yonnie Yunior"* as his friends playfully called him. J.J., as he preferred to call himself, was a good farmer and a hard worker like his dad. Although he did not expand the family farm he was effective at maintaining it and earning a more than adequate income from it for him and his family. It wasn't until the third generation of American Johannsens that trouble reared its ugly head. Johnnie's grandson Tom developed a serious drinking and gambling problem. Over a period of fifteen years Tom successfully managed to gamble away the entire farm except for the original 40 acres which were no longer sufficient in a rapidly modernizing economy to support the financial needs of the family. Finally with no other options left to him Tom sold the remaining acreage to a neighbor and went off to work in a factory.

THIRD GENERATION THROWAWAY

A sad story? True. A true story? More often than most of us would like to admit. There is a pattern found in humanity that I call **Third Generation Throwaway.** It is best exemplified by the story of David's family tree.

David started out as a little Hebrew boy who was the seventh son of Jesse, a normal kind of guy from a normal kind of town named Bethlehem. Through a remarkable series of events engineered by the Lord he ended up as king over all Israel. Under his dynamic leadership Israel waged a series of wars which drove its enemies back and off of lands that had been promised to the descendants of Abraham, Isaac and Jacob. Just like Johnnie the son of Johann in Minnesota, David the son of Jesse did pretty good for himself, by golly! His son Solomon took the efforts of his father and skillfully consolidated them, turning Israel into the gem of the Middle East, the wealthiest and most opulent nation of its day, where iron and brass were considered too commonplace to even bother to count. Everything seemed to be going just fine. And then along came the grandson of David, a snot-nosed, arrogant little twerp born with a silver spoon in his mouth and no brain in his head named Rehoboam (the Retard). What his grandfather David had built out of his sweat and blood and his father Solomon had labored so hard to consolidate, Rehoboam the Retard threw away in a three day period at the beginning of his kingship. We won't go into the gory details of his stupidity, but by the end of the third day, Solomon's former advisor, Jeroboam (the Jerk) had walked off with the ten northern tribes tucked under his belt, and Rehoboam (the Retard) was left with only three tribes: Judah, Benjamin and Levi.

I have seen this pattern repeated time and time again in people's lives. The grandfather will work hard and long and build something of substance for himself and for his progeny, exemplifying the kind of morality and work ethic which once made America great. The son who lived through the hard times as a little boy will continue on in his father's footsteps, working hard and consolidating the efforts of his father. But when it is time for the grandson (or granddaughter, for that matter) to take the reins of authority something goes dreadfully wrong. In many cases this grandchild has never known adversity, lack or want. They have grown up, just as Rehoboam the Retard did, in the lap of relative luxury. They often feel *"entitled"*, a phrase we hear so often today about our own young people. They do not understand what it means to work hard for a living. They lack the ambition or motivation to either create or consolidate a kingdom of their own. They are content like the Paris Hiltons of the world to squander their family wealth in a show of carnal, shallow, opulent foolishness. Unfortunately for many of them, sooner or later they end up sitting with the pigs that they acted like for so very long. Some of them come to their senses, but by that time many of them have not only squandered their share of their father's inheritance, they have managed to lose the entire farm just like Johnnie's grandson Tom. By the way, Solomon probably saw the disaster coming. In writing Ecclesiastes he bemoaned that who knew if the son who came after him would be a fool. (I suspect he already knew!) No wonder he exclaimed, *"Vanity, all is vanity!"*

In both cases, the kingdom was lost. For one son, it was five hundred acres and some darn fine John Deere equipment, not to mention some prize-winning Holsteins. For the other son it was the chance to become the dominant nation in the Middle East for a very long period of time. In both cases the damage was irretrievable. But what if the same situation had happened under the economic guidelines laid down by the Lord God of Hosts? Would things have been different?

WHAT IF LITTLE JOHNNIE HAD BEEN JEWISH???

If Johnnie had been born Hebrew, in the tribe of Dan, for example, and the guidelines laid out by the Lord had been implemented and in place, here's what would have happened. The original plot of ground, all forty acres and the mule, would have been registered under his family name as their rightful property, subleased from God. Those forty acres would have been **non-negotiable** and irrefutably his. No matter what happened in the future that land would **always belong to his family.** As he expanded, he would have sub-leased land from other families around him. Even though his contract stipulated that he was managing the property for them it would have remained in their family name. Nothing would have stopped Johnnie from expanding to his U.S. size of five hundred acres plus John Deere equipment and Holsteins. Things for his son J.J. would have been the same in both the U.S. and Israel. And the grandson Tom would have thrown the farm away in both countries as well. But it would have been in the **fourth generation** that things would have changed drastically. Remember that Israel was instructed to return all property to the original family ownership at the end of every fifty years, the **Year of Jubilee.** In America, because property is actually bought and sold irretrievably and without recourse, Tom's son, whom we will call Johnnie III after his great-grandfather would be stuck with the apartment that his dad lived in while he worked that factory job. Everything that his great-grandfather had worked so hard for was gone forever. **But not in Israel.** In Israel, when the fifty-year reset of the economic production base occurred, restoring the land ownership to the original family regardless of what had happened in the past, young Johnnie, the great-grandson, would receive notice in the mail that his **great-grandfather's family farm, all 40 acres, was being returned to him.** He could assume ownership again within two weeks. They even had a mule left over that the previous owners were willing to leave behind!

In America and the rest of the world, Johnnie the great-grandson was just plain out of luck. So sad, too bad! You snooze, you lose! **But not in Israel.** In Israel, the young blonde-headed Swede from the tribe of Dan would have been able to **start fresh all over again because the family farm would NEVER stop being the family farm.** For all eternity once every fifty years all properties would reset and return to their original ownership. Can you now begin to understand the massive ramifications of this single difference in how land ownership was viewed in Israel versus the rest of the world?

TEN THINGS THE YEAR OF JUBILEE WOULD DO

This simple difference in how property ownership was viewed would have had massive implications for personal and corporate usage of land and would have helped to shape the kind of industrial base formed in any country that would implement it. Here are some snapshots of how it would work in different situations:

1. In the case of the third or fourth generation family member whose predecessors had ruined everything and sold the family farm off it meant **automatic redemption** and a **chance to start over every fifty years**.

2. It would therefore be almost completely **impossible for the poor to stay poor forever.** Sooner or later a fifty-year reset would coincide with someone

with a little ambition and gumption and they would pull the family out of poverty simply by having the opportunity presented to them.

3. This would **decrease** the number of individuals and families **living in poverty** and **increase** the number of families living in **relative prosperity**.

4. This increase in the number of families living in relative prosperity would also **increase** the **relative stability of the political system** resting on this kind of economy.

5. On the flip side, it would **discourage** the development of vast amounts of personal wealth based on property since property would always revert every fifty years to the original landowner.

6. If someone had been subleasing the property and wanted to do so for the next fifty years or less it would necessitate **renegotiating the terms of the sub-lease with the original owners**. If the original owners did not want to renegotiate the sub-lease the property would automatically revert to them with no legal recourse for the former leasers of the property.

7. This kind of ownership structure would **encourage** the development of **small, individual entrepreneurial operations** and **discourage** the development of **massive super-corporations**.

8. Just as with the seven-year cancellation of debt loop, this 50-year restoration of land as the basis of income would favor the **strong, self-reliant, hard-working individual who owned his own business**, be it farming or small job shop.

9. It would **discourage the development of large corporations employing large numbers of anonymous employees** and having no sense of community loyalty or responsibility.
10. It would **defuse feelings of frustration and rage because of inequality** since everyone would know that they would get a fresh start every 50 years.

With these two business models in place economic crashes would be virtually impossible. Strict controls on lending would impose boundaries on speculative banking and investing, two of the major contributors in any crash. Inflation would also be virtually impossible due to a fiscally conservative mindset. Any country implementing this kind of economy would eventually become a nation of strong, self-reliant, hard-working small businessmen with a solid moral foundation and a save-and-fix mindset rather than a trash-and-spend mindset. Big government would also become impossible to sustain, federal government would find itself being downsized and regional and local government would find itself being expanded to take up the slack. **Only in a nation of individuals working for someone else can big government flourish**. When someone yields ownership of their income to someone else they will be willing to yield ownership of their political future to someone else as well. **When a man is responsible for his own economic welfare, he will also tend to be responsible for his own political welfare.** This also applies, by the way, to spiritual matters as well.

Individuals in such an economy will tend to be better educated, better read, better thinkers, better debaters, better leaders, better fathers and husbands and better Christians. They will be more community minded, more sensitive to the needs of others and more willing to pitch in to help. Imagine, if you will, the community work ethic and unity of the Amish and Mennonites, coupled with the best of the free enterprise system envisioned by Adam Smith. It would be a privilege to live and work in such a country. Above all else, **the moral character of such a country would be very strong.**

PROCLAIMING LIBERTY THROUGHOUT THE LAND

There is one more aspect of the fifty-year Jubilee Cycle that deserves a few moments of our time. Unlike the United States of today, Israel had slaves and bond-servants. **It would be grossly unfair to provide a man with the opportunity for economic freedom and a fresh start without granting him a corresponding political and personal fresh start.** For that reason if anyone had fallen so far as to not only have sold the family farm but also have placed themselves into indentured servitude, they would receive their own personal freedom at the same time that their property also gained its freedom. Right now that doesn't seem like such a big deal, but the Lord has dealt with me that **there will come a time in America where slavery in the form of indentured servants will exist once again.** This existed in America during Colonial Times. It will happen again during the Final Great Crash. I will deal with this issue in detail in **Chapter 5 – The Days of Joseph.**

EXPLAIN TO ME ONE MORE TIME HOW THIS STUFF WORKS

All of this can tend to become very confusing and hard to understand. Interest rates, land ownership, philosophy, economics, religion and heaven knows what else have been encapsulated into this book. Don't feel bad if you are feeling somewhat lost at this point in time. Explain to me one more time how this stuff works, you say.

Often, when I try to explain how property values and buying and selling property works in this kind of economy, I see people's eyes roll back in their heads. At the risk of throwing some of my readers into shock, I'd like to spend a little time illustrating how values for property were assigned using a fifty-year economic cycle. Let's refer back to Leviticus Chapter 25 once again:

" [13] *In this Year of Jubilee,* **each of you shall return to his possession**. [14] *And if you sell anything to your neighbor or buy from your neighbor's hand, you shall not oppress one another.* [15] **According to the number of years after the Jubilee you shall buy from your neighbor, and according to the number of years of crops he shall sell to you.** [16] *According to the multitude of years you shall increase its price, and according to the fewer number of years you shall*

> *diminish its price; for **he sells to you according to the number of the years of the crops**.*"

— *Leviticus 25:13-16*

I marvel at how the Bible can pack a complex theological, economic or spiritual principle into a single line and then just kind of shrug its shoulders and go on its merry way. Leviticus says that *"according to the number of years after the Jubilee you shall buy from your neighbor, and according to the number of years of crops he shall sell to you."* What exactly are they referring to, anyway? Now, for the third time, we run into a way of looking at things that is at total variance with the way the world sees and does things. This vastly different way of seeing things has to do with the assigning of **property values.**

APPRECIATION FOR DOING NOTHING...

For the last fifty years or more we have been in a real estate market in which property values have been steadily **appreciating.** That is to say that even with **no change to the actual property itself** property values have been going up steadily due largely to inflation and an almost relentless demand for more developed land and available housing. When I first wrote this book in 2006 it appeared that the Real Estate Bubble might have finally started to burst. Fortunes have been made all across the U.S. for years by simply finding a piece of land with some potential for development and then simply **sitting on it** until the developers caught up with the purchase. The whole Fix-and-Flip industry is based on buying a piece of property that is undervalued, performing some minimal level of cosmetic surgery on it and then *"flipping"* the property back out on the market for a quick-kill profit varying from a few thousand dollars to tens, hundreds of thousands of dollars or even more. On the other hand, the longer you hold onto a property the more the property is worth. I bought my first house in downtown Evansville, Indiana in 1973. It was rundown and was definitely a *"fixer-upper"*. We didn't have a lot of money, but we had a lot of *"sweat equity"* and worked hard to turn it into a house that we would be proud to live in. We had originally set up a ten-year plan to upgrade the house. But four years into the ten year plan an opportunity arose to relocate to a different community for a much better job offer. In only four years, our little home had increased in value by $13,500 to about $21,000 in value. The increase in property value was our walk-away profit almost to the penny and it also became our down payment on a much larger, much more beautiful home that we purchased in our new community. We lived in that new home for many years after that.

Then, in 2009, for the first time in a very long time housing values started to go down. It was inevitable. Housing had been massively overpriced for at least twenty years and it was only a matter of time before the hyperinflation bubble in housing had to release, in this case, violently. Three years after I originally wrote this book, in 2009, the housing bubble didn't just burst. It exploded with real estate values collapsing all across the country at levels varying anywhere from 25 percent to 50 percent or even higher in some regions. Southern California, Detroit and parts of Florida were the most severely devastated, along with Las Vegas. I know that in the community in which we now live house after house sat empty with *For Sale* signs on them. The current owners, often the bank to whom the original homeowners defaulted their mortgage, had more tied up in the home that it was worth on the market at that point in time. Now they were faced with a serious financial dilemma. Did they absorb the financial beating they often deserved and sell the house below the debt linked to it, swallowing the difference and a whole lot of pride or did they hold onto the home in the hopes that the values in the housing market would in some mystical way rebound? I originally thought that this was not very likely to happen, at least not in the near future. We were probably looking at a twenty-year period of deflation until property values returned to rational levels again. That meant that homeowners and investors were going to take a huge pounding for a very long time. In fact, one Sunday quite some time ago while I was coming home from church I spied a yard sale sign that intrigued me. It was only a few blocks away from our house so I swung by. I picked up a few little items in the process. But while I was there I struck up a conversation with one of the ladies who were handling the yard sale.

Everything in the home was for sale, from knick-knacks to wall hangings to furniture. I asked the lady about who had lived there. It turned out that the home had belonged to their grandparents who had at that time both passed away. I then asked them what they were going to do with the house itself. Would they fix it up and sell it or perhaps retain it as a rental property? It turned out that neither option was viable for them. Why? Because even in 2015, seven years after the explosive bursting of the housing bubble, the debt on the home was still more than the home was worth on the current real estate market. The solution for the heirs? To simply let the house return to the original lenders, the bank and let **THEM** deal with the headaches involved. Because of situations like this the Federal Government talked about buying up all the *"bad paper"*, defaulted mortgages and loans which were uncollectible and putting them into a Federal *"Bad Bank"*, further socializing and collectivizing our economy and tragically and mindlessly plunging our nation even further into inescapable debt.

Amazing enough, property values rebounded more quickly than I thought possible and once again, property values are rapidly escalating, often beyond reason,  because of irresponsible policy decisions being made by a *"Tax and Spend"* Democratic administration that sees no possible evil in uncontrolled inflation. Even our own hometown of Jeffersonville has been guilty of much the same monumental escalation in property values. For decades the community and the county in which we live struggled along under a self-franchised *"Good Ole Boy"* Democratic network of politicians who were great at feeding themselves from the public trough but not nearly so good at tending to the general welfare of the population and the city at large. Roads were a constant disgrace. Public infrastructure was badly neglected. Jeffersonville was considered a trampy, sleazy place to live. In county government, where I worked for several years as the Systems Administrator, trying to make 25 separate officeholders in their private little kingdoms happy, there were three almost lifetime politicians who worked out a brilliant scheme to stay in power. In our county government scheme (And believe me, scheming was a very large part of what they did!), officeholders were elected to a term of four years. They could then, just like the President of the United States, be elected for another four years. After eight years, they were no longer eligible to run for that office for a minimum of four years. That approach was designed to prevent career politicians from using the county offices as their own private domains. But these three politicos hatched an ingenious but highly unethical scheme to keep all three of them in office **PERMANENTLY**! How did they do it? Simple! Once they had arrived at their master plan, they waited until **ALL THREE OF THEM** were coming up on the end of their respective eight year terms in their various offices of Clerk, Treasurer and Auditor. Those three offices were the most important offices in the county system, wielded the most power and enabled them to exert the most control over **ALL** of the political processes in the county. They then made a pact with each other to **SWAP OFFICES** with each other in the upcoming elections. What do I mean by that? Well, let's take the office of County Clerk, for example. He knew that he couldn't run for office as the Clerk again for a minimum of four years. But nothing kept him from running for office as Treasurer! In turn, nothing kept the current person occupying the office of Treasurer from running for County Clerk, even though they knew that they had to wait four more years to be eligible to run as Treasurer. Head spinning yet? Oh, my friends, it gets better! The three conspirators laid out their plans as to the three-office rotation scheme and then calmly ran for the different offices that everyone knew they were eligible to run for. Since the county was strongly Democrat at that time, there were no Republican challengers to try and break the scheme up. And so for **DECADES**, these three Democratic officeholders would run for, win and stay in each of their respective offices for the eight years they were eligible for. And then, per the pre-planned rotational scheme they had concocted, they simply **SWITCHED OFFICES** for another eight years, then switched again and again and again…

THE BIG BREAKTHROUGH FOR MY HOME TOWN

This was the state of the city and the county until the Republican Party made some significant breakthroughs in the Mayor's Office for the city. A series of innovative, smart, largely selfless men were able to start a real turnaround in the city proper, but the county still languished under the Good Ole Boy network's control. But when Donald Trump ran for office, a remarkable thing occurred. An incredible number of Democratic moderates who were frankly disgusted at the mismanagement of the county decided to jump ship and vote Republican. Once they did so, they found themselves liking the results. And then came the big breakthrough. Way back in World War II, a huge tract of land lying between the Ohio River and the major local highway between Jeffersonville and Charlestown, a city with even more squalor than our own, had been used to test military weaponry, particularly shells to see if they would explode when they were supposed to. Needless to say, many didn't and so the old "Testing Grounds", as it was called, languished unused because the Good Ole Boy network didn't have the vision to run final tests over the ground to make sure that no unexploded shells remained beneath the soil. There was one more problem that stood in the way of the development of the tract of land and it was political but not the doing of those in local power. Almost every major city in the U.S. has a series of superhighways crossing it going largely north and south (odd numbered superhighways like I-65 and I-67 in Indiana) and east and west (even-numbered superhighways like I-70 and I-80). Most of those roads were built through the impetus of President Eisenhower and his immediate successors. As a General in World War II, Eisenhower saw the remarkable capabilities of the *AutoBahn*, the German superhighway built by Hitler to expedite rapid movement of military armament from the Eastern Front to the Western Front and vice versa. When he became president creating such a network of superhighways became a major goal of his administration. A decade or two later another need arose to assist those north/south and east/west routes. A need for a **LOOP** around most major cities became obvious. The explosion of superhighways triggered a corresponding growth in the trucking industry which triggered an equivalent growth in the availability of retail goods and services to American consumers. Without a loop around major cities, trucks and pedestrian vehicles were all forced into the downtown heart of the city and once again, major traffic congestion occurred. I remember as a boy of 16 traveling from Eastern Pennsylvania to visit a friend of dad's who lived in Central Illinois for our summer vacation. I also remember that it took us **EIGHT HOURS** to get through Wheeling, West Virginia because traffic was stacked end to end for dozens of miles on either side of the city. I remember it so vividly because it was the middle of summer, over 90 degrees, no clouds in sight and car radiator after car radiator blew up under the strain. In response to that need, bypasses, almost all of them ending in the number "5" began to be built. Indianapolis has I-465 as an example, Cincinnati has I-275 and Louisville, Jeffersonville being a satellite community, has I-265, with one notable exception. Because of the lack of vision on the part of Southern Indiana politicians and resistance from wealthy east side Louisville residents who didn't want their property claimed under the right of Eminent Domain, the final leg of I-265 from the Ohio River to north of our city had never been built. Finally, under urging by a new generation of politicians, the final leg was constructed. Prior to that, there had been no way for trucks and personal vehicles to travel effectively in and out of the area of the old Testing Grounds. But with the completion of the I-265 loop, that huge parcel of ground suddenly became very tempting for new industries looking for a fresh place to build a corporate headquarters, warehousing facility or factory and so almost overnight, with land made available inexpensively and with tax advantages provided by visionary city and county leaders, new companies began to flood into the previously abandoned and neglected piece of land. Since nothing occurs in a vacuum, the building of new corporations hiring large numbers of people led to a rapid influx of workers and their families, many of whom fell into the middle and upper-middle class range. They, in turn, needed stores to buy goods from, restaurants to eat in and, most importantly, homes to live in. There really wasn't any room for growth in old Jeffersonville, but Charlestown, on the other hand, had large tracts of land available for the building of homes. Suddenly a city which had frankly been a festering sore in Southern Indiana became the upscale place to build your home and, because the number of new workers pouring into the area outnumbered the housing available and new construction couldn't keep up, housing values in our area suddenly skyrocketed. Houses that would have sold in downtown Jeffersonville for $150,000 found themselves priced at $350,000 in the Charlestown area and even higher. I'm honestly not sure about how much the housing industry has rebounded in those ensuing years nationally, but I can tell you that as an ironic byproduct of growth and progress, housing in our area is vastly overpriced. The building, selling and marketing enthusiasm created by all of that will, of course, eventually run far past the need and accordingly, another mini-bubble will pop and suddenly there will be houses available and empty, prices lower and housing agents groaning in agony.

Inflation isn't the only factor in determining property values. Location is also huge. The old adage about real estate is that there are three important factors involved: location, location and location. The right house in the wrong neighborhood will be seriously devalued. A junker in a high income neighborhood will be worth three times what it should be. What I just described in the Jeffersonville and surrounding area is a classic example of that.

Housing values are seldom totally rational. But the market hasn't been largely rational for a long time. In ancient Israel, a totally different method was used in determining what a piece of property was worth. As we did earlier, let's look at several examples:

HOW MUCH IS THAT FARM IN THE WINDOW?

Let's go back to Johnnie Johannsen for a moment. Let's say that the 40-acre farm of his was truly located in

Israel, in the allotment for the Tribe of Dan. How would we determine how much that farm was worth?

The first thing that we would have to do was to determine what the **net annual profitability of the farm was.** How would we determine that? It's actually pretty simple. Let's say that we could grow a nice crop of corn on those forty acres, and that we could get one hundred thousand dollars a year for the crops that we could grow there. That would be our starting point. Then we would have to calculate the expenses associated with the same plot of ground. That would include seed, fertilizer, amortization for farm equipment and a wide variety of other factors, most of which should be safely left to the hands of a competent accountant. After all the smoke cleared, let's say for sake of argument that the total annual expenses associated with that plot of ground would amount to fifty thousand dollars. That would mean that the **net annual profitability of the farm would also be fifty thousand dollars** (one hundred thousand dollars of income minus fifty thousand dollars of expense).

Now that we would have calculated the net profitability of the farm on an annual basis we would need to determine **how many years were left before the next Year of Jubilee.** Let's say that the **last** Year of Jubilee had been in 2000. That would mean that the **next** Year of Jubilee would be in 2050. And let's further say that the year in which the calculation was being made was 2029. That would mean that there were at that moment in time about **twenty-one years of profitability left before the property would be returned to the original owner.** Now the math gets simple. If the property was capable of creating a net profit of fifty thousand dollars a year and we could keep sub-leasing the property for another twenty-one years the total value of the property **at that moment in time** would have been $50,000/year x 21 years or **ONE MILLION FIFTY THOUSAND DOLLARS!** You wanna buy my farm? **That** is what it will cost you! Obviously the further you were from the next Year of Jubilee the more the property would be worth. The closer you were to the next Year of Jubilee the less the property would be worth. That may seem strange to us but remember, at the end of the 50-year period the farm would go back to Johnnie Johannsen and his descendants, unlike our own economic system. So calculating a value for property in ancient Israel would have used a totally different set of assumptions than the rest of the world does. When God says that His thoughts are not our thoughts and His ways are not our ways, He isn't kidding! And when He says that they are higher, He isn't kidding, either!

That's how you would do the calculation for farmland. What if it were a suburban home? You would simply take what the house could be rented or leased for on a monthly basis and multiply it by twelve to get the annual value. Let's say that a home could be rented for one thousand dollars a month. That would make the annual rental value of the house twelve thousand dollars. Then just multiply that amount by the number of years remaining till the Year of Jubilee and you would have your selling price!

If it were a factory you would have to calculate the net profitability and off you would go again. Once you get a feel for this it really turns out to be pretty simple and a whole lot easier to understand than the dreadful Rule of 78's that we looked at earlier.

There are a few more things that we have to look at before we close this chapter on the Perfect Economy. Even though we have looked at some of the reasons why land is the basis of all prosperity, there are some additional reasons worth considering.

WHY IS LAND OWNERSHIP THE BASIS FOR ALL WEALTH AND PROSPERITY?

1. **It eliminates the largest source of consumer debt – <u>rent and mortgages</u>.**

How much do you spend on your rent, lease or mortgage? More importantly, what percentage of your monthly spendable income do you have to use up in order to keep the Big Bad Wolf away from your door or even to have a door to keep the Big Bad Wolf away from for that matter? According to the Federal Fannie Mae Corporation, you should never spend more than forty percent of your net income on housing. I know many people who spend far more than that just to have a roof over their heads. Many of them are on fixed incomes and really don't have a choice. Given the kind of games that bankers play with mortgages, it is becoming increasingly difficult to own a home **debt free.** Now bankers are offering Senior Citizens something called a **Reverse Mortgage.** This is great for the banker because he will end up getting your house for next to nothing when you pass on. If you don't have any living relatives that you would like to pass the house on to or if you simply have no other way of paying all your bills because of limited retirement income then it's not necessarily a bad deal for the older person. It allows them to draw on the equity in the home to cover monthly expenses not covered by disability, Medicare, retirement and other forms of senior-related income. The Senior Citizen is betting the bank that they will live long enough to exhaust all the equity in the house and then go to their eternal reward, leaving the bank with an asset with no real asset value. If the bank wins it ends up with a nice little piece of property that it can fix and flip. The truly bad news is that it takes an often completely paid piece of property and puts it back under a mortgage, making the bank the true owner again, one monthly payment at a time.

2. **It reduces the stress of <u>living and housing environments</u>.**

Years ago a major university on the West Coast did a fascinating and rather morbid experiment with rats and rat *"culture"*. The skeptic may say that it is rather doubtful that rats have any culture at all. On the contrary, it turns out that rats have a very complex and orderly society with strict *"moral"* boundaries of ethical rat conduct that are rarely ever violated. But then the scientists changed one variable in the rat culture. They increased the amount of crowding until it approximated the population density of a major U.S. city like New York or L.A. When the scientists increased the density of the rat population to equal that of the human population of a major city the moral structure of the rat culture began to completely break down. Gangs of rats began to form and attack individual rats. Gang rape of females also began to occur. Rat homosexuality also manifested itself, something that is never found in a normal rat population. The entire rat society broke down and began to manifest all the moral and social ills that our human urban cultures evidence. Why did this happen? It all has to do with **personal space.** Every creature has personal space. Different species have different tolerances for closeness. The more aggressive the species, the more personal space is required. Herbivores generally congregate in large herds - the larger the better, in order to protect themselves from predators. Carnivores also group together but generally in smaller units like lion prides. Carnivores are also far more aggressive. What is true for whole species is also true for individuals within that species. It even goes as far down as gender. Men tend to be more aggressive than women. As such, most men do not feel comfortable within the confines of large groups and tend not to seek such things as consensus. Male dominated organizations typically feature solitary leaders surrounded by those who implement their wishes. Female dominated organizations tend to make decisions in large groups, always seeking consensus usually while sitting in a circle. I have been in both kinds of organizations in my professional career and it is both fascinating and humorous to see how short a distance we have traveled from our primitive heritage when men hunted in small groups or alone and women gathered protectively in circles around the fire to grind meal, sew clothes or discuss the events of the day. Davey Crockett is once supposed to have said that when he could see the smoke from his neighbor's chimney in the sky it was time to move on. Given the extremely aggressive nature of our species, it is no small wonder that before the Flood, given a probable minimum surface population of between eight and twelve billion that men's hearts were continually focused on nothing but evil. The constant violation of our personal space caused a complete societal breakdown. It is also not surprising that after the Flood the Lord was absolutely insistent on mankind spreading out over the globe rather than focusing our attention and living space into one tightly congested area like the region surrounding the Tower of Babel. So important was this issue to the Almighty that two generations after the Tower of Babel in the days of Peleg the **earth itself was divided**, breaking the super-continent that geologists call *Pangea* into the seven continents that we know today. This isolated different groups of humanity from one another and prevented, at least for about six thousand years, a repeat of the conditions just prior to the Flood.

Families also require personal space. If a family does not own its own property and its own home it forces the members of that family into a proximity that will inevitably produce conflict because the individual members of that family are having their private space violated on a regular basis by other members of the family. The worst possible scenario in America is for two untidy teenage girls to have to share the same bedroom and wear the same size clothes. The opportunities for conflict are literally infinite. Let's take this a step further. Let's say that this same family does not own its own home or even rent a home but has been pushed by economic necessity into an apartment environment. Now not only are the members of the family potentially in conflict with one another but they are also potentially in conflict with those who live next door to them. Suddenly we have an irate neighbor pounding on the wall complaining about the noise being created by the argument between those two teenage daughters. Multiply this by an entire apartment complex and you are working on a police incident. Multiply this by an entire housing project with limited economic opportunity and clearly perceived inequality created by a TV that presents an affluent, largely white population to a poverty-stricken, largely African-American or Hispanic minority population and you have a ready-made recipe for riots, drugs, sexual immorality and eventually ethnic genocide. Having pastored both all White and all Black congregations and having worked in inner city areas I can see how obvious this housing crush coupled with economic inequality is. It does no good to preach to young Black men that they should all behave and be good little boys when our culture and our media constantly present to them a picture that tauntingly says, *"This is what we have and what you can never have!"* I know that in saying this I will offend some of my Indo-European readers. I can only reply that I, if anyone, was born and raised as a WASP (<u>W</u>hite <u>A</u>nglo-<u>S</u>axon <u>P</u>rotestant) with a totally Republican political orientation. I am not a liberal today but without abandoning my cultural and economic heritage I still must say that **until America provides significant economic change for its minorities any attempt at true spiritual revival will be hindered.** It is not without significance that the great Wesleyan Revival which is part of my spiritual heritage included not only heart-rending repentance for individuals but also massive social and economic change for England and America, the two nations in which it occurred. When all individuals and families are provided with their own land which they can manage as they see fit, hostility within and between families is greatly reduced. It can also be powerfully argued that in the same way war itself can be largely eliminated if the distribution of natural resources is perceived as being relatively equal between countries.

3. **It provides the <u>natural resources</u> for manufacturing of all raw and finished goods.**

As we mentioned earlier, during the 1970's, one of the favorite TV sitcoms in America was *"The Beverly Hillbillies"*, an apocryphal tale of a dirt poor Appalachian family that discovered oil on their land. The financial revenues from that discovery catapulted Jed Clampett and his unlikely clan into the totally alien existence of Beverly Hills and provided many generations of Americans with some great slapstick humor. The resources contained on or in the land drive the economies of the world. Even Solomon said that money is the answer to everything. Let me share a true story with you. Many years ago while serving as a Lay Minister in the United Methodist Church I had the privilege of pastoring some little country churches in Warrick County, Indiana. One of them named Fletcher Chapel was located like so many little Methodist country churches in the middle of a series of cornfields at the intersection of two little country roads. Over the passing of time church membership had both aged and dwindled until the church was reaching a point where it was no longer viable. The older members loved the church and couldn't bear to see it torn down. And then the Lord and a major coal company intervened. It just so happened that rich coal deposits were discovered in the immediate area. Many local farmers had sold their farms or subleased them to the coal company and were living off of the significant royalties of the natural resources located just under the surface of their fields. The coal company had been systematically buying up property all around Fletcher Chapel. Finally the inevitable occurred. The coal company made a very attractive offer to the little congregation. But the little congregation turned it down. They could not bear to see their precious little church torn to the ground so they made a counter offer to the coal company, a very interesting and unusual one. The company pondered the offer for a while. Then one day the fateful call came. The company had agreed to the unusual requests. What had the little congregation asked for? They had asked for three things:

a. That the coal company would provide up-front funds for the little congregation so that it could purchase a small piece of property on the main road that traveled from Boonville, the county capital, and I-64, the major interstate in the area and build a replacement church on that property, thus ensuring that the little congregation would have a chance to survive.

b. That the coal company would provide an ongoing royalty payment to the little congregation, thus helping it with its financial stability.

c. And most importantly, that the coal company would pay for all expenses involved in moving the precious little country church all the way to Boonville to a place called Thresherman's Park, a historical preservation area dedicated to protecting and retaining many of the historical aspects of the local region, and that they would pay for the complete renovation of the church, inside and out, restoring the building to its original glory.

A few years after these events transpired I had the privilege of driving back down to Warrick County to see how it had all worked out. Sure enough, as I drove down Highway 62, the connector road between Boonville and I-64, there stood the new Fletcher's Chapel, a tidy little brick church with a modern look to it, apparently still going strong. And then when I reached Boonville I pulled into Thresherman's Park. There was the little country church, perfectly restored including the highly unusual church-in-the-round pew arrangement that had been the primary reason for preserving it. It has since been placed on the Historical Register as one of a kind in the whole Midwest.

Even though I was the only one in the church at the time I could still feel the presence of the Holy Spirit lingering in the building. In this case, ownership of the land and the resources it contained had proven invaluable. Even though they did not retain ownership of the ground and it is today part of a massive strip mine, everything of value on the land was rescued including both the building and the necessary function that it had played. It was clearly a win-win situation for everyone involved.

Now take this incident and play it back, generation after generation, in an economy that regularly returns the basis of all natural resources to the family that originally owned the land. With control of natural resources back in the hands of the individual instead of some corporate conglomerate, wealth flows backwards toward decentralization, making economic prosperity more uniform with the rich getting poorer and the poor getting richer, again providing balance in all things.

4. **It provides all <u>precious gems and metals</u>.**

How would you like to own a diamond mine? How about a gold or silver mine? Would doing so change your economic perspective? Obviously. As in the example listed previously with natural resources, the ownership of almost all gems and precious metals is once again found in the hands of large, multi-national corporations. With the return of baseline ownership of the land to families and individuals it puts control of the land and those assets back into the hands of the people. At this point I probably sound like one of those *"Power to the People, Man!"*-style hippies of the '60s and '70s. Guess what? I was! At one point in my life I had shoulder-length hair and a full beard, dude! But even now it only makes economic sense for the individual and not the corporation to control the economy. Economic manipulation in the form of subtle psychological advertising would become a thing of the past. If Mega-Corp wanted access to the south 40, then, by golly, they would have to pay a pretty penny for the right to dig in the ground out there, and, oh yes, they would have to put everything back where they found it and in better condition than they found it when they were done with it at the end of the 50-year cycle or somebody else would get a shot at it the next time around. We cannot begin to grasp what returning the land to the people would do to our entire economic infrastructure. As I have written this book more and more things have occurred to me as logical implications of what God has said we were to do and I marvel more and more at His infinite wisdom and knowledge.

5. **It controls all <u>transportation and movement</u> of goods and services.**

Remember that I just mentioned that when I was sixteen my parents and I took a trip from Nazareth, Pennsylvania all the way to Flora, Illinois in the middle of summer. Several images from that trip stand out in my mind to this day. The first image was the amazing Pennsylvania Turnpike where vehicles could go up to 60 MPH on four lanes of **almost** repaired highway for six hours, the full length of the state. I remember the Howard Johnson restaurants along the way, with terribly inflated gas prices (thirty cents a gallon!) and the worst food in the world. I also remember spending those eight horrible hours stuck in Wheeling, West Virginia where all east-west traffic came to a halting bottleneck because of the mountains. I also remember passing a four-door sedan in Illinois with one minor flaw – no doors! Things have changed a lot since then. Only one thing has remained constant – the Pennsylvania Turnpike is **still** under construction. It will remain under construction during the entire Millennium for all I know. Now, as we mentioned, vast superhighways crisscross our nation and have revolutionized the transportation industry. But all of those good and services which cross our nation on these six-lane wonders have one thing in common: the land on which they rest once belonged to someone. In some cases the owners of those properties were forced to sell their land for ridiculously low prices. In some cases states simply claimed the right of Eminent Domain and seized the property from their owners. But what if the Biblical model of land ownership was in place in the U.S.? It would be impossible for land owners to be forced to sell or to have their property seized out of hand. We might still have the superhighway network we have today but individual landowners would be profiting on a continual basis from the fact that those highways ran over top of their right of way. Since individual ownership of property is one of the most foundational rights of Biblical law violation of that law as it has been done in the United States would never be allowed to happen.

6. **It provides all <u>food</u> and <u>water</u> consumed.**

When informed that the peasants of Paris were starving and had no bread, Marie Antoinette supposedly said with flippant unconcern, *"Let them eat cake!"* According to legend that callous remark triggered the French Revolution. It wasn't the only war or revolution to ever be triggered by food and water shortages. Although we grow a pittance of our foodstuffs hydroponically the overwhelming percentage of all our food comes from the land and always will. As the population of our planet burgeons toward the explosion point of eight billion, the availability of food becomes increasingly more important. In fact, the 3rd Seal in Revelation involves the collapse of the wheat and barley crops in the Northern Hemisphere of our planet. This is followed by the 4th Seal of plague and famine, which in turn triggers the 5th Seal, the global persecution of Christians referred to by Jesus as the Tribulation. I know that's probably not what you have been taught from the pulpits of the churches you have attended. Just read Revelation for yourself for a change, just like I did and see what conclusions you draw if you approach the subject with a clear mind, clear heart and no previous assumptions. I think the exercise will rock your world.

Think food isn't important? Consider the following Biblical fact as well: near the end of the 7th Seal, the Euphrates River literally dries up into seven small streams and then completely evaporates so that men can cross over the dry riverbed. When Turkey and Iraq drew up plans some years ago to create a massive series of dams to gather the waters of the Euphrates into an exclusive property by creating what is now called the Ataturk Dam, Iran, downstream from them, threatened to go to war over the water that they would then be denied. We know from the Biblical account in Revelation that the sun will scorch the earth during the 4th Bowl Judgment. Whether this means an increase of solar activity or a change in the earth's orbit, either way, it will have devastating effects on the availability of water. It is not without significance that the total drying up of the Euphrates River comes just two Bowl Judgments later in the Sixth Bowl Judgment. We say that we need many things, but, if the truth be known, all we really need are four things: food, water, clothing and shelter. He who controls land ownership controls all four of those constants.

When all is said and done the implementation of these two seemingly simple laws in our world would have astronomical impact on the economy of the world. Unfortunately Israel never bothered to model the full program to us so that we could all see how wonderfully it worked for all parties involved. But take heart. As I have been studying the Millennial Reign of Jesus Christ, the 1,000 year period of time where Christ personally rules over the whole world, I have come to some interesting conclusions. One of those conclusions is that all of these wonderful economic models will finally be implemented during that time. It will be a time of great peace, prosperity and unity. With the threat of war removed and temptation in the form of the devil and his unholy crew safely locked up in the Abyss the monies which our world has had to devote to military and police activities will be fully available for the reclamation of our planet in a near-perfect world utilizing a near-perfect economy. Having said all of that, however, we must now turn our attention to the **rest** of the story, as Paul Harvey used to say. Now we must deal with what has happened in our world in general and in the U.S. in particular because we have not followed these simple economic rules. Now we must look at **Chapter 3 – K-Waves and the Coming Crash.**

K-Waves And The Coming Crash

Chapter 3 | K-Waves And
The Coming Crash

S o far this little book has been a pleasant trip down the placid river of theory. Chapter One was dedicated to helping you understand what **biorhythms** are all about, including their basic nature and the inevitability of their occurrence. Chapter Two was all about what might have been if Israel had actually obeyed the Word of God and modeled God's perfect community and **perfect economy** to the rest of the Gentile world. And so far, none of this should have been very threatening to you. But now things are going to suddenly get ugly. The storm clouds are going to gather. Lightning is going to strike. **And disaster is going to come.** Because when we are done exploring what are called **K-Waves** you will know beyond a shadow of a doubt that not only **can** another crash occur but that it **will** occur within our lifetimes and when it does it will **trigger the first truly global economic collapse of mankind's history.** You will also understand beyond a shadow of a doubt that this massive global economic collapse will be accompanied by an equally massive **global crop failure, located primarily in the Northern Hemisphere.** These two events, paralleling the Great Depression of 1929 and the Dust Bowl of the 1930s, will turn the world against the Christian community and trigger a global persecution of all Christians and Jews which the Gospel of Matthew and the Revelation of Jesus Christ both label as the

Tribulation. This will occur during the **5th Seal** in Revelation and be followed by the cataclysmic events of the time referred to in both Matthew and Revelation as the **Great Tribulation** or **6th Seal**. Only at the end of the horrific events of the 6th Seal will the prepared portion of the church be removed in the event which all of us have come to know as the **Rapture.**

Still reading? Haven't run away shouting *"Heresy! Heresy!"* at the top of your lungs? Good. Now sit down if you aren't already sitting and get a notebook out to write on or please feel free to make notes all over this book since you bought it (borrowers, beware!). What we are going to be discussing is going to be technical in nature and I am going to run a great many facts and concepts past you in this chapter. You don't have to understand **everything** we say here but you must understand the **core concepts** in order for you to be able to tie all of this together. Now let's roll up our sleeves and get to the task at hand!

Nikolai D. Kondratieff 1892-1938

WHAT'S A K-WAVE?

After the Bolshevik Revolution in Russia in 1917 and the accompanying Russian Civil War from 1917-1920 the newly formed Communist government set about to try and prove its economic theories. Among the things which Vladimir Lenin and his cohorts wanted to prove was that capitalism as an economic system was doomed and would eventually wither away and be replaced by a classless worker's society. In order to do so they enlisted the help of a Russian economist named Nikolai Kondratieff. His job was to research economic patterns all over the world in order to prove that communism's basic tenets were correct. Unfortunately for both the Bolsheviks and Kondratieff they hired an honest man.

Being a diligent man, Kondratieff began to study world economic behavior all the way back to 1789. As he began to analyze the data that he had in front of him several things became increasingly apparent. Despite the doctrines of his employers the facts of the matter proved conclusively **that there would never be a collapse of capitalism and the free enterprise system.** Instead his research proved that **world** and **regional** economies behaved in what he called self-correcting **Long Waves.** These Long Waves involved regular patterns of alternating cycles involving rapid growth, plateaus and crashes. It seemed that if left to itself capitalism would **never** fade away and that this idyllic worker's paradise envisioned by Lenin, et al would never come to pass except at the point of a gun barrel. When Kondratieff presented his findings to his superiors their reaction was predictable. The incredible truth that he had discovered was quickly suppressed and Kondratieff was rewarded for his diligence and honesty with a *"promotion"* to a new and more challenging academic opportunity in **Siberia!** Poor Nikolai was unprepared for such adversity and his health eventually gave way. He died in exile sometime in the 1930s, a victim of ignorance and brutality.

Somehow Kondratieff's work survived him and his Long Waves eventually became known as **Kondratieff Waves** or simply **K-Waves.** What Kondratieff had discovered by accident was the incredible fact that although Israel and the world had never accepted the 7-year and 50-year economic cycles found in the Bible those cycles were running the world economy **with or**

without their approval. What Kondratieff discovered was that economies around the world tended to reset themselves **violently in the form of a crash every 53-56 years.** Had he been a student of the Holy Scriptures he would have automatically recognized the **Year of Jubilee** as the driving force behind these cyclical crashes. Simply put, if we had done what God had told us to do and instituted the 7-year releases of debt and 50-year return of property ownership it would have reset the economy in a **controlled fashion** instead of a **violent one.** I can still remember when the Lord showed me the connection between these two events. I was surfing the net for something, heaven only knows what and I stumbled across K-Waves. As I began to read and study more about them I immediately saw the connection. I tell people that I have the **revelation by inspiration, but the confirmation by investigation.** And that's exactly what I did, pouring through everything I could find on K-Waves. What I discovered was fascinating. It was also disturbing. I found that the Great Crash of 1929 and the following Great Depression were not the only time these events had happened in the U.S. In fact, it was the **third time that the economy of our country had crashed, all in cyclical patterns involving a gap of slightly more than 50 years!** I also discovered that K-Waves were **inevitable and absolute.** They had nothing to do with politics, speeches, programs or any other such nonsense. Not even the mighty Alan Greenspan could stop the inexorable tide of time. These were matters such as were described by Solomon in Ecclesiastes. These patterns were part of a plan which was grander than the lifespan of mankind, they were **Biblical Biorhythms.** In fact even as we speak we are overdue by over 40 years for the next crash. Why the delay? We will get into that in **Chapter 4 – The Alpha Female.** Suffice it to say that when this 4th crash does come it will be with a violence and scope unprecedented in the history of civilization. It will not only impact America, it will impact the entire world. How do I know all this? We will discover how as we walk through the pages of this book. For right now, let's get back to the topic at hand, K-Waves.

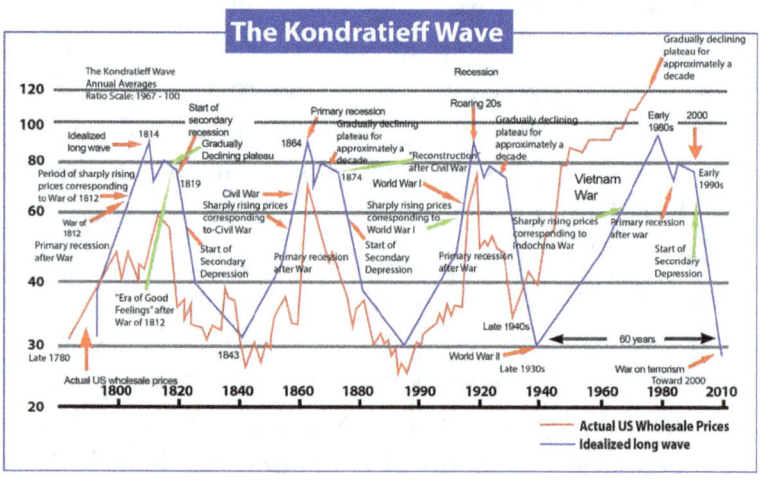

WHAT DOES A K-WAVE LOOK LIKE?

There's an old Chinese proverb that says that one picture is worth a thousand words. So in keeping with that thought here is a very interesting graph I found comparing ideal K-Wave cycles with the actual K-Wave cycles that the United States has experienced. You will find it to be very educational and, in a certain sense, also very disturbing and more than a little chilling once you realize the implications of the two cycles.

In the graph the ideal K-wave is represented by the blue line. You can see that it rises and falls in absolutely perfect symmetry. That kind of result **NEVER** happens in the real world because of other outside factors including other K-Waves elsewhere in the world whose actions impact the K-Wave being studied. The red line represents the actual K-Waves that have occurred in the history of the United States. This is typical of nature and the real world. There is always a theoretical, perfect model and then there is real life. Because cycles in real life are affected by a million different factors they are never perfect but are always predictable. That's because the driving forces behind these basic biorhythmic cycles are so immense that they cannot be prevented by other temporal factors, only altered slightly around the edges, if you will. My basic understanding of these super-massive cycles actually comes from the pages of one of the greatest of all science fiction writers, the late great Dr. Isaac Asimov, inventor of the now-famous Three Laws of Robotics and possibly the author of more great science fiction short stories and novels than any other writer in the history of the genre. Among those brilliant works was a trilogy called, respectively, ***Foundation***, ***Foundation and Empire*** and ***Second Foundation***. The novels trace the rise of a new field of science called ***Psycho-History*** created by a brilliant researcher named

Hari Seldon. Seldon's premise was that the history of mankind and, for that matter, all history, was shaped by certain inexorable patterns which were predictable not only in grand terms but also eventually in terms of actual human lives. The development of this new discipline would eventually take thousands of years. Seldon saw the coming inevitable destruction of the Galactic Empire of which he was a part, followed by a devastating ten thousand year Dark Ages period similar to what happened after the fall of the Roman Empire on Earth. Seldon's research indicated that if small strategic changes were made along the way it could shorten this impending Galactic Dark Age from ten thousand years in duration to a *"mere"* one thousand years. The three novels center around a mysterious organization called ***The Foundation*** whose job it is to bring about these necessary changes and to prevent any future such crashes. Does this bear a vague resemblance to a subject that we have just been talking about? As always, great science fiction always borrows its themes directly from the Bible. I was captivated by the scope of the novels and intrigued by the concept that such super-cycles could exist and exert such an influence over mankind. Equally intriguing was the thought that these cycles could be **analyzed**, **predicted** and **proactively anticipated**, thus altering or bending slightly such cycles. Although at that point in my life I had neither the tools nor the Biblical insight necessary to understand what was happening there was something on the inside of me in what I now know to be my spirit man that instinctively, intuitively responded to this concept as being **foundationally** and **fundamentally true** (forgive the bad play on words!).

Later on as I became a serious student of history I began to see common threads in the rise and fall of all the great world empires. There were indeed common patterns which were present when any nation rose to world power and there were also other, different patterns that were just as predictable when a nation began its inevitable decline into the dust of history. The more I studied the matter the more firmly I became convinced that **something** had to be behind all of these patterns driving them. At that point in my life I somewhat jokingly say that I was not yet fully converted. I had received Christ as my personal Savior when I was 7 and had a personal supernatural revelation of Him when I was 16 but then lapsed into a period of about 9 years where I was on the run from Him. After turning back to Him again when I was 25 and being baptized in the Holy Spirit when I was 29 I embarked on a major campaign to make up for lost time. I read the Bible constantly. I underlined, double-underlined, circled, margin noted and commented on the Scriptures so much that during my peak period of learning, I had to give my Bible away every two years and get a new one, because I had underlined all the *"good parts"* by that time. Then I would take a new Bible, usually a different translation and pen and ruler in hand gleefully begin the process all over again. It was during one of these learning frenzies that I stumbled across the two key driving economic cycles of 7 and 50 years. Suddenly I understood why Asimov's work and the writings of such great men as Adam Smith had such an appeal to me. All of them were quietly, calmly pointing the way back to the Word of God and the Eternal Principles outlined by the Eternal God which would stay in place for all eternity, because that's where they originated from.

Before we move on to an analysis of the various components of a K-Wave I want us to turn back to the chart we just looked at a few minutes ago. In fact, for the sake of ease of reading and to avoid having to flip back and forth constantly between two pages, let's look at that same chart again, only more closely. I chose to have this book printed in color because many of the charts and maps rely on color to be more readable. In addition, the full Kondratieff Wave chart is very hard to read. When printed in 5"x7" book size, the lettering is totally unreadable and that is unacceptable. As a result, I have divided the graph into four separate mini-graphs, three for the full K-Wave cycles that our nation has already experienced and a fourth for the current, much, much larger K-Wave that we currently find ourselves in. Why is this fourth wave so much larger? Ah, my dear friends, that is what we are about to find out!

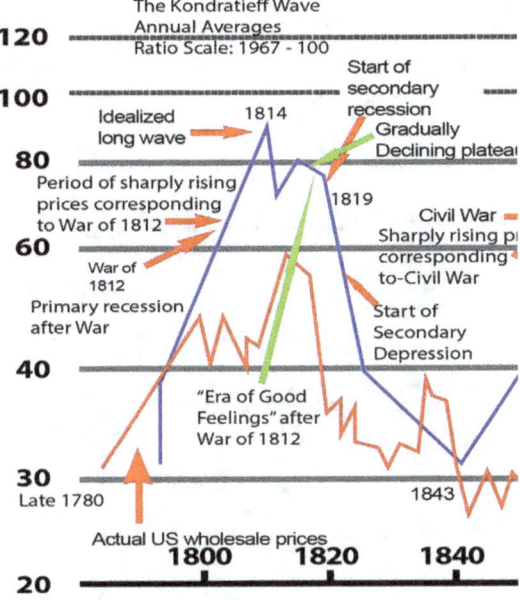

The Kondratieff Wave
Annual Averages
Ratio Scale: 1967 - 100

120

100

80

60

40

30

20

Idealized
long wave

1814

Start of
secondary
recession

Gradually
Declining plateau

Period of sharply rising
prices corresponding
to War of 1812

1819

Civil War

Sharply rising pr
corresponding
to Civil War

War of
1812

Primary recession
after War

Start of
Secondary
Depression

"Era of Good
Feelings" after
War of 1812

Late 1780

1843

Actual US wholesale prices

1800   1820   1840

Notice that in the first K-Wave that the U.S. experienced the actual wave was slightly out of sync with the ideal wave and had kind of a hiccup as it moved toward its peak. There was also another hiccup on the way into the depths of the crash which followed. Since the U.S. was relatively small and weak in terms of the world economy it was possible for **outside factors** to influence the cycle, creating **anomalies** along the edges of the cycle but not **preventing** the cycle from occurring. This first cycle centered on the **War of 1812** when America was beginning to assert itself on the North American continent. As such, other cyclical patterns occurring in other dominant nations such as England and France would have played a major role in influencing our own economic cycle. Remember that critical fact. It will play a major role later on in this book in explaining why the fourth crash has been delayed and why it will be so much larger.

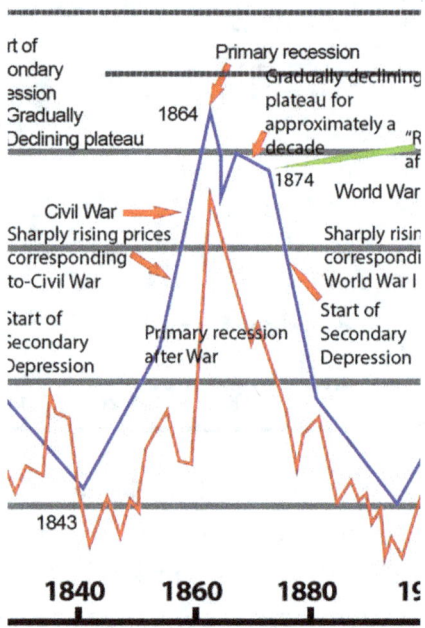

In the second K-Wave centering on the **Civil War** notice that the behavior of the actual K-Wave is much closer to that of a *"pure"* K-Wave. The reason should be obvious: America now was the **dominant economic and political power in the Western Hemisphere.** The War of 1812 had effectively ended Britain's attempt to retain dominance over North America and Spanish and Portuguese influences in South America were waning rapidly. The only issue left for America to decide on was whether or not we would expand toward the Pacific Ocean divided and in a state of constant internecine warfare between the North and the South or united with a single mind and purpose. In the next chapter we will discuss the enormous impact of the Civil War in determining America's destiny. Once it was determined that the United States of America would stay united our own K-Wave cycle became dominant for us with virtually no outside influences. Instead, our own cycle now became strong enough to become influential in the K-Wave cycles of other nations surrounding us. Our **Sphere of Influence** began to grow. America had already issued the **Monroe Doctrine** in 1823, telling the European powers to keep their noses out of the Western Hemisphere. In the document, we essentially told them it was now **our** backyard and no longer their concern.

When we encounter the third K-Wave, we find an unusual variance in the pattern. Once the crash with which we are all familiar occurred our economy went into a tailspin just as it had in the two previous crashes. But if you study the graph closely you will find that it didn't plunge to the depths of the two previous crashes. We'd like to think that things were bad during the 1930s. *"Buddy, can you spare a dime?"* was the theme of the times. Yet, as bad as it was it wasn't as bad as the two previous crashes. The recovery period began much more quickly. And most importantly there has been no fourth crash, which should have occurred in about 1980. What happened? Why was the Great Depression cut short? Why has the inevitable fourth crash been delayed? We'll find out why in our next chapter. But don't jump ahead just yet. Resist the temptation to jump to the next chapter to find out. We'll discover how Flash Gordon survives the crash of his spaceship. But before we do, we need to do some of that **confirmation by investigation** stuff that I talked about earlier.

WHAT ARE THE CHARACTERISTICS OF A K-WAVE?

Trying to see a K-Wave is kind of like walking up to a painting and putting your nose directly on the canvas. If you are too close all you can see are smudges of paint. It's only when you step back away from the picture that it starts to come into focus. Suddenly you can see that those smudges of paint are actually houses with windows and roofs and little chimneys with smoke curling up out of them. The same is true of K-Waves. They are easier to see on a global scale than on a national or regional scale. Although such smaller loops exist they are much milder. In fact **the size and impact of a K-Wave is directly proportional to the political and economic clout of the nation that is experiencing it.** As an example if we went back to a time where there were no dominant nations in Europe during the Bronze Age the K-Waves would have been very small and regional in nature, centering on such city-states as Athens, Carthage and Troy. As such, the Athenian K-Wave would have been occurring at variance with the Carthaginian K-Wave and also out of sync with the Trojan K-Wave. But when the city-state of Rome began to dominate the area surrounding the Mediterranean Ocean, its combined military, political and economic might began to synchronize all of these other mini K-Waves into one combined heartbeat. After the collapse of the Roman Empire, things once again fractured and became virtually invisible again. The more we move toward a global economy based on the economic well-being of a single Alpha-dominant nation, the more obvious and visible the K-Wave associated with that nation becomes. When America was still just thirteen colonies struggling to survive it barely had an economic heartbeat of its own. It was instead dependent on the umbilical cord of its mother, England. As such, it was controlled and dominated by the nation that nurtured it. But by the War of 1812 the child had been born and was strong enough to have an economic heartbeat of its own.

A SLOW START-UP PERIOD / WARS AND RUMORS OF WARS

K-Waves always take the general shape of an **S-shaped growth curve**. There is always a **slow start-up period** as the next wave begins to gather strength and a little momentum. **Wars and revolutions** are more likely during this period of time. Sometimes this period is referred to as the *"Springtime"* sub-cycle, generally taking about 13 years to complete. Perhaps you have already noticed that each of our three previous K-Waves center around a **major defining war** in our nation's history. The **first** K-Wave included the **War of 1812.** The **second** K-Wave included the **Civil War.** The **third** K-Wave included **World War I**. Also please notice that in regard our own country that **each successive K-Wave has triggered a war of increasing violence, scope and intensity.** What does that tell you about what will be associated with the fourth and final K-Wave in the history of our planet? Can you say **Armageddon?** Consider the following: America is currently the dominant nation in the world. Most of the world's economy is based on our own. When we go down everyone else goes down with us with a few significant exceptions. **And the magnitude of the war that follows will be equal to the magnitude of the economies that crashed at the same time.** If you are not genuinely concerned at this point then I am genuinely concerned for you. Perhaps you just haven't been listening. It's not a matter of **if.** It's a matter of **when, how bad** and **how long.** Yes, the **Final Great Crash** will trigger the **Final Great Awakening** which will trigger the **Final Great Persecution** which will trigger the **Final Great Escape** which will trigger the **Final Great Takeover** which will trigger the **Final Great Battle** which will trigger the **Final Great Victory.** For those of you who think that I am an unbridled pessimist, please understand. I am neither a pessimist nor an optimist. I am a **realist.** Benjamin Franklin put it this way: *"Optimists are doomed to eternal disappointment. I, on the other hand, expect only the worst, and then, when it does not occur, am delightfully surprised!"* Despite Ben's tongue-in-cheek comments it does no good for us to stick our heads in the sand and pretend that these things are not going to come upon us. The Pollyanna-ish attitude that the

America church has toward suffering causes me great concern. Because I am in frequent contact with the 3rd World I know the true extent of the global persecution of the church and I also know that it is increasing, not decreasing. There will come a day and not too far away when being a Christian in America will be politically incorrect to the point of imprisonment and execution. Civil liberties in America are rapidly becoming a thing of the past. There will come a time when words like *"God"*, *"freedom"* and *"liberty"* will be stricken from our government. How do I know that? By revelation. Through inspiration. But confirmed by investigation. Bear in mind that I wrote these words all the way back in 2006. Now, over 17 years later in this updated version, the events I predicted are already well on their way to complete fulfillment. When I first began preaching and teaching about these matters, I was often laughed to scorn by those around me who were supposed to be *"in the know"*. I actually had one so-called *"Spirit-filled"* individual stick his fingers in his ears and start shouting, *"La, la, la, la!!!"* as loud as he could when I was trying to tell him what was coming. Years later he would be murdered by his drug-addicted son because he wouldn't give him his drug money as usual. Such is the price for compromising the Gospel of Jesus Christ and His Holy Word. And such is also the price for being a prophetic voice. You see things coming that others, blinded by the activities that swirl around them, cannot. I'll be honest. It hurts. A lot. But I knew what God had shown me and, like the prophets of old, there was a fire burning in my heart that would not be quenched unless I spoke out regardless of the response I received to what I said. But in the last ten years or so, I have noticed a distinct change in the spiritual atmosphere of the American Church. Pastors that for decades had been pounding their pulpits espousing the doctrine of a Pre-Tribulation Rapture have suddenly now begun to speak of impending persecution and have amazingly finally remembered that our Lord Himself said that in this world we would have tribulation but to be of good cheer because He had overcome the world. And now, after 40 years, as the Babylonian armies began to surround Jerusalem, Jeremiah was suddenly no longer some crazy old fool. Now the very king who had burned the scrolls containing his prophecies was meeting with him in secret pleading for some sort of prophetic word to help him escape his demise. Sorry, my friend! It's not gonna happen! **I TOLD YOU SO**, didn't I??? Please forgive me. These issues burn so strongly in my heart that I sometimes get off topic. But this is not just a treatise designed to move your **head**. It is an impassioned plea with enough facts to, God willing, move your **heart.**

Having said all of that, let's get back on course. During the slow start-up period wars and revolutions are more likely to occur. The nation or group of nations experiencing this part of the cycle will have a sense of **youthful vigor** much like a teenage boy with **more energy than sense**. There will also often be a sense of **Manifest Destiny** associated with this period. The nation involved will see itself as destined to rule, expand and control by God or the gods or nature or natural selection or the universe or whatever force they acknowledge as being in general control of their lives. When we went into World War II many of our boys had belt buckles with *"God is With Us"* inscribed on them. When we began to capture Germans as prisoners of war and confiscate their personal belongings we were shocked to find their belt buckles were inscribed with the German phrase, *"Gott mit uns!"* For those of you who don't know any German, it means *"God is With Us"*. Sadly, both sides were firmly convinced that God had sovereignly ordained them to carry out their divine destiny. Ironically it may well be that both sides were actually right in a bizarre sort of way. Here's a troubling thought to chew on: Without World War II there would be no Nazi Final Solution. Without the Nazi Final Solution there would be no concentration camps, no gas ovens and no slaughter of six million innocent Jews. Without the slaughter of six million innocent Jews there would be no gripping moral conviction in Europe and America that we must somehow make amends for letting all of this happen. And without any gripping moral conviction in Europe and America there would have been no nation of Israel created in 1948 in a single day just as Isaiah had prophesied. Do yourself a big favor. Don't linger over this train of thought too long. You are probably staring at a truth that is too big and too disturbing for the average person to deal with. There is always a necessary chain of events which must take place for a certain result to be obtained.

Sometimes the turn in the direction of the chariot of time requires just a gentle nudge. Sometimes it takes a whack across the side of the head with a two-by-four. The Nazi abomination was the whack that it took to birth Israel out of America and Europe. We had been jointly incubating her for a long time just as Egypt had incubated her once before during her initial birth. Now in her second and final birth before the return of the Messiah another slap was necessary to separate the child from the womb and start it breathing on its own. We are in very deep water here, dear friends. I may be handing you more meat than you are prepared to chew on just yet in your walk with God. If that is the case, then simply put aside what I just told you, wrap it up in an air-tight Ziploc bag and stick it in your spiritual freezer until your teeth come in fully and you are able to chew and digest something a little stronger than milk. I must tell you this: the further I go into writing this book the more revelation the Holy Spirit is pouring out to me. There is no telling where all of this will lead. We are on a journey of exploration together. And there are times when I have no more idea what is going to happen next than you do. Let's find out together what the Spirit has to say to the churches.

A PERIOD OF RAPID GROWTH

At the same time that wars and revolutions are occurring, a period of **rapid growth** also occurs. Again, the parallel between the nation involved in this process and a teenage boy is absolutely uncanny. I can remember when I hit my growth spurt. As a freshman in high school I was a little butterball. I was five feet, four inches tall and 185 pounds. I went out for football and had my left knee destroyed on the third day of practice when a 230-pounder fell on it sideways. Everyone called me a quitter. I never underwent surgery but I used 125 pounds of weights, a barbell, a couple of dumbbells, a piano bench and Strength & Health Magazine to rebuild my body. At the same time I was working out privately at home I began to grow. Dramatically. I would come home and drink an entire gallon of milk straight out of the refrigerator. In one year I grew seven inches. I reported for football the next year at five feet eleven inches tall and 185 pounds but now I was seven inches taller and solid muscle instead of wobbly flab. The head coach came up to me and said, *"Who are you?"* I replied, obviously, *"I'm Ray Young!"* The coach looked me up and down carefully, and then said, *"No, you're not!"* It's true! I'm not making this story up! It really happened! It took me several minutes to convince him that I was who I said I was. I won't comment about what that says about some sports coaches but in retrospect I can kind of see why he might have had his doubts. Given the dramatic change that had occurred in me over a single year, I am sure that the coach envisioned me at about six feet, six inches tall and 260 pounds by the time I was a senior. Sadly, that never happened. I never grew another inch in my life. After a close loss to a heavily favored opponent in my senior year during which I had played a supposed all-state lineman to a draw, the coach took me aside, congratulated me for my performance on the field and then said, plaintively, *"Youngie, why the h*** didn't you ever grow?"* Unfortunately for both of us, I had no answer to the question. I did end up being the only member of my graduating class to play college ball on scholarship, so it all ended well.

A LEVELING OFF PERIOD

After the period of fast growth a **leveling off period** occurs. The parallels between K-Waves and the human growth cycle are simply amazing! After I grew like a weed I stopped. Period. That leveling off period will last for a variable length of time but it will always be followed by a period where things start to **slowly decline** with no means of stopping the slide. A young man will grow like a weed from about the age of twelve to the age of twenty or so. He will then stop growing. From the age of twenty till about the age of thirty his relative strength and stamina will stay the same. He will probably gain a little weight. His cardiovascular health may decline due to decreased physical activity. He will become more injury prone. Oddly, a man's physical strength will continue to grow during this period and even extend into his forties and fifties if he maintains a strict regimen of exercise. All the great power lifters tend to be in their thirties and forties whereas sports that require speed, agility and eye-hand coordination tend to peak in the range of their twenties and thirties. Someone like baseball's Barry Bonds was an extreme rarity, no doubt enhanced by steroids. And just like a man a nation will eventually begin to decline in vitality and no amount of exercise and no number of nutritional supplements will stem the tide. This period of time is often referred to as the *"Summer"* phase of the K-Wave and often also runs for approximately thirteen years.

A PANIC

Eventually, a trigger event will cause a **panic.** In 1929, it was the failure of a single rogue bank in Chicago that had made way too many speculative loans to debtors who had little or no prospects of ever paying them off. Frightened by the obvious instability of the bank, depositors made a run on the bank demanding their deposits back in full. But the bank was critically overextended and had nowhere near the cash on hand necessary to satisfy them. The bank went to its principle financier hoping that he would bail them out. But, typical robber baron of the times that he was, he callously told them that they had made their bed and that they now needed to lie in it. They had made the high-risk loans even though they knew better. Now the time to pay the piper had come and there was no escape. In the same way, America was living an equally risky lifestyle and She knew it.

She had been brought up properly and knew better. She knew right from wrong. She knew that flappers and bathtub gin were not exactly pleasing to the Almighty. Even though She was having a good time during the Roaring Twenties, there was a general sense of uneasiness about it all. It was almost as if She were living in denial, but continuing to party even though She knew that morning would bring a man to the door who would demand that She pay the price for her sins. Adolf Hitler would be the piper She would have to pay. And since **financial stability in an economy not based on a gold standard is built solely on confidence in that economy** when one solitary bank crashed it triggered a ripple of fear through the American psyche. Suddenly every bank was experiencing runs on it even if its financial lending policies were soundly conservative. None of the banks had the cash on hand in the vault to cover a complete refund demand. Most of their monies were out on loan making money for the banks. That's how banks do business. They use **your** money to make **their** money. It's a well-known principle in the financial community and it even has an acronym associated with it: **OPM** or **Other People's Money.** The panic in the world financial community in 2009 was almost equal to the level of fear that gripped the country in 1929, over ninety years ago. The difference between then and now? **Federal involvement**. In 1929 the Federal Government did little or nothing to assist the banking industry, leaving it to rise or fall on its own strength. From 1929 to 1933, **40 percent** of the nation's banks failed while the Federal Reserve remained aloof, allowing a harsh recession to cascade into a banking collapse and a disastrous drop in the money supply of our nation. Cash plus bank deposits dropped by more than one-third nationally. Out of that calamity came such things as the FDIC (Federal Deposit Insurance Corporation) and FSLIC (Federal Savings and Loan Insurance Corporation), mandating that the first one hundred thousand dollars of any investor's deposits were automatically guaranteed by the Federal Reserve and also mandating that the banks hold a larger share of investor's deposits in house to weather any potential banking run. As a part of the stimulus package under Obama that one hundred thousand dollar guarantee was boosted to two hundred and fifty thousand dollars in an attempt to calm panicky investors and depositors. Unfortunately, even that **787 billion** dollar stimulus bill would only **temporarily** stabilize the financial marketplace. As hard as the U.S. was hit, foreign banks and markets were hit even harder. It is estimated that global stock markets lost over **6.5 trillion** dollars on October sixth and seventh of 2008. Hard to imagine?

Iceland, a nation whose entire financial structure and economy are built on their international banking business and who had carefully crafted itself as an international banking center, nearly had to declare bankruptcy **as a nation!** European markets plummeted **38 percent**, Latin American markets dropped **40 percent**, Asian markets dropped a staggering **60 percent** and Russian markets fell an astounding **67 percent!**

I would not want a nation as unstable as Russia is right now with its whole arsenal of nuclear weapons armed and ready at all times to undergo a financial meltdown. Heaven only knows who would rise to power in such a situation. As of this current update, an arrogant, often bare-chested, macho leader holds sway in Russia, a man known as Vladimir Putin. In February of 2022, he launched an invasion into the Ukraine, which was once part of the greater U.S.S.R. The Ukraine is the breadbasket of Europe with the same black, loamy Chernozem soil that we find in the U.S. and Canada, ideal for growing wheat. Remember, dear friends, what crops will fail in the 3rd Seal. Can you say **wheat** and **barley**??? The Ukraine also contains vast deposits of many other natural resources, something that Mother Russia does not have and desperately needs. Putin thought that the war would be over quickly, a *"one and done"* kind of affair, but the Ukrainians, proud of what their nation has been able to achieve since they gained their freedom back in 1991 when the U.S.S.R. collapsed, have actually fought back with such intensity and fervor that the unorganized, unprepared young men that Russia hurled into battle untrained and unmotivated have literally collapsed back on themselves. Now, much to Putin's dismay, the battle is raging in the other direction. It is our fervent hope and prayer that God grant the Ukraine total victory and that they regain every inch of ground seized by the Russians, in the Mighty Name of Jesus! Why would we be so intensely interested in the Ukraine? First of all, because the Ukraine has a higher percentage of Jewish people than any other nation in Europe. Massive efforts on the part of Israel have been undertaken to fly as many of them to safety as possible because Israel all too well remembers that violent persecution of the Jews came not only from Nazi Germany but also from Russia. That persecution is a central theme of the world-famous play and movie, *"The Fiddler on the Roof"*. Second of all, because as I write these words, a major revival is breaking out in the Ukraine. Christianity shines the brightest when the world around it is the darkest and times of crisis are used by God to bring people to Christ. Such is the situation there right now. Finally, because it is the same exact tactic that Adolph Hitler used when he invaded Poland and Czechoslovakia, claiming the German people needed **lebensraum** (Literally, *"living room"*), defined on the web as *"The territory that a state or nation believes is needed for its natural development, especially associated with Nazi Germany."* If the frightening similarity between the two men and the two nations does not make your blood run cold, you have not been listening. Go back and read what I wrote again. And again. And again.

The last time something like this happened Hitler rose to power in an economically devastated Germany and precipitated Europe and America into the most devastating war in the history of the planet. As time has gone on the European Union has seen a disturbingly high number of member nations come frighteningly close to bankruptcy. Greece borders on near-insanity, careening between the need for extreme austerity measures and the violent protests of the individuals affected by those measures. Spain isn't much better off. Unfortunately the proponents of universal socialism, where the needs of the individual from cradle to grave are handled by the society in which they live, are finding out much to their dismay that you have to **PAY** for those privileges. My son-in-law and good friend Ed lived in Europe for over 40 years, working initially as a NATO translator and later on in his own company and finally as the City Manager for a town in Italy of over 30,000. Did Italy have cradle to grave health insurance? Yes, they did. What did that require from a taxation point of view? How about **50% of your annual income???** That's right! The Italian government takes 50% **or more** of each individual's income in order to provide that kind of support. And yet, even that is not enough. Italy has survived multiple mini economic crises that keep toppling the government in power only to be replaced by a new coalition just as shaky. All of this requires more money and more money which requires higher and higher taxes which in turn strangle individual and corporate initiative which then **REDUCE** the amount of cash available to tax which triggers violent protests which inevitably produce a totalitarian state with limited amounts of cash and perpetual, universal poverty except for the privileged few. In a well-intentioned attempt to take care of **EVERYBODY** the society ends up taking care of virtually **NOBODY**.

A CRASH

And so the panic turns into a **crash**. Once the course has been laid in there is no turning back. The economy has spent itself to the point of no return and now it enters into a period of rapidly declining health eventually leading to economic death or at least a serious coma. After the cycle has reached the bottom of the loop the process begins all over again, this time with a new set of players who usually know nothing about the previous cycle and so are doomed to replay the same events over and over again, mindlessly making the same mistakes. This cycle takes between **50 and 60 years** to play out only to crash again and then rebuild again and again and again. Only with knowledge of the characteristics of a K-Wave can we begin to anticipate and recognize these trends so that we can at least be prepared when these events come to pass. To be **forewarned** is to be **forearmed**. And as a prophet it is my unfortunate job to tell you what I see coming toward the city from my vantage point atop the watchtower. My greatest heartache is that most of those I warn will take no heed to what is being said to them. All they can see is the marketplace around them. Times are good. There is much merchandise to sell. But when the soldiers break down the gates of the city there will be no goods to sell and no buyers to buy them. That's why being a prophet is such a lonely business. A true prophet of God tells the people what they **need** to hear rather than what they **want** to hear. But down in the streets there are many who claim to be prophets of God Most High. They too say that they have been to the watchtower. But they have spent no time in solitude staring out into the desert night. Their eyes and ears are not trained to sense the subtle changes in the wind nor to pick up the distant sounds of men shouting and horse's hooves pounding on the road miles away. And so these men who call themselves prophets tell the people what they want to hear. That all is well. That the economy will expand forever. That prosperity can be continuous even though history stands in mute rebuke of their lies. As the Holy Spirit cries out for repentance, America and the church move blindly on toward the edge of the precipice unaware and unconcerned about the abyss which lies yawning in front of them. Eyes that cannot see. Ears that cannot hear. Hearts that have hardened themselves toward the Still Small Voice that could prepare them for what is to come. I pray as we continue this message that your heart is open, your mind is ready and your ears are listening. Because even though these things must come to pass it is still possible for you, dear reader, to prepare yourself and your family for the inevitable, **to have a plan which can rescue you while others around you perish.**

Please forgive me. I have tried so hard to make this into a purely economic work but the Holy Spirit will not let me do so. In the final analysis, **everything is Spiritual.** And so this book will be a strange blend of Adam Smith and Nikolai Kondratieff and Isaac Asimov and Moses and Jesus and Heaven only knows who else. But I will guarantee you two things: **(1) everything I tell you will be Gospel truth and (2) these things will surely come to pass.** Let the others tickle your ears. **I am here to save your soul.** Now, having preached to you as the Holy Spirit dictated that I should do, let's move on and look at K-Waves more closely.

WHAT ARE THE PHASES OF A K-WAVE?

1. **The Expansion Phase (The Spring – 13 years)**

   ✓ New technology is rapidly put into use
   ✓ Production of goods increases

- ✓ Greater prosperity
- ✓ Higher prices
- ✓ New satellite countries are brought into the "loop"
- ✓ Produces an increasingly global economy
- ✓ Changes occur in gold production and monetary circulation
- ✓ Most wars and revolutions occur during this phase
- ✓ Unemployment falls
- ✓ Production increases
- ✓ Wages and productivity rise
- ✓ Accumulation of wealth and high consumer spending
- ✓ Technology is refined and absorbed
- ✓ There is an increase in new construction and the availability of durable goods
- ✓ Trough War – "Inspired" and limited war early in the Expansion Phase
- ✓ Peak War – Result of the government trying to stimulate the economy - defense spending
- ✓ "Guns and Butter" Economy

It doesn't take a great deal of insight to see how these patterns clearly apply to the United States. If you look at the economic history of our country since the turn of the 20th Century you can see these patterns at work as the U.S. grew and began to exert a global influence both politically and economically. It is at this time in the K-Wave that any nation feels robust and energized. Things are good. Wages are up. Productivity is up. We are finally beginning to realize the Great American Dream of a three-bedroom, two-car garage ranch-style home in suburbia. I was born in 1948 just after the end of World War II and in the same year that Israel was born. As I look at the points in history which have occurred since then I can see my own life pass by. And with a little help from the history books I can travel back in time to look at the most significant Peak War in recent history, World War II. Remember that earlier I mentioned that the Crash of 1929 didn't stay *"crashed"* long enough to fit the chart? There were two reasons for that and both of them are disturbing. When an economy has stalled and can't restart government steps in to lend a hand. That's how it was in the Great Depression. The U.S. government began to spend money it didn't have in order to create public works projects. These projects were designed to put many of the men who were unemployed back to work in some kind of quasi-meaningful job. I had the unexpected privilege of encountering one of those WPA-created projects as I was walking along the Ohio River one day. Before we moved back to Jeffersonville from the Cincinnati area we decided to visit our family there. While there, I decided to take a little stroll along the Ohio River through downtown Jeffersonville. As I was entering into a new area which was still under construction I came across a plaque on a pedestal. I paused for a second to read it and was astonished. All along the walkway were beautifully chiseled stones, perhaps three feet wide by five feet long by one inch thick. It seems that in the 1930s the Federal Government had initiated a project to cut these stones out and use them for a landing area where the local ferry came across the river from Louisville. I paused in my reading of the inscription on the stone and smiled. It was hard for me to imagine only a single ferry boat servicing the metropolitan Louisville area when today there are four bridges servicing the area with several more planned as I write these words. Here was unexpected, mute testimony of the very thing I had been writing about just the day before. Unlike the current generation who seem quite content to sit and do absolutely nothing while on the public dole, men in that day defined themselves as providers and breadwinners by working for a living. Even the Bible says that if a man will not work he shall not eat. Sadly that concept seems to have gone by the wayside in today's culture. As I drive through Jeffersonville and neighboring communities, I see *"Now Hiring"* signs **EVERYWHERE**. Driven partially by the fear of Covid and partially by repeated government handouts of free cash, many individuals seem to have lost all desire to hold down even a part-time job. I find that reprehensible and irresponsible. When I was in college I sometimes worked as many as **THREE** jobs at the same time. Did I eventually collapse from exhaustion? Yes, of course. But even when I worked for others in the computer industry and particularly when I had my **OWN** company, I often put in an 80 hour work week. I have worked as a pastor with any number of job retraining organizations and their common complaint is that it is difficult to get people who want to work anymore. I personally know of situations in the inner city where we have three or even four generations of families who have never worked a day in their lives and who have absolutely no desire or intention to work so long as public monies are provided to them. This is equally true for Christians and non-Christians, sad to say. I know of way too many women who attend church regularly, shout for the Lord and then go out and continue to have child after child out of wedlock because it is financially to their advantage to have a child periodically and thus stay eligible for public assistance. All protestations notwithstanding, if you sit down with the average inner city pastor and ask him what the chief sins of his congregation are, sexual immorality will rank right up there with drugs and crime.

But in the 1930s most men still had a certain amount of self-respect and wanted to work. So the government created jobs. Lots of low-paying, menial jobs which could easily have been done with far fewer men and a little heavy equipment. But it was not efficiency that the government was after. It was trying to provide a sense of self-worth to a great many very frustrated men. There was a Catch-22 in all of this well-meaning WPA style employment, though. You see, government should only spend money that it has available to it. That money comes from taxes on the American worker and the American corporation. But what if the company is bankrupt and the worker is unemployed? Where then does the money come from? If you are an individual it is a difficult thing to deal with because historically you can't spend what you don't have. But not so with a government. If there isn't enough money to fund a project all you have to do is **print some new**

money! Suddenly you have enough in the budget to fund all those public works projects. It seemed like a perfectly reasonable solution to the problem. Unfortunately all it did was to create a cycle which we are still paying for today. It triggered the beginning of an inflationary spiral which we are still living in. I can clearly remember the first Arab Oil Embargo in 1973. Prices for gasoline rose to the obscene level of **seventy-three cents a gallon!** At that point America should have awakened to smell the coffee and actually done something about the situation. Instead, as soon as the crisis abated, our legislators slipped back into their usual mindless bickering and squabbling and accomplished nothing. As a result gas prices have risen steadily since that time until we have the highway robbery that we are enduring today. For a brief period of time gas prices skyrocketed in this country all the way to four dollars a gallon and more. But we did not have it as bad as many European countries, some of whom were paying as much as seven to ten dollars a gallon. The destabilization of the world financial markets temporarily suspended this exorbitant and unethical boosting of prices and when I edited this section of the book back in 2003 prices had dropped back to slightly more than two dollars a gallon. Those prices continued to escalate until by 2014 the average price of gasoline had risen to $3.37. The price then abruptly dropped for two years and then began to climb rapidly again. In a web article by the New York Post on November 15th, 2022, they reported that under the Democrat Biden administration gas prices had **doubled** since Biden took office in January of 2021. Prices skyrocketed to $4.86 a gallon, twice the price of gas when Biden took office at $2.39. As of this current update and the day in which I am writing this, the national average price for gas is $3.77, but on the West Coast, prices range from $4.09 a gallon to $5.43. In the Northeast it's not much better, with prices ranging from $3.84 to $4.08. Now stop and think. Americans were outraged back in 1973 when the price of gas skyrocketed to **seventy-three cents a gallon!** What should be our reaction today to what is happening, not just to the price of gasoline but to every single thing we need to live? Should this be tolerated? We have been led down the road to slaughter by a bizarre combination of Big Oil betrayal and irrational far-left policies. Big Oil's unholy alliance with the Arab nations has betrayed the very country that gave them birth. Their profit-driven actions are close to treasonous. And in our own generation two Presidents from the great state of Texas have failed to rebuke or curb them because their own pockets were lined with oil money.

By printing more money, the US government also created a serious problem with the value of the US dollar. Up until 1973 the US dollar was based to a certain extent on a one-to-one ratio with equal gold assets supposedly located in Fort Knox. But Richard Milhous Nixon finished taking us off that gold standard and did permanent, irreparable damage to the viability of our currency in the world exchange system. As long as one paper dollar was backed up by one dollar's worth of gold our currency was invulnerable to outside influences. But after the dollar was disengaged from a physical, tangible asset of equal monetary value it meant that **our currency was only based on confidence in the economy that produced that currency**. That's why there are exchange rates for every currency in the world. The exchange rate between the US dollar and the India rupee is currently running at an exchange rate of about 81 to 1. That means that one US dollar is equal to eighty-one Indian rupees. That's great if you're sending money from the US to India. It makes us all look very rich to folks over there. As a contrast, we have friends who live in Australia. Their exchange rate runs about forty-five to one so one Aussie dollar (and they use dollars, not pounds like England!) is worth about forty-five Indian rupees. As you can clearly tell our economy is far stronger than India's economy and slightly stronger than Australia's economy. But all of those factors are recalculated constantly and are all based on the world's perceptions of the relative strengths of each of the economies involved. Now suppose that a crash were to strike the United States. Since our dollar is no longer tethered to a gold anchor it is free to float or sink based on how the world views us. An economic crash would destroy the value of the U.S. dollar in the marketplace. Things which are readily available to us for next to nothing because they are made overseas would suddenly become much, much more expensive. It is these disparities in relative economic strength that have driven much of the manufacturing process overseas in the last few decades. In fact, and we will talk about this elsewhere in the book, China's "Long Game" is to replace the U.S. dollar with the Chinese Yuan (their version of the dollar) as the international currency base. Back in 2013 they took their very first step in that plan by teaming up with India to form a Far Eastern version of the IMF, the International Monetary Fund. Within two years of the announcement of their plan, 57 nations had signed onto their project including Britain, Germany, Australia and South Korea.

Printing money without a foundation of precious metals to back it up wasn't the only problem, though. Once our government had established a pattern of spending money it didn't have it was only a matter of time until the US taxpayer followed suit. We will explore the enormity of the Federal Debt and the equal enormity of US personal debt in detail later on in this book. The truth still remains the same. We simply followed the lead of our government. Almost all financial decisions, both governmental and personal, are based on impulse and short-term need and not on long-term economic wisdom. We have totally disenfranchised ourselves as a nation in just over fifty years by simply spending money that we did not have. How did American taxpayers follow the lead of their tax-and-spend governmental leaders? We couldn't just print extra money although I personally know of one backslidden pastor's son who actually set up a counterfeiting ring in the office of his dad's abandoned church. What mechanism did the American public use? **Credit cards!** A huge percentage of the American public are living beyond their means, spending more than they make by simply charging the overage onto one of their dozen or so credit cards. I don't want to steal the thunder of an upcoming chapter, though, so I'll stop right here on that subject.

The other factor that helped the U.S. recover prematurely was that fact that we **went to war.** It would be ludicrous to suggest that the United States somehow fomented World War II to help get us out of the financial ditch we were in. Former Russian demagogue Vladimir Zhirinovsky, who died recently in April of 2022, suggested that this is what actually happened in his violently Anti-Semitic book, *The Last Break* (or *Dash*) *Southward*. If you want your blood to run cold, go online to *Wikipedia.com*, look him up and read his bio, his quotes and his theology/philosophy. Anyone who lost a son or a daughter in that horrible war would be justifiably outraged by such a suggestion as would any member of the world Jewish community. But what **did** happen was that it pushed the US into a **guns and butter economy.** For those of you who are unfamiliar with that term, it refers to the fact that the U.S. manufacturing community, which was largely moribund after the Crash of 1929, was galvanized back into life by the need for military armament, hence the term **guns.** The **butter** part of the phrase refers to the basic foodstuffs required in the civilian and military economy. Ironically, the origination of the phrase goes all the back to World War I, Woodrow Wilson and famed orator Williams Jennings Bryan when a conflict arose regarding whether monies should be spent on the military (guns) or domestic concerns (butter). Once the manufacturing community in the U.S. had been galvanized back into life by the military needs of the war it kept right on running. All the Public Works deficit spending of the 1930s never really solved the problem. In fact, if not for World War II it might have taken an extra 20 or 30 years for the US to fully recover from the crash. In another one of those perverse twists of history we actually created and *"solved"* our own problem. What do I mean? Follow this chain of events carefully. It is another one of those very disturbing trains of thought that I will introduce to you periodically throughout this book. During the Roaring Twenties America was living in willful disobedience to God. It's one thing for any nation to live in rebellion to God. Many have in the past and still do today. However when a nation is **founded** on the principles of the Bible and says that it is **one nation under God** and has **In God We Trust** printed on its currency it's another matter altogether. We have said for over two hundred years that we are God's nation. No other nations have ever made that statement in the history of the world except Israel, England for a period of time and surprisingly the African nation of Zambia, which categorically states that they are a Christian nation in their own Constitution. When a nation claims that it belongs to God and actually makes a reasonable attempt to live for God it will receive certain inevitable blessings. America has been greatly blessed during its history, more so than any nation in history other than Israel. But when a nation says that it belongs to God it also garners to itself certain responsibilities toward God. If a child is misbehaving in the grocery store and that child belongs to someone else it is irritating but it is not your problem. However if that child is **your** child then it becomes your responsibility. By saying that we belonged to God, we then created a situation where disciplining us became God's responsibility. And in the Roaring Twenties we were being a very bad child. As such the Lord struck us twice, first with the Stock Market Crash and second with the Dust Bowl era of the 1930s. After about ten years America became duly repentant and experienced a time of significant revival. It's a good thing that it did for America's moral fiber would be severely tested in the 1940s by the Second World War. If America had not been morally right with God going into that war, we would have lost. It not a widely known fact, but the Germans almost had the A-bomb before us. They had the computer before us as well as the V-2 rocket and the first jet fighters. The decisive battle of the war, the Battle of the Bulge, hung in the balance and was decided by a very small band of highly courageous soldiers who held the line against the German counteroffensive. Two of my uncles were in that battle and I remember the tales that they told. If the truth were known we were very close to defeat time and time again. What if a German U-boat on a suicide mission had surfaced in New York City harbor with an A-bomb strapped on its back? What if it had been the Big Apple that had gotten nuked instead of Hiroshima? How would that have changed the outcome of the war? And what if it had happened again just a few weeks later in Washington, D.C., located conveniently on the Potomac River, just off the Atlantic Ocean? Like I said earlier, I will introduce some disturbing thoughts into your mind during this book. Stop for just a moment to shudder and then move on. Let's leave that thought for just a moment, though and roll the film backwards in time to the crash of '29. I have said before that America was to some extent indirectly responsible for World War II. How could that be true? Because when our own economy collapsed in 1929 it aggravated the hyperinflation already in effect in Europe courtesy of the onerous financial pressures put on Germany after World War I to repay their *"debt"* to England and France for the cost of the war. In 1920 one U.S. dollar was equal to 64.80 German marks. Only three years later that ratio had skyrocketed to **four trillion, two hundred billion** marks for a single U.S. dollar! Yes, you read that correctly! Despite U.S. counsel to the contrary, in May of 1921 England demanded reparations in gold to be paid by Germany in annual installments of **two billion gold marks plus 26 percent of the value of Germany's exports!** No nation could sustain such an enormous financial drain. It forced Germany off of the gold standard. Once its base currency was disengaged from a tangible asset like gold the value of the mark immediately collapsed taking the German economy with it. By 1923 prices in Germany were **doubling every forty-nine hours!** German workers began to demand that they be paid daily and not weekly because of the rapid drop in the value of their money. As the collapse escalated workers demanded that they be paid **twice a day** so that they could go out at lunch to buy food for the evening meal. Why the rush? Because by the end of the day the value of their wages would have been **cut in half as prices doubled.** That hyperinflation destabilized the Weimar Republic in Germany and led to the eventual rise of Adolf Hitler, who brought the horrors of World War II into our lives. If America had been living right during the 20's perhaps the crash of the 30's would not have happened or might have been much less devastating. If that had occurred instead, Europe and Germany might not have been turned upside down. If there had been a stable German economy the Weimar Republic would have been strong enough to crush an unstable ex-paperhanger's political dreams. However, that did not happen. Hitler did arise. America was forced into World War II. Our economy was kick-started by the need for guns and butter. It's as if the Lord said to us, *"You can do this the easy way, or you can do this the hard way. It's up to you."* Sadly, America chose the more difficult of the two roads that diverged in a snowy woods just as most of us tend to do.

2. **The Peak Phase (Summer – 13 years)**

   ✓ Affluence causes a shortage of goods
   ✓ Production becomes strained

- ✓ Work attitudes change, for the worse
- ✓ Prices go up
- ✓ Profits go down
- ✓ There are economic strains and rapid inflation
- ✓ Economic stagnation sets in
- ✓ The economic mood becomes much more conservative

Most of you who will read this book will be younger than me. As I edit this current update, I am 74 years of age. So many of the things that I have talked about in the present tense may seem like ancient history to you and may be difficult for you to identify with. They may seem like the ramblings of an old man. That may be so for the moment but you may find yourself changing your mind when they begin to happen all over again, as they surely will. In fact, the characteristics of the Peak Phase have to strike a chord of familiarity in your hearts because you have experienced them in just the last twenty years. Let's go through the checklist and see if I am telling you the truth. Has affluence caused a shortage of goods? Not really until recently when consistently illogical economic policy decisions by a deluded Democrat administration have plunged the entire nation into shortages in every possible category from toilet paper to foodstuffs. Up until recently, we were able to dodge shortages in goods because we have been able to outsource most of our production into the Third World. As a result from a **global** perspective there has been no shortage of goods flowing into the United States and globally production has not become strained. But within the United States work attitudes have changed, drastically, for the worse. I don't have to go back to the 50's in order to track the erosion in work attitudes. All I have to do is walk into the personnel office of any corporation in the U.S. and talk to the Personnel Director. I had my own computer company for twelve years. During that twelve year period I employed many students from my own university computer science program where I was also a tenured faculty member and Associate Professor of Computer Programming Technology for eighteen years. I also taught business classes at a university level and as a result I approached the writing of this book from both a business and a ministry standpoint. But back to those students. I hired only the brightest and the best out of the computer program at the university. I hired individuals that I thought had a reasonable level of moral integrity. But in all of those twelve years I only had **two employees that I felt I could trust with the keys to the front door and the cash drawer.**

Finding employees who think about the good of the company first and themselves last is close to an impossibility and has been for the last twenty years or so. Now, stop and think about your last ten retail experiences. Have they been positive? Have the individuals who attended to your needs been concerned, committed, clean and competent? C'mon, now, be honest! How many times have you walked out of a retail location vowing to never do business with them again because of the total lack of professionalism and concern in the people that you had to do business with? When I both had my own company and was also teaching at a university level I called it the ***Chimps, Chumps and Champs Principle.*** It has been my experience that ninety percent of the people that I dealt with in the computer industry were either ***Chimps*** or ***Chumps***. They either **didn't know** or **didn't care** about my problem and in many cases successfully combined both characteristics yet still somehow managed to retain their jobs. Only in ten percent of the individuals I encountered did I find a ***Champ***, someone who **cared about their job and knew what they were talking about.** Every time I found an individual like that I immediately got their full name, their phone extension, a direct phone line number if at all possible and an email address. Why such a frenzy of activity? Because they are so hard to find, even more so today in our modern *"Slacker"* culture. In solving a problem the last thing I want to do is to wade through nine people who don't have a clue or give a care until I finally find a new Champ. No sir! No thank you! By the way, there's a corollary rule to all of this which I call the ***90-10 Rule.*** It has also been my experience as I have studied history and dealt with people in business, education and ministry that **ten percent of the people in this world cause ninety percent of the problems and ten percent of the people in this world create ninety percent of the good.** The other eighty percent of the world's population are just along for the ride, neither significantly contributing to nor significantly diminishing the well-being of this planet. That may seem a bit harsh but take a look at your own life. Of all the individuals you have met how many of them have significantly impacted your life either positively or negatively? In the ***Screwtape Letters*** by famed Christian author C.S. Lewis, the demon writing the letters complains that there are hardly any good, meaty souls around anymore, great saints or great sinners and that everyone is just so **bland and tasteless** as the demon devours their souls. (By the way, I highly recommend that book for reading. Even though it is technically fiction, I strongly suspect that many of the ways, means and motivations of the demonic realm have been properly analyzed by C. S. Lewis. As I compare my own experiences with demons, and yes, I have had a good many of them, to what he writes, I find us in almost complete and total agreement. You can easily find the book online.)

So much for work attitudes. Now let's look at some things that need no explanation or documentation. **Have prices continued to escalate?** Yes? **Have profits continued to go down?** Yes? In the last decade have we seen **economic strains** and **rapid inflation?** Yes, except for the brief but dramatic resuscitation of the American economy under President Donald Trump. Has **economic stagnation** started to set in? Yes again? And has the mood of the country started to become much more **conservative?** Unfortunately, that last sentence is a loaded question. The **HEART** of America, the central portion of our country along with the South and much of the Southwest, has definitely become more conservative. Common sense still generally rules in our part of the world, my wife and I being residents of the State of Indiana. While other regions of the country are effectively bankrupt, the State of Indiana **ONCE AGAIN RAN A SURPLUS**, spending **LESS** than it took in, using the money wisely and, amazingly, **RETURNING A PORTION OF THAT SURPLUS TO ITS CITIZENS ONCE THE FISCAL YEAR HAD ENDED**. For those of you who live in states that are less wisely run, I invite you to come to Indiana. We run our state government on what we legitimately receive in taxation, both from individuals and corporations. We do not run the state on an irrational *"tax and spend"* or *"print extra money you don't have"* policy. For a long time, the state has been run wisely by either conservative Democrats or Republicans. As a result, once our state pays all the bills and takes care of all the projects, **THERE IS MONEY LEFT OVER**. And wisely, since that money **CAME** from the good people of the state, it only stands to reason that that same state should **RETURN THE MONEY TO WHERE IT CAME FROM**. Friends, I call that good business!

The flip side of that loaded question is that the East and West Coasts of our country have become money pits, swallowing up not only what their own citizens produce but also constantly trying to eat into the legitimate revenues of other parts of the country. Much of California and the surrounding area has become a giant welfare state, with undocumented and illegal aliens comprising a large portion of the population. New York, Pennsylvania (the eastern, urban part) and the surrounding region on the East Coast have followed the same mindless, irrational path. Unfortunately, the masses that live in urban areas on the East and West Coast who have become used to generations of public assistance, living on the federal dole, have no desire or inclination to work. And since Democrat administrations have for decades gained office by giving away money, often to those who really don't deserve it, these same people readily vote Democrats back into office again and again, knowing that the public trough will be open as long as that party stays in office.

As a result, our nation has developed a split personality. One personality is conservative, works a job and tries to live by common sense rules, often by those found in the Word of God. The other personality is a far-left, radical personality built on the principle of ***"No Absolutes!"*** Everything to them is **RELATIVE**. That makes the assignment of values in a situation a **TOTALLY SUBJECTIVE MATTER**. To them, there are no Ten Commandments, not even *"Ten Suggestions"*! There are no black and white rules of conduct. Anything anyone does is acceptable as long as it seems right to them. Without realizing it, their portion of America has ironically reverted itself right back to that old Black Book of Standards that they deplore, right back to the chaotic time of the Judges in the Old Testament. In Judges 21:25, it says that *"In those days there was no* *king in Israel;* (No central, unifying standard and no individual to enforce that standard) ***everyone did what seemed right in his own eyes"***. That describes the morality (or lack thereof!) of the Radical Left to a *"T"*. Part of America is trying desperately to get its foot on the brake pedal because it can see us running right off the edge of the cliff. The other part? Gleefully stomping on the gas pedal and shouting, *"Full Speed Ahead!"* Knowing what I know now, I shudder to think how all of this will end. I do need to apologize for something, though. Sometimes I wander far afield in my discussions and writing. I become involved in a story and that leads to another story which leads to yet another. Please bear with me. Every story I tell, every side comment I make, I do so in order to share with you some of the things that the Lord and hard experience have taught me over the years. Now, back to K-Waves!

As things start to become stretched beyond the ability of the economic surge to carry them forward people begin to sense that something is wrong. At first it isn't an alarmist kind of thing. It's just a general uneasiness, a sense that things are starting to head in the wrong direction. It is also accompanied by a general awareness that something needs to be done. Perhaps we need to stop living so high off the hog. Maybe we need to start paying off those credit cards. Unfortunately, this response, while valid, will prove to be **too little and too late** when all is said and done. Because our political leadership is a classic salute to situational ethics and the quick fix we can expect no significant political

Moses to arise from that direction. After then-President Obama was elected, he repeatedly told Americans that they would have to *"put away childish things"*. It soon became obvious how little authority or impact this new austerity message would carry when it found itself facing entrenched, established *"Good Ole Boy"* networks, replete with Pork Barrel politics and ear-marked projects by the hundreds, if not thousands, which always end up in any proposed budget.

In the early days of American politics ministers of the Gospel played a major role in every aspect of our political spectrum. Pulpits thundered with sermons espousing or castigating one political view or another. Unfortunately most pastors today are so overwhelmed with trying to keep the church mortgage current and keep the offerings and membership up that there will be little visionary support from that direction. Add to that the fact that most pastors are horribly ignorant of economic issues and you can see why very few voices of leadership arise from within the religious community. Sometime pastors will become politically involved but without the underlying economic understanding required to know what to do if they actually get elected. Even if they do, our current Cancel Culture, established by the far left, has made it an offence to voice any opinion not solidly in line with the current political *"RightSpeak"*. We have become disturbingly similar to George Orwell's novel *"1984"*. It would appear that Orwell was truly prophetic in what he said. It's just taken a little longer for America to go off the rails and into the ditch.

Sadly, quick fixes and situational ethics will not solve what is wrong with America. What is wrong with America is moral and religious in nature. It is called **Sin.** There is only one answer to sin. **Repentance.** There is only one thing that will force repentance. **Crisis.** Again, I urge you to think about your own life. Are you a Christian today because everything went so wonderfully in your life? Or are you, just like me, a believer today because after trying to let you do it the easy way God was forced to let you deal with the consequences of your own immature and unwise actions, perhaps for the first time in your life? When that happened you were forced to drop to your knees and admit that you couldn't do it on your own and that the mess that you were in was largely of your own making. It was then that you finally truly realized that you were a **sinner**, that you had **sinned**, and that you needed a **Savior**. In order to find that Savior you needed to repent of what you had done in the past and turn control of your life over to a Person other than yourself. **As it is with individuals so it is with nations and empires.** They are, after all, made up of people, aren't they? If they are made up of people why would it be surprising if they would behave collectively in the same fashion? They are made up of organic creatures. It should not be surprising then that they behave organically, being born, growing, living, aging and eventually dying.

3. The First Adjustment Phase

- ✓ In US, occurred in 1816, 1867 and 1920
- ✓ High rate of government debt
- ✓ Labor shortages

Because of an awareness that something needs to be done, something actually is done. As I've said earlier, it will be too little and too late but it will temporarily forestall the inevitable. Aware of the fact that things are headed in the wrong direction, **the Federal Government will begin to accrue huge amounts of debt, trying to reignite the economy through deficit spending.** Nothing could be worse for what ails the economy at this point in time. While it gives the appearance of restarting the economy it is just like the ill-fated ship Titanic, taking on water faster and faster and unable to stop the process. The burden of this additional debt will cause the government to become more and more unable to function effectively. You can never permanently solve a problem by spending money that you don't have. In every single case it produces **debt** which then produces **interest** which **must be paid**. At some critical juncture the rate of economic bleeding becomes greater than the ability of the government to bring additional revenues in through higher taxes. America passed this point of no return a very long time ago. To give you an idea how bad it really is and how completely out of control it is I did some research online. In 2006 when I first began my investigation the total U.S. National Debt stood at **$8,836,471,817,425.11.** Now, for those of us (like me!) who have problems with dollar amounts with more than one comma in them, that's **eight <u>trillion</u>, eight hundred thirty six <u>billion</u>, four hundred seventy one <u>million</u>, eight hundred seventeen <u>thousand</u>, four hundred twenty five dollars, and, oh yes, <u>eleven cents</u>.** Tell you what. I'm good for the eleven cents. Can you cover the rest for me??? With a population of over 301 million at that time, it meant that each of us was responsible for over **twenty nine thousand dollars personally.** In addition, the National Debt was increasing by an average of **1.57 BILLION dollars A DAY.** But then three more years passed. By then, in March of 2009, the National Debt had skyrocketed to, are you ready for this? – **10 TRILLLION, 891 BILLION, 114 MILLION, 737 THOUSAND, 729 DOLLARS AND 56 CENTS!** Again, I think I've got the fifty-six cents. Maybe you can write a check or something for the balance. Our individual share of that debt had increased from the mere $29,000.00 figure quoted just a few sentences ago to **$35,622.62! But wait! There's more!!!** By September 29, 2015, the national debt had cascaded to **18 TRILLLION, 153 BILLION, 320 MILLION, 8 THOUSAND, 913 DOLLARS AND 23 CENTS!!!** The estimated population of the United States was **321,479,143** as of that date so each citizen's share of this debt had jumped to **$56,468.11**. In addition, the National Debt was continuing to increase by an average of **$1.91 billion dollars per day.** Now, in our most recent update, the wheels have completely come off the car and we are gleefully skidding off the edge of the cliff, hands held high in the air, yelling *"Whee!!!"* gleefully as we do so. At the end of the Fiscal Year of 2022, it is estimated that the National Debt will have grown to, brace yourselves, **THIRTY TRILLION, EIGHT HUNDRED BILLION DOLLARS** and, oh yeah, just a random couple of hundred million and thousand dollars and cents or so. Again, I'm good for the loose change.

That's a lot of numbers, and I can just see your head swimming at this point, so let's recap. In 2006, our National Debt was almost **nine trillion dollars.** By 2009, that figure had jumped to almost **eleven trillion dollars.** By 2015, the National Debt had now swollen to a staggering **eighteen trillion dollars!** And, as of the date that I write these words in 2022, our National Debt is projected to be in excess of **thirty trillion dollars!!!** In 2006, you and I were **PERSONALLY** responsible for over **$29,000.00** of the National Debt. By 2009, our responsibility had jumped to over **$35,000.00**. By

2015 you and I owed everyone else in the world over **$56,000.00.** And of this 4ᵗʰ Edition in 2022, we now each have a staggering personal share of the National Debt of **$93,980.00.** If, by this time, you can't see all the symptoms of a runaway train with no brakes, I can't help you. Throw this book away and turn on the TV and watch the WWE and MMA or turn on the cartoon channel and watch SpongeBob and Patrick and hide your head in the sand. When the crash comes, you will be destroyed along with all those others who blindly refused to look at the cold, hard facts, but at least you will be blissfully ignorant of your destruction until the moment that the blade falls. If that sounds harsh, it's not meant to be. It is, however a sad, resigned acknowledgment of the degree of self-deception that America has fallen into and the staggering degree of hardness of heart that we have acquired by failing to listen to the Still Small Voice of the Holy Spirit warning us to exercise a little common sense and wisdom both individually and collectively as a nation.

Can you see why I say that we are already way too far over the edge? There is no way humanly possible for the US government to **ever** pay off a debt of this staggering magnitude or even slow down the accumulation of that debt. And yet we continue to dig ourselves deeper and deeper into debt like an alcoholic on one last binge before he drives the car off the cliff and into the sea. It is sheer madness to think that we can right this and it is beyond belief that we have let ourselves come to this point in time financially and economically.

4. The Plateau Phase (Fall – 13 Years)

- ✓ Final "Blow Off" period
- ✓ Referred to as Euphoric Times
- ✓ 1815-23 – "Era Of Good Feeling"
- ✓ 1867-72 – "The Gilded Age"
- ✓ 1922-29 – "The Roaring Twenties"
- ✓ Start of a 7-10 year economic decline
- ✓ Relative stability
- ✓ Loosening of morals, increase in gambling
- ✓ Dramatic increase in consumer spending, debt
- ✓ New technologies developed
- ✓ Strong feelings of euphoria
- ✓ Increases in business failures and foreclosures

Whenever I write a book dedicated to apocalyptic events, the inevitable question asked is, *"All this is well and good, but **where are we right now** in this timetable of events?"* People want to wait until the last possible minute to repent so they can cram as much quality sinning in as possible. Sound negative? Then you have never pastored a Full Gospel church. In over thirty years of ministry, I am hard pressed to recall the names of a dozen people who came to me and said, *"Pastor, show me how I can live in as much righteousness and holiness as possible."* On the other hand, I can recount literally thousands of so-called Christians who are constantly trying to find out **how much they can get away with** rather than find out **how much they can accomplish for Christ and His Gospel.** People are obsessed in this era of *"All Grace!"* with determining how close to Hell they can skate before the wheels of their roller skates melt off. When the Resurrection and Rapture come, they will be part of the Five Foolish Virgins that Jesus talked about who were not ready and who were excluded for all eternity from entering into the Wedding Feast of the Lamb.

All of that aside, *"Where are we right now?"* is a good question even if you're living right. Where we are right now is in the **Plateau Phase.** Now, the word plateau indicates a flat area often associated with a mountain. There are many plateaus located in the West, the most famous of which is perhaps Devil's Peak, popularized by the classic science fiction movie, *"Close Encounters of the Third Kind"*. What does a plateau look like? Well, if you were climbing toward a plateau, you would climb up one side of the mountain or incline. Then you would come to a large flat area, as if the peak of the mountain had been carved off. This would go on for a period of time, followed by an equally rapid descent to the bottom of the mountain. Remember, plateaus are always **preceded** by a rapid **ascent** and are always **succeeded** by a rapid **descent.** Economically, we are describing the **boom** and **bust** phases of the K-Wave. How can I be sure we are in the Plateau Phase? Well, let's compare the current condition of our economy to the standard characteristics of a Plateau Phase.

THE FINAL "BLOW OFF"

People have a natural, sinful habit of splurging one final time before repentance, hard times or the tightening of the belt comes. It is not without significance that one of the most sinful holidays in the entire world, Mardi Gras, comes just before Lent. The idea is that since we are going to have to be good for forty days, let's get all the quality sinning in we can just before that so we'll have some really good sins to repent of. I know of too many people who have gone on one last binge on Saturday night before coming to the altar to repent on Sunday morning. This final blow-off period always contains the illusion that somehow it will always last forever. Since the only things that will last forever will be the New Jerusalem and the Lake of Fire, located in the New Heavens and the New Earth, we can say with reasonable assurance that this, too, will come to an end. In fact, it will come to an end all too soon. But it always carries with it this kind of free-fall moment of euphoria.

REFERRED TO AS EUPHORIC TIMES

In this euphoric period there is the sense that it is *"all good"* and that we can do whatever we want without consequences. The church would better understand it as the false doctrine of *"All Grace"*. Most of us conduct our lives and businesses as if there will be no consequences for our actions. We have, after all, been riding on a long wave of increasing economic prosperity. At some point in this exhilarating ride we have come to the conclusion that it will never end. We are such time-delimited beings. We think if anything lasts more than a year or two that it will last forever. We also begin to think that there is no connection between our behavior and our future. As I look at the doctrines that have permeated the American church over the last fifty years, they bear the unmistakable mark of this kind of self-deluded euphoria. We are right because we are America because we are right. We are right because we are Christians because we are right. This kind of self-justifying logic is always wrong. Alexis de Tocqueville, the great French historian whose portrait is shown on the previous page said it best: ***"America is great because America is good. And when America ceases to be good, she will also cease to be great".*** We have not yet come to an understanding of this in our country, no more than ancient Israel and Judah did in their day. The prophets bewailed the fact that even though God's people were no longer conducting themselves as God's people they still continued to think that they would enjoy God's favor.

Here is another riveting quote that I ran across recently from a great American Quaker leader and the founder of the state of Pennsylvania early in the history of our country. It expresses the same thought but it is so powerful that it warrants inclusion in this book:

> *"Wherefore governments rather depend upon men, than men upon governments. <u>Let men be good</u>, and the government <u>cannot be bad</u>; if it be ill, they will cure it. But, <u>if men be bad</u>, let the government be never so good, <u>they will endeavour to warp and spoil it to their turn.</u>"*

> – WILLIAM PENN, 1682

Although what I am about to say is not an economic principle, per se, it always carries economic ramifications with it. There is a standard, historical, Biblical pattern or biorhythm which goes something like this:

a. The people of God are in a terrible state. They are oppressed by other nations and in horrible economic distress, slavery and servitude. Everything is going wrong in their lives. Finally, in desperation, **they call out to God** with prayer, supplication, fasting and true repentance and vow that **if God will deliver them they will amend their ways and serve and worship Him and Him only.**

b. God, in His infinite wisdom and mercy, **hears these prayers of desperation** and comes and forgives the people for their sins. He pours His Holy Spirit out on them and **transforms them from the inside out**. As a result, they begin to conduct themselves in a totally different manner, with truth, integrity, justice, fairness and mercy. This new way of conduct inevitably leads to a new way of conducting themselves economically as hard work, integrity and honesty become the foundation of a **new economic system.** This new economic system then logically produces a **new wave of economic prosperity** as the final link in a chain reaction of events. And so for a season the people rejoice in their new-found liberty and prosperity and give appropriate thanks to God who has made all this possible by **changing them and the way that they conduct their lives.**

c. After a period of time, the people begin to feel that that they are not only **empowered** but also **entitled** to their blessings and begin to take those blessings and prosperity **for granted.** This is precisely what the K-Wave cycle calls *"Euphoric Times"*. They no longer remember the terrible times their ancestors went through perhaps only two generations previously. They forget that their **current prosperity** is directly connected by **linear cause and effect** to the **repentance and righteous living** that had permeated the lives of their **fathers and grandfathers.** And so they begin to relax the standards and morals of the previous generation, believing erroneously that their current peace and prosperity will continue **no matter what they do.**

d. Since all things are tied together by cause and effect the negative actions of their generation do not necessarily adversely affect **that** generation but rather manifest themselves in the **next** generation. Those few who do understand this principle selfishly conclude that it is all right since it won't impact them but rather those who come after them. This is precisely why generation after generation of conscience-less legislators have continued to pile more and more onto the National Debt, willing to penalize their children for the sins of the fathers. Eventually the chain of cause and effect leads the political and economic conditions so far down the road to disaster that the events of destruction that will follow become unavoidable and inalterable. The nation crashes into despair and defeat. Their enemies come in and conquer them, subjugating them to slavery, poverty and misery. We have now come full cycle in this spiritual biorhythm. In this condition of desperation we once again cry out to God, returning to step one to repeat the cycle all over again. This was the pattern during the time of the Judges and it ran in cycles of three generations, almost without fail.

The Bible isn't the only authoritative source to notice this frustrating pattern, either. Scottish jurist and historian Sir Alex Fraser Tytler also made some telling observations about this cyclical behavior. Taken from the 1801 Collection of his Lectures, listen to two truly profound statements he made. Compare what he said over 200 years ago with our current version of reality. Here is the first one:

> *"A democracy cannot exist as a permanent form of government. It can exist only until the voters discover that they can **vote themselves largess from the public treasury**. From that time on, the majority always votes for the candidates promising the most benefits from the public treasury, with the result that a democracy always collapses over **loose fiscal policy**, always followed by a **dictatorship**."*

Wow! Tell me that doesn't describe American Pork Barrel politics to a *"T"*! The only thing that holds this kind of financial insanity in check in a mechanism which is almost unique to American politics, something we take for granted but which doesn't exist in any other country I know of, the **two party system.** Most countries with some form of democracy have three or more parties, often many more. This produces political chaos and constantly unstable government. Italy, for example, has had well over fifty governments form and collapse since the end of World War II. Two strong parties act as a check and balance on the fiscal policies of one another, causing a pendulum kind of effect in political and fiscal orientation. The Republicans have always been noted for being partial to business and industry and for having a tight fiscal policy. The Democrats, on the other hand, have typically been associated with some form or another of populism and a *"tax and spend"* mindset. If you trace the political history of our country you will find that a balance of power exists between the two parties, voters affections swinging first one way and then another.

Tytler's first comment is powerful but his second is electrifying. I can think of no other statement I have ever heard which so succinctly captures the very essence of this entire book:

> *"The average age of the world's great civilizations has been **200 years**. These nations have progressed through this sequence: from **bondage** to **spiritual faith**; from spiritual faith to **great courage**; from great courage to **liberty**; from liberty to **abundance**; from abundance to **selfishness**; from selfishness to **complacency**; from complacency to **apathy**; from apathy to **dependency**; from dependency back again into **bondage**."*

Let's make this into a list to improve its readability:

1. Bondage ==> Spiritual Faith
2. Spiritual Faith ==> Great Courage
3. Great Courage ==> Liberty
4. Liberty ==> Abundance
5. Abundance ==> Selfishness
6. Selfishness ==> Complacency
7. Complacency ==> Apathy
8. Apathy ==> Dependency
9. Dependency ==> Bondage

Pretty scary, huh? Now, here's the ugly question that you have to answer for yourself. **Exactly where is America in this cycle?** What? Don't like the answer? Friend, neither do I. That's why I wrote this book.

America is on its way back into bondage, servitude and despair. And there is no way to reverse the trend. In fact, American civilization may be far more fragile than we think due to the complexity of our economic infrastructure. Michael Shermer, writing in a column for *Scientific American*, researched sixty civilizations, both ancient and modern. His goal was to discover the life span of the average civilization. For each extinct culture he calculated how long it remained in existence. For those still in existence he used their current age. Shermer concluded that the average life span of a civilization is only 421 years. Even more troubling is the fact that modern civilizations do not last as long as ancient ones. In viewing the twenty-eight most recent civilizations that have existed since the fall of Rome the average age of a culture is only **305 years.** America is currently **246** years old. If we were a human being with an expected life span of **seventy** that would mean that our country is **fifty-six years old**. Perhaps a better way of helping you understand the ratio is to say that if America is typical of most modern empires it has already expended **80 percent** of its life-force. The paunch is starting to show. We no longer have the national vitality that we once had. I was sixty years old when I first wrote these words. Over the last fourteen years, I have watched my physical vitality wane. After my bout with cancer and a heart attack, I found it very difficult to regain my core strength and muscle mass. The old gray guy ain't what he used to be. Ironically, I don't look 74 at all. Most of my friends tell me I look a dynamic 60. If only I **felt** that young! (Oh, wait! That **is** my last name, isn't it?)

These very same patterns have been true in America as well. If you will remember, I said that America has experienced three crashes. It has also experienced three periods of Euphoric Times. The first occurred in **1815-23** and was called *"The Era of Good Feeling"*. The second occurred in **1867-72** and was called *"The Gilded Age"*. The most recent of the three occurred in **1922-29** and was called, as we all know, *"The Roaring Twenties"*. Fascinating, isn't it, how these cycles appear every fifty to sixty years, visiting us again and again. In every single case, it marked the **start of a seven to ten year economic decline;** a gentle slope or sort of skid but not the kind of thing which would generate a serious sense of alarm. The reason for this lack of concern was that during these final transitional periods, there was a period of **relative stability.** Because this stability seemed to be independent of the moral conduct of the people, as we discussed just a few paragraphs ago, there was always a **loosening of morals.** Another pragmatic observation from over forty years in ministry is that people will only be as good as they absolutely have to be. And once having loosened the moral collar around their necks without a sudden jerk back on the leash by their Master they are encouraged to do so again and again. Believing that they can now do anything they want without fear of reprisal or punishment there is an increase in the reckless spending of money without thought to the consequences, creating an **increase in gambling** and a **dramatic increase in consumer spending and debt.** The negative impact of these actions is somewhat mollified by the **development of new technologies**, which create an artificial boost in the prosperity of the era. As we mentioned earlier, the dominant characteristic of times such as these is a **strong feeling of euphoria** despite the fact that there is a dramatic **increase in business failures and foreclosures.**

Now, dear reader, **you tell me.** Are these the sign of the times in which we live? Tell me that we are not looking straight into a mirror and seeing ourselves. Which of these characteristics have not marked the period of time in which we find ourselves? The only difference is that our period of time has stretched far beyond the seven to ten year boundary normally associated with Euphoric Times. There is a good reason for all of this and we will discuss it in the next chapter. Since the 1950s, America has been steadily eroding away, economically, politically and spiritually. We have gone from being the richest nation in the world to the greatest debtor nation in the world, all in the span of three generations. We have moved from being the most righteous nation in the world to being the most perverse, carnal and ungodly nation in the world, all in the span of three generations. How did this happen? Because we forgot that whatsoever a man soweth, that also shall he reap. We deluded ourselves into thinking that peace and prosperity would continue unabated no matter what our conduct was. And now we have positioned ourselves for the next dreadful phase in our Biblical Biorhythm.

10. **The Panic Phase**

- ✓ Businesses continue to fail
- ✓ Banks begin to fail
- ✓ One Trigger Event leads to a reversal of Public Confidence
- ✓ Economic collapse
- ✓ This is slowed only by an economic inertia created by the fact that individual businesses want to survive and stay in business
- ✓ Price structures collapse over a 3-year period
- ✓ Farmers in particular go through a difficult time

Remember that in the previous phase we had begun to see an increasing number of business failures. This process now suddenly escalates and begins to trigger a funnel-shaped drain on the economy. Once again a chain reaction begins to take place. A business strained beyond its ability to endure profitably suddenly closes its doors. This puts all of its employees out on the street seeking new employment. Normally the failure of an individual business in and of itself is not a traumatic thing to the economy at large. Statistics indicate that by the ten-year mark well over 90 percent of the businesses started ten years prior to that point have either gone out of business, merged or been bought out by larger, more cash-rich companies. The fact that my own company survived for twelve years makes me feel pretty good. We never set the world on fire but we managed to stay afloat and generate a little profit every now and then. So, when one company folds and places its workers back into the job marketplace, there will generally be another company to employ them. It's a case of musical chairs and in times of great prosperity companies can afford to offer extraordinary job security, benefit plans, health insurance, 401-K's, Golden Parachutes to their high paid executives and generally high wages to all their employees. Employees can afford to jump from one job opportunity to another without consequences because they know that another company is earnestly seeking their services, regardless of their past lack of corporate loyalty. I clearly remember when we sent one of our salesmen to Comdex, the computer industry's largest annual convention. When he came back from the convention he took me aside and related a story to me. It seems that he had been in a workshop on some sort of marketing topic and the speaker had asked the assembled group of salesmen how many of them had been at their current job for more than one year. Not one person in that room could answer in the affirmative! As long as things are good you can get away with this kind of bunny rabbit disloyalty, hippety-hopping from one job to another. But not so in an economy that has begun its inevitable downward spiral.

Now, with multiple companies failing, job opportunities suddenly begin to dry up. Benefit packages suddenly begin to feel the squeeze. Insurance premiums begin to increase and correlated insurance benefits begin to decrease. The number of days you can spend in a hospital for a given operation decrease. Suddenly outpatient services include surgeries, pregnancies and other medically-related events which would have put you in the hospital for weeks in times past. Wages begin to shrink. People who were full-time are suddenly put on almost-but-not-quite-full-time status so that companies don't have to pay health and insurance benefits to them. The mass merchandisers such as Sears, Wal-Mart, Target, K-Mart and the like have made a living out of doing this. It seems that no one is employed full time at such stores any more. Why? Because then the company would be obligated to pay full-time benefits, per federal mandates. In our own particular scenario, American employers have added fuel to the fire by not only closing or downsizing their American manufacturing facilities but by also sending those jobs overseas to other countries such as Mexico, China, Malaysia, Indonesia, the Philippines, Taiwan and other Third World nations. I had to make a run to the store the other day to pick up a few items because my precious wife Beverly wasn't feeling well. As I walked through the store I had to take a short cut through the women's apparel section. Out of curiosity, I decided to check on some of the garment tags to see where those good were manufactured. Many were, of course, made in China. Some were made in alternate Third World Far East countries. Some were made in South America. **BUT NONE WERE MADE IN AMERICA!** Virtually 100 percent of these companies were birthed in the United States and still have their corporate headquarters here yet they have chosen to betray the nation that permitted them to be birthed and enjoy the rights of free enterprise. I find this to be unconscionable. There should be a penalty for companies that show this lack of loyalty. In fact, perhaps it is time for some restrictive tariffs to be put back in place to put a premium on foreign imports. I have had serious reservations about NAFTA for quite some time now and with the massive disloyalty of American corporations it only serves to drive the point home. In attempting to globalize themselves and make themselves crash-proof they only serve to hasten the demise of the very economy to which they are inexorably bound. As a passing note, I have to take mention that President Donald Trump enforced just such trade mandates while he was in office. As a result of that decision, along with a number of other good business practice actions, the United States experienced a remarkable bounce-back economically. Businesses in the U.S. were booming during his administration, despite the fact that Covid 19 caused serious problems in all aspects of our lives. Had the 2020 election not been deliberately stolen by the Democratic Party (and I have personally reviewed an incredible amount of documentation concerning these facts!), it is entirely possible that our country could have experienced an economic revival of sorts. When the election was stolen, it doomed us to even more tax-and-spend politics, resulting in the disastrous National Debt increases which I documented not too long ago.

As more and more companies fail suddenly workers can no longer simply relocate and become re-employed. Now they too are out of business. They are no longer generating an income and so they stop spending. Suddenly more companies that depended on their purchases go out of business. As a result, more workers are put out on the street and they stop spending. Then more companies go out of business. And the funnel cloud begins to suck more and more individuals and corporations down the economic drain. And…And… And…

At a certain point in time, this encroaching whirlpool reaches the banking industry itself. America experienced a near-miss in the 1980's with the Whitewater S&L Scandal. Based on research I have done, I have come to the conclusion that we came perilously close to a collapse of the Savings and Loan industry. If Whitewater had failed, it might have triggered a panic and a run on the S&L industry and then the banking industry in general. In theory, the banking industry is supposed to be protected by the FDIC or Federal Deposit Insurance Corporation. The savings and loan industry is supposed to be protected by a similar mechanism, the FSLIC or Federal Savings and

Loan Insurance Corporation. In both situations a certain percentage of all deposits are supposed to be retained on hand in order to protect against the kind of runs on banks that permeated 1929. But in reality neither organization provides protection against a true crash. Here's how it's supposed to work. The FDIC and FSLIC are supposed to retain 10 percent of all deposits made against the possibility of a bank or S&L crashing. And that principle works fine as long as the entity crashing is a single bank. If the theoretical Watchnetockee Bank of Upper Long Island went belly up, the FDIC could step in and refund 100 percent of all the deposits made in that individual bank. The same would be true of an individual savings and loan. But that mechanism was put in place long ago, after the Great Depression when almost 100% of all banks and savings and loans were locally owned. Since then a great many things have changed. At first all banks were individually owned and local in nature with a real sense of responsibility to the local community which they served. Think of *"It's a Wonderful Life"* with Jimmy Stewart and his little savings and loan company as a classic example of that kind of community involvement and commitment. But then some banks began to grow significantly larger than those around them and began buying up many of the smaller banks. These banks began to evolve into regional banks, serving an entire state or group of states. Eventually some of those regional banks began to grow bigger than their britches and decided that they needed to become national entities so they began to buy up the regional banks around them.

Finally some of those banks decided that they wanted to become multinational or international and so they began to buy up some of the national banks around them. This process of big fish swallowing little fish has been going on for the last seventy years or so. In doing so they have placed the small local bank in danger of extinction. I had a very strange experience many years ago that really drove this fact home to me. I still had my own computer company and we were trying to compete with the computer retailers around us so we were renting a building with about two thousand square feet of storefront space. One day a fairly nondescript gentleman wearing a flannel shirt strolled into my store and walked up to the counter. It was a slow day and I was hoping for some business so I paid extra attention to him. It turns out that he wasn't there to buy anything. Instead, he was there to give me an education that I would never forget. *"I'm a millionaire!"* he exclaimed. *"Would you like to know how I did it?"* I looked at him with a jaundiced, skeptical eye. This guy sure didn't **look** like a millionaire. But it was a slow afternoon and I was bored. *"Sure"*, I replied, *"Tell me. I'd **love** to know how you did it!"*

For the next hour and a half this unlikely millionaire proceeded to tell me his story. Sure enough, he was really a millionaire. Why had he chosen to stop at my store and tell me his story? Heaven only knows. I'm sure glad he did. Perhaps it was so that **his** story could become a part of **this** story so that you could read it and learn from it. Once I had agreed to listen, he told me to wait for a few moments and then went out to his car. He brought back a huge computer printout in a binder and opened it up in front of me. *"This"*, he said, *"is the secret to my success. It is a printout of every small bank in America, a breakout of all its assets, and what its financial health is. Every month I get a new printout and I watch very carefully to see which small banks are slowly slipping into a financial position from which they cannot recover. When I see one about to slip into receivership or bankruptcy, I simply wait and watch. When it folds, all of its 'paper' goes up for sales for pennies on the dollar"*. At this point, I interrupted. *"I don't understand what you mean when you say, 'paper'. Please explain this to me."* *"When I say 'paper'"*, he replied, *"what I mean are the various notes, loans and other documents of financial lending that a bank has, such as home mortgages, car loans, notes receivable from businesses and the like"*. I finally understood and nodded in agreement. He continued, *"When those documents become available in a bankruptcy sale, I can buy them for pennies on the dollar"*. *"I understand all that"*, I said, *"but how do you make money off of the transaction?"* *"Simple."* he replied. *"Let's say that you have a car loan with that bank for* *say, ten thousand dollars. And let's further say that I can purchase that same loan from the bank for one thousand dollars. Let's further stipulate that I have purchased several hundred or even several thousand loans, notes, mortgages and other pieces of financial paper, all for ten cents on the dollar. Now, I put all the information on each of those documents into my computer; name, address, type of loan, amount owed and so on. The next thing I do is to send a simple one page letter to each individual who owes the bank money. Actually, since I bought their paper they no longer owe that money to the bank. They owe it to me. I am now legally their lender. In that letter I make them the deal of a lifetime. Let's go back to that ten thousand dollar car loan for a second. Remember that I bought it for one thousand dollars. In my letter I make you a simple offer. I offer to reduce your amount owed from **ten** thousand dollars to **five** thousand dollars **if** you will pay the loan off in the next 30 days. Otherwise I will sell your note at pretty much full price to another lending institution who will then assume responsibility for the note and your indebtedness. I know very few people who will turn that kind of offer down. They will beg, borrow or steal the five thousand dollars to pay the loan off. They could actually go to another lending institution themselves to get the five thousand dollars. I don't care how they get it, only that they do it within the thirty day deadline. I don't want to carry their note. I just want to profit off of it. Now comes the really great part".* His eyes glistened as he came to the *coup 'de grace.* "You save five thousand dollars on your car loan so it's a win for you. You reduce your total *indebtedness by five thousand dollars. **Nobody** turns me down on this deal unless they absolutely can't get a loan anywhere else. It's rare, but it happens. But now it's **my** turn. Remember, I bought the loan for **one** thousand dollars. I just sold that self-same loan for **five** thousand dollars and put the title of the car or home or whatever it is back into the hands of the previous debtor. I turned a cool profit of **four thousand dollars** on the deal or a **four hundred percent** profit, **all for the cost of one piece of paper, an envelope and a stamp**."*

I sat there dumbfounded. It was so obvious, so simple. Yet I would never have thought of it in a million years. I gratefully thanked the man for sharing his secret with me. After all of these years, I still don't know why he did it. He didn't seem like he was interested in any partners, although I hinted around about the possibility.

That was many years ago. Things are much worse for the small banks today than they were back then. Pressure to compete with regional, national and multinational banks has forced most small banks to sell out, merge or fold because they cannot offer the services and rates that the larger banks can. And if a multinational bank decides that it wants a specific local bank out of business it can offer such brutally competitive rates that it becomes almost impossible for the little guy to compete.

That is exactly what happened to me and my company. I had carefully analyzed our own business patterns over a ten year period. We would go through a three year period of growth and then have a one-year setback. Then we would go through another three year period of growth followed by a one-year setback. We were just coming off of our third period of setback and sales had already started to skyrocket. Things were going well. I figured if we were ever going to change our paradigm, this was the time. I had my own internal patterns figured out pretty well. Unfortunately, what I didn't account for were the external patterns that were going on in the marketplace at large. I decided to move from being what is called a **value-added reseller**, operating out of a modest office in a basement at a low, low overhead to being a **computer retailer**, operating in a high-overhead, high rent, visible location. At the very same time as I made that decision the market made a major paradigm swing **away** from selling computers strictly through computer retailer outlets and began selling them for the first time through **mass merchandisers.** Today this is a common practice, even the preferred method. Back then it was revolutionary. But what was devastating to me was the fact that these mass merchandisers were able to sell their products, the same products that I was trying to sell, at prices **below my cost!** There was simply no way that I could compete. If I kept my prices at a level which protected the necessary profit margin that any retailer must have in order to survive, I got killed in deal after deal. If I dropped my prices so low that I could be competitive, I had to sacrifice virtually every penny of profit and made myself terribly vulnerable if anything should go wrong with whatever it was I was selling. I found out, much to my horror, that hardware sales accounted for only ten percent of my profit, but ninety percent of my headaches. I was trapped between a rock and a hard place and it eventually wore me out and put me out of business.

This same trend, by the way, was happening all over America in virtually every type of business. The small, independent local businessman was slowly but surely being squeezed out of business by the large regional or multinational chain whose prices they could not compete with. I have watched the assassination of the small businessman in America over the last fifty years. Small farmers were put out of business by large corporate farm conglomerates. Small retailers whose shops had graced the downtown area for as much as one hundred years were systematically eliminated by chains like Sears, K-Mart, Wal-Mart and the like. Small bankers were replaced by mega-banks spanning the whole globe. Small grocery stores were ground into the ground by their regional and national competitors, chains like Kroger and Winn Dixie. Small family restaurants have been replaced with national chains such as Golden Corral, Wendy's, McDonalds and the like. If you drive through any retail strip in America you will find them all to be disturbingly the same. Do it sometime just for fun. Drive or walk through your local strip mall or mall complex and do a simple tally. Count the number of franchises or chains versus the number of locally owned shops and then compare the tallies. There has been silent murder going on all over America for the last fifty years. Corporate America has killed the small businessman. There has been one area of compromise, however. Some franchises allow for local ownership and operation of their stores. But that store must be run to the same exacting specifications as the corporate stores are. They must file the same reports, order from the same suppliers and do everything according to corporate guidelines. All of this was done in the name of competition, better prices and greater selection. And we have gained all those things. We now have better prices and better selection. We also have much poorer service because a miniscule profit margin per item will not allow mass merchandisers to provide such support. Instead, we get minimum wage clerks with *"Let me help YOU!"* stickers on their vests who have absolutely no clue about how the products they are selling work or even how one might **find** the product in question in their megalithic store. They think it **might** be in aisle seventeen but they're not sure. Let me tell you a true story to back this statement up. In doing so, I will reveal a deep, dark secret of my life. All my life, I've had problems going to the bathroom. For some reason the Lord designed me with a chute that can handle 10 pound packages and a production system that produces 15 pound packages. I'll let you figure out the implications of that. Ouch! As a result, for over 20 years, I have employed good ole *Phillips Milk of Magnesia* to lubricate the gears. Just the other day, my wife went to Wal-Mart to pick up some items. As it turned out, milk of magnesia was on her list. She couldn't find it initially, so she asked a female employee who was working near the pharmacy area where it was located. *"Oh!"* the young clerk said, **"We don't have that anymore. I don't even think that they make it anymore!"** My wife just stared at her in astonishment. She then went on a mission of her own to find the product that supposedly didn't exist anymore. Sure enough, there it was, right in the place where other similar products were located! My wife gleefully grabbed a bottle of it and went in search of the young employee. When she found her, she triumphantly held up the bottle of milk of magnesia and said, **"Honey, here is the very product that you said NO LONGER EVEN EXISTED!** *Now I'm going to take you to the place where this 'non-existent' product is conveniently shelved so that the **next time somebody asks you about it** you'll be able to answer accurately!"* Wasn't she nice??? The sad but simple truth is that every gain has its corresponding loss. Whenever you gain something you always have to give up something else in order to get it. Another disturbing side effect of the rise of the mass merchandiser is the homogenization of American culture. I've been across a fair percentage of the East Coast and the Midwest. Everywhere I go, it's always the same. The stores are the same, the designs of the malls are the same and the way that the people dress is the same. We have lost to a great degree the ethnic and regional flavors that our country once had. Now thanks to TV and the mass merchandisers we all look, act and think just the same. We have become Clones-R-Us!

America is also ready to pay a far greater price for this mass merchandising than it has ever had to in its history. If you will remember, the Great Depression was triggered when **a single bank** overextended itself. At that point in time almost all businesses in America were in the form of small, independent owners. The crash was slowed and softened by the fact that there were a lot of tough minded private business owners out there who were darned if they were going to go down without a fight. They had invested their own sweat and blood in their company. It was actually like a child to them. And they were not about to let a member of the family die. Today, the picture is much different. The small business owner is gone. Now, we simply have a manager of a store who is employed by the corporate headquarters. The will to save the local outlet is not as strong. All of these regional and multinational corporations are now tied together in a domino fashion. In 1929 when a single store failed, a single store failed. Today if a chain fails hundreds or even thousands of outlets will all fail at the same time just as Circuit City, a major electronics and computer retailer did some years ago. The ramifications are staggering. Untold thousands of employees will lose their jobs all at the same time. Imagine if you will what would happen if Wal-Mart were to go out of business suddenly. What would the impact on the US economy be? Would the US be able to absorb the impact? What if several chains failed at once? Remember, all of these outlets are connected together. If one goes down they **all** go down at the same time.

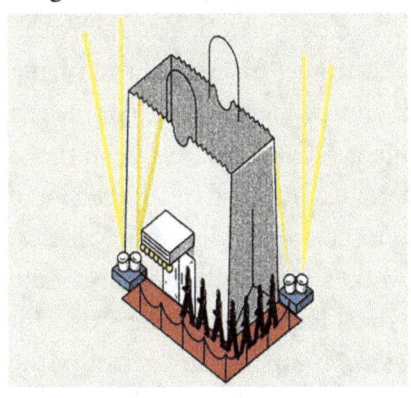

In fact, this economic chain reaction collapse will even have greater ramifications because of what are called **Flagship** retail operations and **Boutique** retail operations. What do I mean by that? Let me give you a real, live example of what has recently happened in my very own home community. The Kroger grocery chain happens to have a superstore located close to where we live. Founded by Bernard Kroger in 1883 in Cincinnati, Ohio, Kroger operates 2,721 grocery retail stores under its various banners and divisions in 35 states and the District of Columbia. Kroger, along with other retail giants like Wal-Mart, Target and the like, build what are generally referred to as **Flagship** retail locations. What, then, is a *"Flagship"*? According to the Merriam-Webster Online Dictionary and Thesaurus, there are two common meanings for the word *"Flagship"*; (1) - the ship that carries the commander of a fleet or subdivision of a fleet and flies the commander's flag or (2) - the finest, largest, or most important one of a group of things (such as products, stores, etc.). In the retail world, the term *"Flagship"* is generally reserved for large mass-merchandizers such as Kroger, Wal-Mart and the like. They carry a broad spectrum of retail goods. Our own Kroger superstore is just such a location. Yes, they carry groceries, obviously. But the new superstore also carries clothing, birthday cards and a wide variety of completely non-edible items for sale. It only stands to reason that a mass merchandizer like Kroger is going to attract a lot of customers. And so in shopping malls all across America, when layout planning is done for malls like this, room is made, not just for the Flagship store but also for a large number of *"Boutique"* operations surrounding the Flagship. Now we have a working definition for *"Flagship"* but we have yet to define *"Boutique"*.

A *Boutique* operation is a smaller, **specialty** store that feeds off of the general merchandise traffic generated by the *Flagship* store. For example, in the surrounding Boutique area around our new Kroger there are, in no particular order, specialized locations like *Body and Brow* (Easy to figure out, right, girls?), *Buff City Soap* (Not totally sure about that one!), *Sports Clips* (One for the guys!), *One Main Financial* (Loans, etc.), *ColdStone Ice Cream* (From personal experience, awesome!), *ProRehab* (Physical therapy), *Spring Street Dental* (Obvious, but, duh! They aren't located on Spring Street anymore!),

ChickfilA (Fast food), *OpenSided MRI* (Self-explanatory) and literally **dozens** of other specialty outlet stores, all **focusing on one type of product or service.** Now here's the catch: **none of them would EVER have moved to the new retail center HAD KROGER NOT MOVED THERE FIRST.** It's almost like a giant sperm whale busy feeding, with untold thousands of tiny marine creatures swarming around the huge beast surviving and even thriving on the **leftovers.** This has been a successful retail mall formula for a very long time and it has been awesome for our community. But every fish in the ocean has a **bigger** fish to follow and our community is no exception. What prompted the development of the new retail mall center? Up until a few years ago the property that the mall is built on had lain dormant and for sale at nearly **any** price without any prospective buyers. What triggered the change? **A BIGGER fish even than Kroger!** A large tract of land originally used by the military during World War II for testing weaponry shells had also remained dormant and unused because the "leaders" of our county had absolutely no vision to develop it until two major events occurred, one triggered by the other. First, after empty promise after empty promise down through the years, a major **bridge** was finally constructed, connecting the prosperous east side of our larger metropolitan area to our side of the Ohio River. Before, there was no easy or practical way to move goods and services from anyone building on our large, undeveloped tract to any other area in the Midwest. Trucks would have had to pass through most of our city on poorly maintained 4-lane roads, dealing with typical town traffic before they finally hit the interstate. No thanks, buddy! Second, after literally decades of squabbling and procrastination, the final leg of the superhighway loop around our larger metropolitan area was finally completed, including easy access (5 miles or less) from any point in the undeveloped tract to the new, completed loop, connecting us with five other metropolitan areas as large or larger than us, all approximately 2 hours away. Suddenly, our little community of 30,000 became one of the most desirable location or relocation spots in the whole country. And locate someone did! The online shopping giant **Amazon** picked our community to build a brand new, massive **Fulfillment Center.** For those of you who are unfamiliar with the term, the Fulfillment Center is actually a **giant shipping and receiving warehouse servicing at the very least, the whole Midwest and theoretically the entire globe!** Before, **no one** wanted a piece of the pie. But after Amazon announced their decision, there was a massive scramble for *Boutique Manufacturing Facilities* to relocate here. Now **everyone** wanted a piece of the pie! Massive entities like the Fulfillment Center create their own manufacturing and distribution boutique network, just like our new Kroger did. So two major economic and transportation decisions by Indiana and Kentucky triggered the most massive growth spurt our city has ever seen. The Amazon decision caused the previously unused military tract to literally blossom with new industries. **New industries** (including, obviously, Amazon itself) meant the need for **new workers.** New workers created the need for **new housing.** New housing created the need for **new retail locations** to fill the refrigerators, living rooms and pools of the new houses being built. Amazon as a Flagship operation triggered **another subsidiary** Flagship operation featuring Kroger to move into the area which in turn created a secondary Boutique network surrounding it. Follow the pattern? The really nice thing for us was that our city has doubled its size, its revenue base, its economic vitality and **finally** been able to afford to pave its streets properly! We and an adjacent community have been the recipients of all of this largess, our own community focusing on new factories, new warehouses, new retail outlets and new service locations, even including an out-branch of our community hospital! Our neighboring community has benefitted by being the location for a seemingly endless number of new, high-feature and even higher-priced houses. Housing in general has **tripled** in cost in the last 5 years.

All of this is wonderful, you say, right??? But there's a catch. In the event of a major economic collapse, the subject of this book, **what happens when that Amazon Fulfillment Center closes its doors???** The cascade effect locally would be absolutely disastrous. With no Fulfillment Center, all of the satellite, Boutique manufacturing and warehousing industries also will close their doors. With their employers now gone, what will the employees do? And once the former employees no longer have money to spend, what will happen to the new Kroger superstore and all of the boutique locations surrounding it? It is just like a stack of dominos, all lined up one after the other. Tip the first domino over and what happens? My greatest fear, if I have one, is that the collapse of our global economy will completely devastate our own home town. Where will we go then? That, dear friends, is the subject of a chapter that is coming up. Stay tuned!

Now that we have firmly established the extremely vulnerable nature of our current economy, we can return to the banking industry to conclude our conversation about the FDIC and FSLIC. Remember, both institutions only hold **ten percent** of the total deposits in reserve. That would have been sufficient in the era of small, independent bank owners. But now if a bank goes down it will be a Fifth/Third Bank, a Bank of America or a Chase Bank. And when **all** of the depositors of such a large institution present their demands **at one time**, tell me again how a measly **ten percent** is going to cover all those deposits. Remember that I mentioned earlier that the Whitewater Scandal almost broke the bank? That was literally true. Had Whitewater gone down a little differently it would have exhausted the financial storehouse of the FSLIC and triggered a panic and a run on other S&L's across the country. Now project an across-the-board collapse of the banking industry as in 1929, and you can see the obvious results. We will witness the complete collapse of the entire lending industry for the first time in the history of the world.

As I was updating this book back in 2009, I found place after place where events predicted in

2006 had already come to pass in 2009, only three years afterwards. Nowhere was this more evident than the near-disaster in the banking industry. US banks lost **26.2 billion dollars** during the final quarter of 2008. Fourteen federally-insured institutions had already failed the following year as I was updating my information, extending a wave of collapses that began in 2008. That previous year's tally of **twenty-five banks** shut down by regulators was more than in the previous five years combined and up from only **three** bank failures in 2007.

Those failures sliced the amount in the deposit insurance fund to $18.9 billion as of December 31 of that year, the lowest level for the fund since 1993, **during the savings and loan crisis.** That compares with a $52.4 billion balance a year earlier. The regulators said there were **252 banks in trouble at the end of 2008**, up from 171 in the third quarter. Because of this enormous financial strain on the FDIC and the steady depletion of its funds, the head of the FDIC, Sheila Blair, sent a letter out to bank chief executives dated March 2, 2009 warning them **that the FDIC could go broke THAT YEAR!!!** The FDIC also estimated that the number of bank failures in 2010 would be much higher than the previous year. Because of this, the FDIC imposed a temporary emergency fee on lenders and raised its regular assessments of banks in the hopes of forestalling **its own bankruptcy.** Please remember that in 2006 I clearly warned that this kind of thing could happen. In 2009 we almost saw yet another event the Lord showed me come to pass. But please also believe this: I take no pleasure in seeing the things I prophesied and predicted come to pass. This is why Jeremiah is often referred to as the *"Weeping Prophet"*. He did not want to see the destruction of Jerusalem and the captivity of his people. Yet he also had no choice but to be obedient to the Lord and issue his warnings, which were then calmly and callously ignored until it was too late. How I understand his torment!

In and of themselves, these numbers and events are mind-boggling yet the end is not in sight nor was this the *"big one"* referred to constantly by Fred Sanford in the old TV comedy, *Sanford and Son*. When the financial crisis erupted my email program and phone line were almost overwhelmed with people wanting to know if this was what I had been predicting. Sadly, the answer is no, not yet. In that most recent crisis the stock market dropped precipitously but only by thirty percent. To most speculators, the word **only** and the figure **thirty percent** had nothing in common with one another. They viewed this as a major crisis. You have to remember, however, that by the low point in the stock market crash of 1929, which came in 1932 four years after the free-fall began, stocks had dropped by almost **ninety percent** from their previous peaks.

We have some good friends in the Cincinnati area who have worked with us in overseas missions. The husband is a retired doctor who carefully watches his stock investments several hours a day. They represent his nest egg and his source of income now that he is no longer actively practicing medicine. Shortly before we left to return to our hometown in Indiana, I felt the strong urge to warn him to sell off a reasonable portion of his stocks and convert them into physical, tangible assets such as gold. I couldn't put my finger on exactly why I felt that way, and, being the analytical man that he is, he discounted my advice and retained all his stocks. Right now he is probably looking at a twenty-five percent or more decrease in his investment. It wasn't just my friend, however, that was in mounting financial trouble. Two of the biggest bank failures in the nation's history occurred that same year. Pasadena-based IndyMac Bank collapsed in July of that year and cost the Federal Deposit Insurance Fund $10.7 billion and Seattle-based Washington Mutual Inc. followed shortly thereafter, accounted for the largest U.S. bank failure ever. WaMu fell in September of that year with around **$307 billion in assets** and was acquired by JPMorgan Chase & Co. for a mere **$1.9 billion** in a deal brokered by the FDIC. Talk about a steal! That's even better than the dime on the dollar deals that my strange friend was making! Who says banks aren't tender-hearted? Add to that such disasters as Bear-Stearns and CitiGroup and you had a potential crash in the making. Only a massive infusion of funds temporarily stayed the execution of the investment industry. Notice I said **temporarily.** In previous collapses the vitality of the private small business owner and small-town banker held the fort against total collapse. But we killed them off a while back in favor of lower prices and better selection, didn't we? Now, we too will have to pay the price and it will be far more than we want to pay.

Hardest hit will be the farmers, upon whose products we depend for our very lives. I will share with you another story which I have garnered down through the years. For eighteen years I taught full time at a university level, teaching computer science and business courses. During one of my courses I was sharing some of these facts and a middle-aged woman in the back of the classroom commented angrily that she knew exactly what I was talking about. I asked her to explain and again I learned a very valuable lesson. Before I tell you her story, though, I would like to pose another theoretical economic problem for you. Let's say that it is the Great Depression and the year is 1935. Two farms in the local area that both have mortgages at your bank have been struggling and have come into receivership, unable to make their payments. You as head of the Loan Department have to decide whether to foreclose on one, the other, both or neither. Here then is your situation: Both properties are worth one hundred thousand dollars in the monetary values of the day, clearly farms worthy of buying or selling. One farm has been very well managed and has only twenty thousand dollars worth of debt on it, giving it an equity value of eighty thousand dollars. The other farm has been poorly managed and has eighty thousand dollars worth of debt on it, giving it an equity value of only twenty thousand dollars. The two farms are clearly reverse mirror images of one another. Now it is your turn. What will your business decision be? Will you foreclose on the farm with eighty thousand dollars worth of debt or the farm with eighty thousand dollars worth of equity? This was the story that this woman in her late fifties related to our class. And she posed that very question to us. Almost every person in the class replied that they would foreclose on the farm which had the greatest amount of debt. And then to our amazement she told us that the bank did **just the opposite!** When we inquired why here's how she explained it:

As a banker you are concerned about turning a profit on every transaction. You make money on other people's money and you don't do deals where you are going to lose your shirt. It is the Depression and so there is even more pressure on you to not lose money for the bank. As you look over the situation, you know that you can resell either farm for about fifty thousand dollars or about fifty cents on the dollar. Not exactly what the property is worth but property values are extremely depressed just like everything else. So you look very closely at the asset/liability ratios of the two properties and you think in hard, cold dollars and sense. If you foreclose on the property that has eighty thousand dollars worth of debt and then resell it for fifty thousand dollars you will take a beating of thirty thousand dollars! The next thing you will do is get a little cardboard box to clean out all of your personal belongings because you will have gotten yourself fired! Nope! As poorly as this farm is being managed, you simply cannot afford to foreclose on them. You will just have to ride out the storm with them, hoping that they will turn things around. **On the other hand** You now turn your attention to the **other** farm, the **profitable** farm, the one with a **sizeable net asset value of eighty thousand dollars!** If you foreclose on **that** farm you only have twenty thousand dollars worth of debt. And if you can turn it around and sell it again for fifty thousand dollars you will make a clear profit of thirty thousand dollars. It was that decision that the bank made, the lady said. They left the poorly managed farm alone because it wasn't worth foreclosing on. But the well managed farm was foreclosed on, destroying the farmer and his family in the process. How did she know these things were true, she asked? Because, in answering her own question, she replied that **her father was the good farmer who was foreclosed on by a local bank in the area who shall forever remain nameless in this book!** We all sat there shocked and appalled. You could see that even after all these years she had never been able to forgive her *"friends"* the bankers who had sold her father down the river for the sake of profit.

In the previous chapter, we pointed out how ownership of land is critical to a stable economy and political system. What will happen when we begin to put the farmers of this nation out in the street and begin to seize their farms? Remember, most of these men still know how to handle firearms.

America is already poised at the edge of the cliff. All that is left is a single **Trigger Event.** What will it be? Only heaven knows and my heavenly sources aren't talking about that subject right now. But I wouldn't be surprised if I am told just before the event. Later on in this book I am going to tell you another true story about my now-deceased friend Orville Martin who was told by the Lord to sell his stock in a company just in time to save his ten thousand dollar stock market profit so that it could be invested in a Christian bookstore. If the Lord could provide such detailed, timely information to a Christian businessman and lay pastor then certainly the Lord is both capable and willing to tell me and other men and women of God who walk in the prophetic when it is about to happen. Surely the Lord our God does **nothing** without revealing it to His servants the prophets!

THE DECLINE PHASE

At this point, the die is cast. The events that will transpire over the next several years will be inexorable, a juggernaut that **no one will be able to stop.** When the crash finally comes, the entire world economy will begin to skid. Only the economy of Mainland China will be spared to some extent, but due to recent financial coupling with the United States, China now **needs us** more than they **hate us**. China is the top holder of US Treasury bills. T-Bills, as they are called, are how we finance the enormous Federal Deficit. We basically **borrow money from other countries to prop up our own financial irresponsibility.** Back in 2009, China owned **$696.2 billion** worth of them. Only six years later, that figure had ballooned to **1.2 TRILLION** dollars. In other words, **in just six short years our debt to China had almost doubled.** According to statistics that I recently looked up, that number has actually decreased slightly but please understand that China is **NOT** our friend. In fact, she would like nothing more than to topple the US dollar from its position as the dominant currency in the world. Most of the strength of the United States economy versus the rest of the world comes from the value of the US dollar in relationship to other national currencies across the world. Historically, we have always had an AAA credit rating with the International Monetary Fund (IMF) who are essentially the world bank for nations. But several credit rating agencies around the world have downgraded their credit ratings of the US federal government, including Standard & Poor's (S&P), which reduced our country's rating from AAA (outstanding) to AA+ (excellent) on August 5, 2011. What are the implications of that? It's actually fairly simple. The better your national credit rating, the more power your currency has in relationship to the rest of the world's currencies. Remember how earlier I pointed out that the dollar to rupee relationship between us and India was in the range of one US dollar to roughly forty-five Indian rupees and how the Australian dollar had a ratio slightly smaller than that? Well, every time that our dollar is devalued, it runs the risk of being removed as the *"gold standard"* by the IMF. If the dollar is replaced by the Euro or the German Mark, or, worse yet, the Chinese Yuan, which is exactly what China would like to see happen, prices in the United States would immediately double overnight! This would produce exactly the impetus needed to cascade the US into the most catastrophic economic collapse in recorded history and also trigger a corresponding worldwide collapse. What keeps this from happening? Why doesn't China simply *"call the note"* on the US and demand payment of the staggering amount that we owe them? Because they, too, have now become ensnared in our economic madness. If they shoot the horse they are riding, they will plummet to their own economic death at the same time. How is this so? Here's why: back in the 1950's and 1960's, America was flooded with cheaply made and cheaply priced items from Japan. *"Made in Japan"* became a standing joke and a symbol of substandard production and quality. But something happened over the next few decades. While American manufacturing either remained at a standstill or continued to slide downhill, Japan was working feverishly to increase her financial strength and the quality of the products that she was producing. Eventually the quality and pricing of products made by Japanese automobile and electronic manufacturers passed their American counterparts and they haven't looked back since. Don't believe me? Just walk around any electronics store like Best Buy and take a good hard look at the names of the manufacturers on the products they carry. Then tell me how many of the names are American names. None? You are absolutely right! Now China is threatening to do the same. Let me share a personal example with you.

Many years ago, my daughter Kathy gave me a Christmas church as a Christmas present. What do I mean by a Christmas church? During the holidays, many people, including our family, decorate the house for Christmas. In fact, we are serious *"Christmaholics"*. We love Christmas and we decorate the house to the max during the Christmas season. The decorations go up the weekend following Thanksgiving and remain in place until shortly before Valentine's Day in February. We absolutely LOVE Christmas and everything that it stands for, particularly the celebration of the Lord's birth. Now, if you're decorating for Christmas, you might have an H-O gauge train set and a Christmas village to go with it. In that Christmas village you might have a school, several houses, a farm, a grocery store and, at least in the past, a church to go with it because every little hamlet in America had one or more churches in the town. Because I have been in the ministry for over 35 years, you know that I have to love the Church of Jesus Christ. As a result of that love of the Church in general, my daughter Kathy gave me a decorative plastic church with an angel that moves back and forth through the front doors as a Christmas present. I really loved the present and decided that I would like to get a few more. I didn't want to spend a lot of money, so I started frequenting Goodwill, the Salvation Army and various other thrift stores and flea markets. Most of the churches I buy cost me less than three dollars each. How many do I have now? Well, based on my most recent inventory, I now have a total of over **800** ceramic, glass, wax, plastic, wood, crocheted, pictures of and heaven-only-knows-what-other-kinds-of decorative Christmas churches. They are scattered throughout the house but most of them are located in the sun room at the front of our house. Many of them are designed for a C7 night light bulb to be inserted in the back and so the sun room glows each and every night with a beauty that will transfix you. Each church has become symbolic of a church that I have either ministered in or will minister in at some time in the future by faith and also of churches and ministries in the 3rd World with which we have frequent contact. Sometimes in the evening I will go into the sun room and touch the spire of each church, praying in the Spirit and thanking God for the ministry opportunities that He is going to give me and the victories and successes that He is going to give them. It used to be that each new Christmas village set that came out in retail stores always included a church but about ten years ago suddenly the churches began to disappear from the new sets being sold by various retailers because we have become ashamed of the Gospel of Jesus Christ. I could no longer buy new ones so I turned again to the thrift shops and began to *"rescue"* all the little cast-aside churches I could get my hands on. It is both practical and symbolic in nature. I don't have to pay much for each of them and each one is a point of contact to pray for the restoration of the true Church in America and across the world.

Why tell you all of this about my churches? Because, almost without fail they all have a tiny sticker on the bottom of them saying, *"Made in China"*. As American manufacturers began to outsource our industrial facilities in the 70's and beyond we traded economic vitality for cheap prices. Now we are totally dependent on nations like China for our merchandise, often produced in sweat shop environments but inexpensive so most Americans turn a blind eye to the inequities involved. We are dependent on China for much of our merchandise. At the same time, much to their dismay, the Chinese have become just as dependent on us to help fund their factories and industrial growth. In many ways, China today is much like America during the Robber Baron era, when economic and industrial growth was king, often at the expense of the ecology around it. China's pollution problems are simply off the chart and many cities require that any individual outside wear a mask of some sort to reduce the inhalation of toxic fumes and smoke. What they would love to do more than anything else is to be able to develop an internal economy capable of absorbing one hundred percent of what they manufacture, making them self-sufficient from a global economic standpoint. Earlier in this book I mentioned that some time ago they engineered, in association with India and other Far Eastern countries, a Far Eastern equivalent of the IMF. China wants to replace us as the leading power in the world and they are on their way to doing it. They are playing a *"long game"* economically and they are winning.

It is not without significance that in the Book of Revelation it speaks of a two hundred million man army coming from what the King James Version calls *"the Kings of the East"*. Unfortunately, that translation is not exactly correct, based on the *Koine* Greek text itself. The actual, literal translation of the Greek text reads, *"The Kings of the Land of the Rising Sun"*. If you know any recent history at all that phrase should immediately bring a shocked response. What nation historically has called itself *"The Land of the Rising Sun"*??? That's right! Japan! Imagine, in the End Times, a Far Eastern hegemony with its own IMF, military prowess and agenda, made up primarily of Japan, China and the satellite Asian countries dependent on them. What is fascinating about the prophecy in Revelation is that at the time that the Lord had John to write it down, there weren't even two hundred million human beings on the entire planet, much less an army of men that large. But now China's population is almost 1.4 billion.

If half of those 1.4 billion people are men then China has a male population of approximately seven hundred million. And it would not be a difficult thing to recruit a two hundred million man army from a pool of seven hundred million men and boys. Now, for the first time in history, a **LITERAL** fulfillment of what God told John the Revelator almost two thousand years ago is not only possible but also highly probable.

China reasons and unfortunately, rightly so, that if they can become economically self-sustaining, consuming everything that they produce in a quasi-capitalistic, quasi-communistic amalgam economy that they won't need our economy to consume their goods any more. If they can achieve that they will call in their T-bill notes effectively bankrupting the United States overnight because we will be totally unable to pay. We are so bankrupt and most of us don't even know it. The only thing that has to happen is for the bank to call the note, just as the real bank did on the poor, struggling farmer we met earlier in this book. Fortunately for us and unfortunately for China, their own economy is struggling at this point and seems unlikely in the immediate future of being capable of coming to a point of self-sufficiency. As long as they don't we can survive to see another day. But when they feel secure enough to pull the plug, they will plunge the entire world, except perhaps for themselves into the most horrible, massive, extended financial collapse in global history.

Japan is actually ahead of China in terms of owning our National Debt and currently holds around

1.3 trillion dollars, over double what we owed them in 2009, when our debt to the Japanese was a mere **$578.3 billion** according to the latest official data from Washington. I shudder when I read those statistics. We now are in debt to the Far East to the tune of roughly **2.5 trillion dollars!** However, the United States is not content to hold the line on those numbers. Some few years ago, then Secretary of State Hilary Clinton made a trip there on behalf of President Obama practically begging the Chinese to buy even more of our debt! It would be disturbing enough if it were merely a matter of finances. Technically, Japan and/or China could ask for their money at any time. To do so would be no different in principle than an investor wanting to sell his stock like my friend Orville Martin or a customer who comes to his local bank branch and asks to withdraw his deposits. But as a minister of the Gospel and a serious student of the End Times, I find it unnerving to the max that we are being held afloat by Japan and China.

Africa will also be spared in the global collapse to a certain extent, but largely because it may well be a corpse continent by that time, ravaged by diseases and ceaseless ethnic, tribal and religious warfare so that its population will be drastically reduced. Its economy could easily become largely non-existent. The entire world will enter into a time of economic devastation unknown in the history of man. Business and industry worldwide will collapse and be unable to rise up. All of the manufacturing plants built outside of the United States will suddenly grow silent because there will be no one left with enough money to buy their products. Shortages of goods and services will sweep throughout the world because we refused to allow small local businessmen to provide those good and services to the local region in which they lived. With no monies available to transport those goods and services the transportation industry will grind to a halt. There will be no eighteen-wheelers plying our superhighways. Airlines will stop flying. Trains will stop moving across the tracks of our country. Starvation, plague and famine will sweep our land. All of this will be coupled with a collapse of the wheat and barley crops in the Northern Hemisphere. This will impact such countries as the US, Canada and the Ukraine. In short, most of the countries with the nukes will be hit the hardest by famine.

You have heard the old phrase, *"Desperate times require desperate measures"*. Never will this be more true. As in Germany during the period after the Crash of 1929 and before World War II, people will desperately search for a strong leader who will promise to lead them out of this terrible time and back into times of peace and prosperity. People will also search for scapegoats to blame for all of this. In Germany, they found the Jews as their scapegoat. And they listened to the words of an unemployed paperhanger named Adolph Hitler, who promised them that if they gave power into his hands, he would lead them into their manifest destiny and establish a one thousand year Reich in which the German people would rule and reign.

One fateful night, the Brownshirts came and destroyed the shops of all the Jewish merchants all across Germany. It was called ***Krystallnacht***, or *the Night of Breaking Glass*, as storefront after storefront was broken into, looted and destroyed. Only this time, it won't only be the Jews who are blamed for this terrible disaster. **It will be the Christians as well.** The catastrophic events of the 3rd and 4th Seals will usher in the greatest period of **Tribulation** the world has ever known, the terrible **5**th **Seal of Revelation.** Christians by the untold millions will have to give their lives for Christ or deny Him to save, at least temporarily, their miserable hides. Only the Swat Team Rescue of the ***Parousia*** or **Rapture** will draw part of the church out of this terrible time. But that will not occur until the end of the **6**th **Seal**, described in Revelation 7:9-11 and confirmed by one of the 24 Elders around the Throne of God in Revelation 7:13-14. This 6th Seal is referred to in both the Olivet Discourse in Matthew 24:21 and in Revelation 7:13-14 as the **Great Tribulation**, a separate and distinct event from the Tribulation itself. Go ahead. Turn to Revelation and read the description of the 5th Seal and tell me that it doesn't match exactly what we describe as the Tribulation. Then read what will happen in the 6th Seal, then read Matthew 24:21-22, Matthew 24:29-31 and try tell me that those events, referred to by both Matthew and Revelation as a **Great Tribulation**, don't match perfectly. And then do me one more favor. Turn to Matthew 24:29 and read that Jesus uses the words, *"immediately AFTER..."* After what? **The Tribulation!** There's so much more, but a great many more events must occur before we can discuss such matters further.

Now, we must return again to the subject of K-Waves. We have looked at a great deal of theory concerning them, but theory must be backed up by fact. That is what the next section of this chapter will deal with; documenting the actual K-Wave crashes that have occurred in the history of the United States.

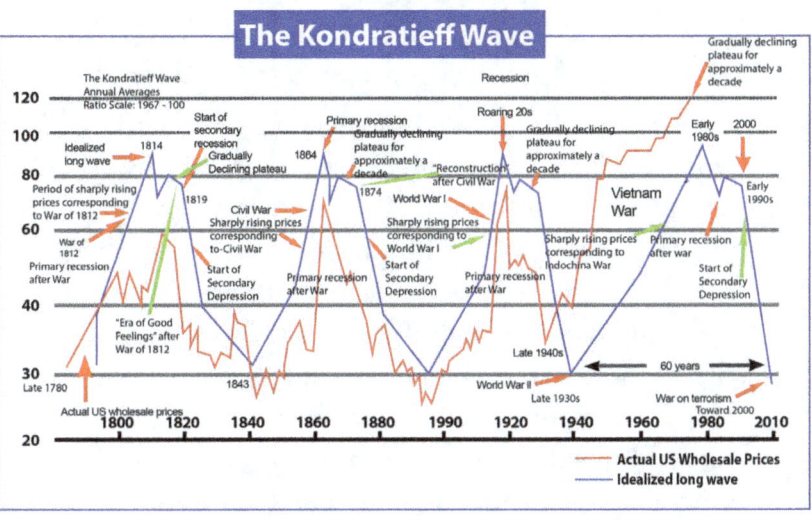

At first, we looked at American K-Waves as a graph and that was very telling and helpful in understanding what a K-Wave looks like and in comparing each successive K-Wave to the previous one in order to understand why changes occurred from one to the other. But when you start to look at the actual numbers that underlie the graph another set of informational nuggets start to reveal themselves.

K-Waves In American History

	1st Cycle	2nd Cycle	3rd Cycle	4th Cycle
Trough	1789	1843	1896	1952
Peak	1814	1864	1920	????
Crash	1825	1872	1929	1980(?)
Depression	1836	1883	1937	????
Recovery	1845	1892	1948	????
Expansion	33 Years	26 Years	28 Years	????
Decline	30 Years	26 Years	28 Years	????
Total Wave	63 Years	52 Years	56 Years	????

First of all, let's define what the row headings represent. The **Trough** is the bottom of the K-Wave. The **Peak** is when the K-Wave reached its period of maximum prosperity. The **Crash** is when everything fell apart. The **Depression** is when things started to get really bad economically. The **Recovery** is when the economy started rallying and began climbing again. The **Expansion** is the number of years that the economy moved in an upward fashion toward increasing prosperity. The **Decline** is the number of years that the economy moved in a downward fashion toward decreasing prosperity and the **Total Wave** represents how long the entire K-Wave lasted, from one trough to another, before we began a new cycle.

HOW LONG IS A K-WAVE?

The first thing we notice is the total length of the respective waves. The first wave lasted sixty-three years, the second only fifty-two and the third, fifty-six. God's economy was meant to be precise and controlled, with seven-year sub-cycles and exact fifty-year major cycles. That way the economy could have had a regular, steady, rhythmic heartbeat. Instead, we find that when we leave the economy to itself we have what heart doctors would call an **arrhythmia** or an irregular heartbeat. It isn't totally off but it isn't totally regular either. None of the waves were less than fifty years but some seemed to go longer than others. The major reason for this was that each cycle was influenced to some extent by cycles that were going on elsewhere which impacted the American cycle. These cycles did not exist in a vacuum. It is much like the weather patterns across the United States. Just as it can sometimes be difficult to be a weather forecaster, so it can sometimes also be difficult to be an economic forecaster. There may be a cold front coming down from Canada but it has to compete with a tropical storm coming up from the Gulf of Mexico. All of these various weather fronts interact with and affect each other. Sometimes it is difficult to predict what that interaction will be. We can know in general terms what will happen from one season to the next but sometimes predicting what will occur on a given day can prove to be problematic. In the same way, it is much easier to predict the broader strokes of an economic cycle than it is to say what will happen in the next year, month or week, much less the daily fluctuations. We simply don't have the tools to do that yet and our understanding of these economic cycles is still far too primitive. It is my hope that this book will stir a greater interest in researching and understanding K-Waves. We have lived in ignorance of the forces around us for far too long.

WHAT GOES UP MUST COME DOWN

The second thing that really jumps out at us is the fact that **it takes as long to go up as it takes to come down.** In the first recorded crash, it took thirty-three years to reach the peak and another thirty years to hit the bottom. In the second recorded crash both

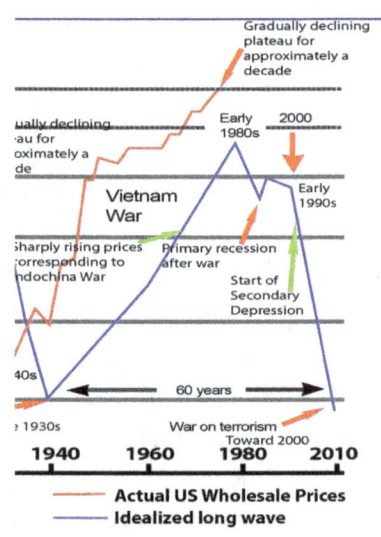

the *"up"* and the *"down"* took twenty-six years and in the third recorded crash it took twenty-eight years for each. There are no shortcuts, no magic formulas and no government programs that can significantly affect the ebb and flow of these magnificent forces of economy. Legend has it that the Persian king Xerxes became outraged when he ordered the tide not to come in and it did anyway. As a *"punishment"*, Xerxes ordered his men to lash the waves with their whips. How ridiculous! How foolish! How totally useless! In the same way, any and all programs that we devise will do nothing more than disrupt the top of the wave and send a few drops of water flailing in some different direction. But our economic whips will have no more influence on changing the tide or preventing it from coming in or going out than the whips of Xerxes's men did in his day.

WHEN IS THE NEXT CRASH COMING?

The third and perhaps most disturbing thing that stands out is **the mysterious absence of the fourth and final crash.** By all rights, using the formulas provided to us by the three previous, predictable crashes, a crash should have occurred in about **1980**. As I have studied K-Waves and crashes, it has become obvious that these cycles are based on the length of **three human generations.** Every fourth generation tends to see a crash. And **when the last member of a generation that has seen a crash finally dies off it is time for a new one**. I can still remember how my mother had my father build rows and rows of shelving on the wall beside the steps that led down to our basement. When I was younger she would often torment me by forcing me to go with her to the grocery store. Even though we had tons of cans of green beans, string beans, peas, corn and the like, every single time that she went to the store she would buy even more of the stuff. Finally, frustrated by what seemed like insanity to me, I blurted out, *"Mom, why in the world are you doing this? We already have* *tons of this stuff at home!"* My mother looked off in the distance and replied, *"Well, you never know!"* It never dawned on me until many years later that she had experienced the crash of 1929 and the Great Depression personally. The terrible scarcity of things that were necessary for life permanently affected her and how she approached things. I found the same thing to be true of my mother-in-law. Even though she was relatively well-to-do later on in her life she had that same economic insecurity based on what she had experienced in her youth. In fact, growing up in Missouri, her family was so poor that they often had nothing to eat but lard sandwiches! How horrible! As a result of this constant infusion of cholesterol into her young body it began to automatically manufacture *"bad"* cholesterol in excessive amounts on its own! Later on in her life she had a constant battle with the problem and had to limit herself to nothing but fat-free foods and ate virtually nothing at meals. Her body was so emaciated that she looked like a survivor from Auschwitz in World War II. But from my generation on till the present we have never experienced lack in our lives. We cannot imagine a time when everyone would be hungry and we would all be having *"Stone Soup"* for lunch, if you will.

If you are not familiar with it, the *"Stone Soup"* story goes as follows: it was a time of great scarcity and want. Almost all the crops had failed and the village in question was facing starvation. All that apparently was left was a large metal pot of water sitting on an open fire. Then one of the villagers had an inspiration.

Walking up to the pot, he proclaimed with a loud voice, *"We are going to have <u>Stone Soup</u> today!"* He then took a large stone he had brought with him and dumped it into the boiling water. *"Now"*, he said to the other villagers, *"What do you have to throw in the pot?"* At first no one moved, but then quietly one person after another left the group, returned to their own home and brought what meager supplies they had to add to the mix. One person had a tomato. Fine! Cut it up and toss it in! Another person brought a single potato. Toss it in! Another, a stalk of celery. In it went! And so it transpired that as each villager brought the little that they did have, far less than what they themselves needed to survive, that the **COMBINED** foodstuffs in the village created a large, nutritious stew that everyone partook of. The village survived only because of the cooperation required to make the Stone Soup. There will come a time when we will have to resort to similar means of cooperative living in order to survive. We will speak more on that subject in a following chapter.

Perhaps it is this **blindness to scarcity that brings about the scarcity itself.** The devil now has a new generation of suckers and rubes to pull his same old tricks on. The last generation that he conned into a crash is now dead. There is now no one left alive to warn the young. But there is another, even more significant cycle of three that also seems to operate in K-Waves. **Just as K-Waves seem to appear in three generation loops**, so **nations and empires seem to last for the span of three K-Waves.** Once a nation or empire has experienced three K-Waves, the fourth wave seems to bring them down. And once they have crashed themselves, they never enter the picture of world domination again. This is a very deep subject and we will return to it later on in this book. All of this has been historically true across the world from the 1700's on. Actually, it has been true all along but Kondratieff only went back that far in his research. But **this time around, something different is happening.** If you refer back to the graphic representation of the K-Waves, you can see how the crash of 1929 was interrupted prematurely by World War II, when a *"Guns and Butter"* economy spurred by the need for military hardware cause the economy to kick start. Once it started back up, it has never stopped climbing. There have been several points at which the economy might have and probably should have crashed but in every case we have dodged the bullet, so to speak and have continued to climb. The reason why this has happened is found in our next chapter, but one thing should be plainly, terrifyingly clear. **The bigger they are, the harder they fall.** Prices and prosperity have been driven to an almost insane level, far higher than in any of the previous waves. This ridiculous height has been driven by forces outside of the American economic loop, as God prepares us and the world for the Final Great Crash that will trigger the events we have discussed earlier. When this Final Great Crash occurs it will drop the entire world to its economic knees. **The length of the crash will be proportionate**

to its ascent. In other words, the time to go back down equals the time that it took to go up. We have been going up since 1952. If we have already peaked, and I think that it can be argued convincingly that we have, we may be looking at a **one hundred year or even larger super-cycle. This K-Wave is a minimum of twice as long and twice as big as any of the previous cycles, much as a tsunami might be compared to a conventional wave.** Based on my understanding of K-Waves the typical ascension period is about **twenty-five to thirty years**. This time it appears that we have an ascension period of roughly **fifty years**. That would put our **peak** at approximately the year **2000**. Again, it is difficult to see where we are in the wave as long as we are actually in the wave itself. Things will be much clearer and easier to see **after the fact.** Unfortunately, we don't have that privilege right now, so we just have to estimate our way through and hope for the best. If the peak of this super-cycle was reached in 2000 then there will be a gradual decline period and temporary plateau twice as long as the normal decline period. If the decline period is also twice as long and it should be then instead of lasting seven to ten years it will last fourteen to twenty years. If I take the midpoint of that range that would have meant that the most likely date for our economy to fall off the edge of the cliff would have been 2016. Obviously, that didn't happen either. To be very truthful, the crash should have already occurred. At this point I **will** share some prophetic information that the Lord gave me over the last few years. Perhaps it will help you to understand how important spiritual things are in impacting economic things.

All of this began back in 1998 when the Lord spoke to me and told me that just as it had been in the days of Joseph in Egypt so it would be in the United States in our day. The Pharaoh had been given a dream. In fact he had been given it in two different forms. Joseph had interpreted those dreams and told the Pharaoh that seven good years of plenty were coming, followed by seven bad years. He also told him that the seven bad years would be so bad that they would *"eat up"* all the remembrance of the seven good years. The Lord then told me that American had **seven good years left.** That was in **1998** and what He told me launched me into an extensive investigation of economic cycles that has eventually led to the writing of this book. *"Aha!"* you say. *"If the Lord spoke to you in 1998 and told you that America had only seven good years left then that would have meant that the Final Great Crash was to have occurred in* **2005!***"* Right you are! And when 2005 came and was nearly gone, I was puzzled and confused. I knew I had heard from God on the matter but I couldn't understand why the crash had not happened. So, I went to the Lord and asked what in the world was going on. I asked Him shortly after the presidential elections had been held and George W. Bush had been re-elected as President of the United States. Here's what He told me: *"America was indeed scheduled to crash in 2005* ***but because***

America has chosen a godly President over an ungodly one, I have decided to delay the crash."

I immediately thought of Jonah, who walked for three days through Nineveh crying *"Yet forty days and Nineveh shall be overthrown!"* After making this **unconditional prophecy**, Jonah calmly settled himself outside the city waiting for the Wrath of God to descend on the Assyrian capital. Much to his consternation, **it didn't happen.** The king of Assyria took the message of destruction to heart and commanded every man and beast in the capital city to fast and pray for three days to see if this judgment could be turned away. Lo and behold, God was merciful and cancelled the judgment, at least for the moment. Assyria would indeed eventually be captured, sacked and burned to the ground by the Babylonians but it didn't happen exactly when Jonah thought it would. I found myself in the same predicament in this case. The Lord had given me what I thought was a firm date, yet He was willing to modify it because our nation made a good choice. As I think back on that election, I marvel at just how close it really was. I lived in the State of Ohio, near Cincinnati during that period of time. Ohio proved to be the pivotal state in the presidential election of that year. I never really understood how just a few votes at the right place and the right time could turn the tide in a critical season and make such an overwhelming difference. We went blindly on our way, unaware of the disaster which we had narrowly averted. I am sure that many of the citizens of Nineveh came out of their fast and said to themselves, *"What the heck was **that** all about? Nothing happened!"* Indeed, nothing **did** happen. But they averted something that **should** have happened and **didn't**. So it was in 2005. We dodged the bullet and didn't even know that it went whizzing past our heads. Since then, the Lord has given me a new date, but for a long time I have had no release from Him to begin talking about it. I have been forced to wait on the watchtower until it is time. If I had announced the coming of the enemy too soon people would have accused me of crying wolf. I will not do that. I will not cry out the date until He tells me it is time. I have announced dates and times and actual full names of individuals in a TV studio audience in the past and they have all come to pass. When it is time and when I finally have a national stance from which to proclaim what God has given me, I will put the trumpet to my mouth and blow it.

I said earlier that America spent fifty years going up. That means that she will probably spend another fifty years coming down. People who have been taught that there will be a nice, quick seven year Tribulation and the supposed *"fact"* that we will be raptured out before any of it happens are going to be in for a real surprise. The folks that have been taught that Jesus could come any second now are going to be in for a real surprise. Based on my study of the Revelation of Jesus Christ, it looks very clear in context that the Wrath of God alone, the 7th Seal, will probably take about forty years to fully come to completion. There is in fact a real seven year period referred to in Daniel, broken into two three-and-one-half-year sub-periods but that seven year period occurs within the context of the Seventh Seal, **after** the Rapture, which occurs at the end of the Sixth Seal. Confused? Not what you've been taught? Troubled? Good! I hope you stay troubled until you go and read the Word of God for yourself, just as I was forced to do fifteen years ago. It troubled me then. It troubles me still. What I found in the Word had very little to do with what was being preached from the pulpits of America at that time. It still has very little in common with what is being preached today. Would it trouble you to know that the 1st Seal, the White Horse of War, began when World War I began? Would it trouble you to know that the 2nd Seal, the Red Horse of Ethnic Genocide, has been opened for a long time as well? Would it trouble you to know that we are currently in at least the 3rd Seal, the Seal of Crop Failure in the Northern Hemisphere and that the Dust Bowl Era of the 1930s may well have been the start of the 3rd Seal itself? I challenge you. Give me one half hour with you and any translation of the Bible that is accurate and authentic. Give me an open mind and a pure heart to receive what I will say. And in one half hour I can **prove to you from Scripture** what I have just been telling you. Only a few weeks ago I sat down with the pastor of the church that we currently attend. His denomination is strongly Pre-Trib, as is he, although he confesses that he himself is not sure about the timing of things. He also has known me for a long time and knew that I had done quite a bit of research on the End Times. So I asked him for a two hour window some weekday morning where he and I could sit down with our Bibles and compare Scripture to Scripture. At the end of the two hours he told me, *"Brother Ray, you have turned everything I thought I knew about the End Times upside down!"* The timetables which we have been given by our so-called prophecy experts are almost all completely wrong. How many promises and predictions have they already made which have not come to pass? When I hear what the body of Christ is being told today, I sigh with frustration and disgust. **Dear friend, it is not going to happen the way they say it is.** God does not count time as we count time. One day with the Lord is the equivalent of one thousand years to man. Not figuratively. Not allegorically. **Literally.** That is totally provable as well. Oh, please don't get me started. There is so much pent up in me. I must speak and tell everyone what God has told me. Yet I have been pent up and held back until my time comes. I pray earnestly that this book is the beginning of my time to speak the Words that the Lord Jesus Christ has given me. And speak them I will, to everyone who will listen.

There is still much that must be said, but not in this chapter. We have accomplished our goal for this chapter, which was to familiarize you with K-Waves in general and how American K-Waves in particular have conducted themselves. We have taken you to the edge of the waterfall and let you look down into the mists into which we must eventually plunge. And we have shown you how God is working in all of this to perform His good, acceptable and perfect will. In Chapter 5, we will look at the mechanisms we must put in place **in order to survive and prosper** (yes, I said prosper!) while everyone else is going to you-know-where in a hand basket. Believe it or not, there is some good news ahead for those who will listen to what God has to say and implement His recovery plan into their lives as quickly as possible.

But we still have an unexplained mystery, and that is why the Fourth Crash didn't occur in the 1980's as predicted. I promised you that I would show you why this happened, and so I will, in **Chapter 4 – The Alpha Female.**

CHAPTER 4

The Alpha Female

Chapter 4 | The Alpha Female

I t all began in 1971 at Wellesley College, an all-female undergraduate institution. A woman named Martha McClintock began doing some research on a strange phenomenon that had been manifesting itself in the student body for some time prior to that. It seemed that if a group of women, all in their child-bearing years, lived with one another for an extended period of time **all of them would begin to experience their monthly periods at the same time.** Generally, **it took about three or four months for their monthly cycles to become synchronized.** The cycles of seven female lifeguards involved in one study were far apart when the women began working together at the start of the summer, but fell within four days of each other three months later. Scientists are not sure what causes this menstrual synchronization but they believe that it may be a female pheromone that in some unknown way triggers the changes in the cycles in others. It has since become known as the **Dormitory Effect.**

Regardless of whether it involves pheromones or not, it is very clear from observing the behavior patterns of all human and animal life on this planet that when a group of individuals come together in some form of social, communal living, an **Alpha Male** or **Alpha Female** arises out of the group as the established leader of the group. Sometimes violence is involved. Often it is not. Among bird species, particularly chickens, it is referred to as the **Pecking Order.** Despite what dear old Lenin wanted to believe, there will never be such a thing as a classless or leaderless society. I can still remember when Russia would send orchestras to America to perform without a conductor. They had taken the concept of a leaderless society to the logical extreme. While it was true that orchestras without a conductor could produce relatively effective music, it was even truer that when an accomplished conductor was added to the mix he was able to take the music to the next level. The Russian government finally gave up and abandoned the experiment, reverting to the accepted method for creating beautiful music. Leadership in any social structure is automatic and assumed. Many people want nothing to do with leadership, while others naturally gravitate to it. Any time I go into a Wal-Mart or some other mass merchandising store, within a matter of minutes someone who is a customer will walk up to me and start asking me questions about where things are located. At first when this happened, I used to react in astonishment. After a while, it became fairly humorous. The "bad widdle boy" in the back of my head used to want to give them ridiculous instructions, just to see if they would follow them. But the big grown up guy in my head would whip the little rascal and send him packing. I would then graciously send them to someone who could help them. Just as there are dominant individuals to whom leadership naturally flows in the social arena, so there are dominant individuals and countries to whom leadership flows in the economic arena. These individuals and countries can be referred to as **Alpha Males** or **Alpha Females.** In America, we tend to see our country as a woman, symbolized by the Statue of Liberty, so I will refer to America as the **Alpha Female** for the entire world as far as economic issues are concerned.

THE UN-UNITED STATES OF AMERICA

In order to understand why the fourth and Final Great Crash has been delayed, we must study the history of our country in order to understand how she was formed, how she grew and how she has come to be the dominant country in the world today. This chapter will contain a lot of maps because in this case a picture is actually worth more than a thousand words. When America was first formed, she was far from an Alpha Country in the world economic community. At first, she was simply **Thirteen Colonies situated along the eastern seacoast** of the North American Continent. Let's take a quick look at what America looked like back then:

In our first wave of growth, we simply clung to the coastline, trying to survive. But as time grew, we began to **expand to the west,** moving toward the Mississippi River, contending with the French and the Indians all along the way. Beyond the Mississippi the rest of the continent was conceded to Spain at the time because she controlled all of South America, Central America and all of the West Coast of North America. Today we take a single, United States as a matter of course but it wouldn't have come out that way without a remarkable series of events, some of which we had no control over. In order to understand what America might have looked like without Divine intervention, let's take a good look at how the entire continent was divided up at the time that America began to expand westward.

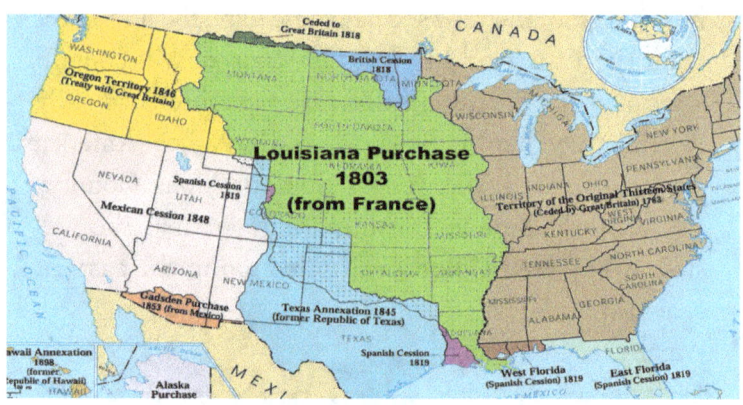

This could be the potential alignment of the **Un-United States** of North America today. As I mentioned earlier in this book, we could have been as many as **nine** different nations or more, much like Europe. Factoring in the Civil War, there would have been a much smaller nation located in the northeastern quadrant of the continent called the **United States of America** but it would have stopped at the Mississippi River and also at the so-called Mason-Dixon Line. South of the line would have been the **Confederated States of America**, which would also have extended to the Mississippi River and then down to the **Republic of Hispaniola**, a composite of Florida, the southernmost tips of Alabama and Mississippi, part of Louisiana up to the Mississippi River, Cuba and the Caribbean Islands. Occupying the center of the continent would have been the **Republic of Louisiana**, a largely French-speaking country, having been successfully settled from the North by the founders of the city of Quebec. This republic would have been bordered on the east by the Mississippi and on the west by the Rocky Mountains. To the south would have been the **Sovereign Republic of Texas**, English speaking but only loosely aligned with either the smaller USA or the CSA located to the east of them. To the west of the Republic of Texas would have been the nation of **Calamexia**, a composite of what we know of today as Mexico, California and most of Central America down to the Isthmus of Panama. And finally, in the Pacific Northwest would be the small but prosperous **Republic of the Palisades**, encompassing what we know today as Washington and Oregon, plus small parts of some of the surrounding states and the Western Coastline of Canada for some distance toward Alaska. Palisades would also be English speaking but with few political ties to anyone else on the continent. In addition, we would have the English speaking giant of the continent, **Canada** and finally, the French speaking nation of **Quebec**, a small but passionately French enclave surrounded by English speaking nations. This would effectively divide the North American continent into **nine separate nations** speaking **three different languages.** None of these nations would begin to wield the kind of political, economic and military power that the United States of America does today. In fact, if we had entered into World War I in this condition, we would have never expanded to be the Alpha Female that we are in the world today and had we entered into World War II in this divided condition it is probable that Hitler would have been effective in his total conquest of Europe and possibly the world. England would have fallen as the last bastion of freedom on the European continent. With no enemy to fight on her western front, the German panzer divisions would have turned their full attention to the Russian threat on her eastern front. It would have only been a matter of time before German tank columns would have rolled into Moscow, Stalingrad and Leningrad and would have crushed forever the fledgling communist regime there. As a side effect of this action, China would never have fallen to Mao Tse Tung, because there would have been no Chinese Communist Party. This would, in turn, have caused massive changes in the power structure of China, the Middle East, Northern Africa, and Central and South America. The Third Reich would still be in power today, along with a series of satellite countries carrying their political doctrines scattered all over the world and a totally unified Europe under the Nazi Swastika would be the most powerful political and military force in the world today. Hitler would have succeeded in his Final Solution and the people known as the Jews would only be a memory today. If you don't think that America appears in the Bible or plays a significant, even critical role in the salvation of the Jewish people and the return of Jesus Christ, please think again! All it would have taken for this scenario to be reality instead of the one we have was for a few minor decisions to have been made or not made here and there. What if the French had not decided to sell the Louisiana Territory to America because Napoleon was low on funds and needed money for his war effort? What if the Civil War had split the United States into two competing nations, fighting against one another every step of the way instead of uniting together to push forward to the Western coastline of the Pacific Ocean? And, oh yes, lest we forget about **Alaska**, let us remember that it was known as **Seward's Folly** when it was first purchased, and was considered to be the act of a madman. After all, it was good for nothing. All we had purchased was a land of ice and snow. Today, it would be a part of the **Grand Republic of Mongolia**, an Asiatic foothold on the North American Continent. **Hawaii** would be a protectorate of the **Imperial Japanese Empire**, who annexed it during the Second World War along with all of **Indonesia, Malaysia, the Philippines, Taiwan, Cambodia, Laos, Vietnam and all the Polynesian Islands.** By adding an Asiatic Alaska and a Japanese Hawaii to the mix, boosting the total to eleven and subtracting Canada and Quebec from the U.S. portion, we come up with a total of **nine different nations** instead of a **single, unified nation** capable of becoming the alpha female for the world. Think America's presence in the world hasn't made a difference? Without us, this world would be a far grimmer, more brutal, less free place. All of Israel would be a graveyard. The Arab world would be a playground for military presences to test out their new killing machines. It is not a world I would want to live in. It would not be a pleasant place to live. There would be no such thing as religious freedom, and slavery would be the common practice in as much as fifty percent of North America.

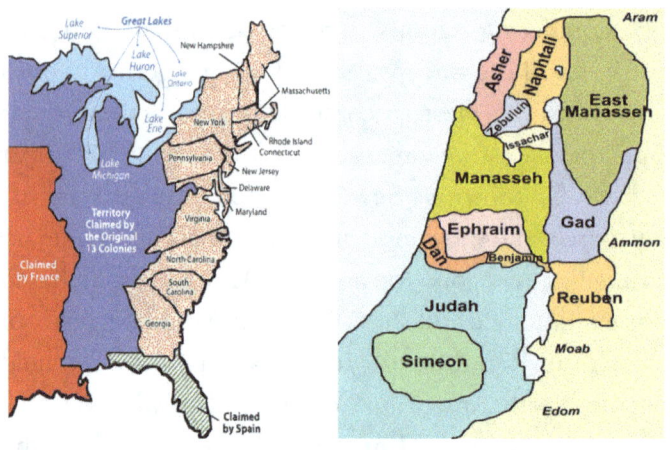

MIRROR IMAGE TWINS

In order to understand America's role as the current Alpha Female for the world economic community, we must go back in time and compare **America** and **Israel** as prime examples of **God's Alpha Countries**, because the parallels between the two are simply amazing. The two countries are actually mirror images of each other, looking exactly alike in some respects but reversed in others. Remember that we told you that the United States had **Thirteen Colonies?** Well, just compare that to the **Thirteen Tribes of Israel.** Yes, I know that Jacob only had twelve sons. But as he neared the end of his life, Joseph came to visit him in Goshen. Jacob then took Manasseh and Ephraim, Joseph's two boys, put them on his knees and officially adopted them as his own children, effectively giving Joseph a **double portion inheritance** and official position as if he were the oldest son. That meant that the descendants of Joseph now counted as **two tribes** and not one, pushing the official number of tribes of Israel from **twelve to thirteen**. Remember how we told you that the United States began on the **Eastern** Shore of a great land mass with a great body of water to the **East,** the **Atlantic Ocean?** Well, consider the fact that Israel began on the **Western** shore of a great land mass with a great body of water to the **West,** the **Mediterranean.** If we take a look at Israel after the conquest of Canaan under Joshua, we can clearly see the tribal land assignments in comparison with the thirteen original colonies with one subtle exception. If you count the actual assignments given to each tribe it turns out that there are thirteen territorial designations but there are a few problems. First of all, **Manasseh** ended up with **two** regions not one and second of all, **Levi** is completely missing! What on earth happened? If you know your Bible, you will recall that when the Children of Israel got ready to cross over the Jordan to enter into their inheritance, **two and one half tribes decided not to cross over.** Reuben, Gad and half of the tribe of Manasseh decided to stay **on the eastern side of the Jordan**. Their decision to do so almost ended up in a civil war between them and the other tribes before the conquest of the land had even begun. The other half of the tribe of Manasseh decided to cross over along with the rest of the tribes, so Manasseh ended up with two large parcels of ground to conquer. That ends up giving us thirteen regions but still doesn't explain what happened to Levi. Again, you need to know your Bible and particularly the Old Testament and a very terrible event surrounding the rash actions of Levi and Reuben. Because their sister Dinah had been raped by a local chieftain's son the boys went on a rampage, slaughtering a whole city. As a result, when Jacob was giving the prophecies over the boys at the end of his life, he said that the descendants of Levi would be scattered and not have a region of their own. However, in the desert after the Exodus, God gracious "recruited" the descendants of Levi to act as priests. While they were scattered across all of Israel, they ended up owning farmland and homes and serving at the Temple in Jerusalem. Once all the smoke had cleared, there were still thirteen American colonies and thirteen Israelite tribes.

Can you see how one is the reverse mirror image of the other? America was planted on the **East Coast** and told to expand to the **West.** Israel was planted on the **West Coast** and told to expand to the **East.** Didn't know that? Let's see what Scripture has to say about what Israel's territorial destiny was **supposed** to be:

> " ¹ *After the death of Moses the servant of the LORD, it came to pass that the LORD spoke to Joshua the son of Nun, Moses' assistant, saying:* ² *'Moses My servant is dead. Now therefore, arise, go over this Jordan, you and all this people,* **to the land which I am giving to them**--*the children of Israel.* ³ *Every place that the sole of your foot will tread upon I have given you, as I said to Moses.* ⁴ **From the wilderness and this Lebanon as far as the great river, the River Euphrates, all the land of the Hittites, and to the Great Sea toward the going down of the sun, shall be your territory.'** "

– JOSHUA 1:1-4

Did you catch what the Lord told Joshua? He told him that the territory of **Israel** was to extend going to the East **all the way to the Euphrates River!** That's a far cry from the Israel we are used to seeing today. Let's take a look below at what Israel gave away by **losing their own Civil War.**

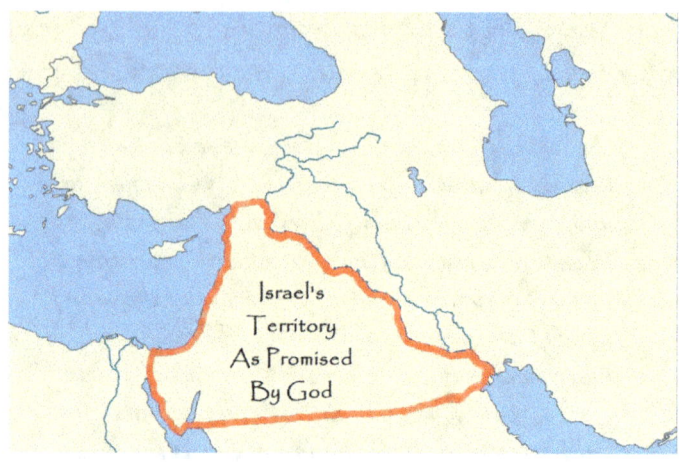

This would have been the **United States of Israel** if only the people of God had obeyed what the Lord told them to do. It would have encompassed modern-day Israel, Syria, Jordan, Lebanon, most of Iraq, a little of Egypt and part of Saudi Arabia. What David had worked so hard to build and Solomon had worked so hard to consolidate, Rehoboam the Retard managed to throw away in just three short days. Had the kingdom not been split in a Civil War which was really never even fought, Israel's efforts would not have been divided by wars between the two kingdoms. Its energies and military might would not have been wasted in constant fighting between the North and the South. And had Israel remained a united kingdom under the descendants of David as was originally intended by God, Israel would have maintained its dramatic push eastward under Solomon having extended its borders all the way to the Euphrates River on the East, encompassing part of Saudi Arabia on the south and flush with the border of Iran on the east, swallowing up their eternal enemies, Ammon, Moab, Mt. Seir, Syria, Lebanon and Jordan. It would have effectively ended the Arab problem and it would have effectively established Israel as one of the most powerful nations in the world. Hitler's Final Solution would never have gotten off the drawing board. Military strike forces from Israel would have dropped the paperhanger dead in his tracks, and I do mean dead! Israel, and not the United States, would be the most powerful, most prosperous nation in the world today, and she, not us, would be the Alpha Female.

But that didn't happen. Israel was split into two warring nations who wore each other out fighting amongst themselves. Because of that, they had no energy left to fight the foes who came at them from the outside, such as the Assyrians, the Babylonians, the Seleucids, the Romans and just about everybody else who decided to ride roughshod through the region. If Israel had been united, none of this would have happened. Israel would have cut through the various nations around it like a hot knife through butter. It would have established its place of international prominence and dominance and would have become the peacekeeper for the world. Instead, the Northern kingdom fell to the Assyrians and the Southern kingdom fell to the Babylonians. What God had originally intended to do was cancelled by the rebellion of his children. For several thousand years, no nation really stepped up to the plate and said, *"God, do for us what You did for them! We will be Your nation, Your people, **one nation under God!"*** Then the Lord smiled, and said to a few fledgling colonies located on the edge of the North American continent, *"All right, let's try it one more time. I will give you a land that you can call your own. I want you to run it according to My statutes and principles, based on My Laws of grace, mercy and holiness. **I will give you the same opportunity that I gave Israel!**"*

America took that opportunity and ran with it. It passed the critical test of Civil War and emerged a unified nation capable within logical limits of moving westward in order to fulfill its manifest destiny to dominate the continent. Out of that emerged the most powerful, most prosperous nation in the history of the world and the nation which has poured more funds into the promotion of the Gospel than any nation in the history of the world except perhaps Great Britain.

Oh, one final interesting mirror statistic. Israel had its capitol in the **South**, and the **North** seceded. America had its capitol in the **North**, and the **South** seceded. Here is a side-by-side comparison of America and Israel. Enjoy!

Israel	America
✓ Founded on Biblical Principles	✓ Founded on Biblical Principles
✓ 13 Tribes	✓ 13 States
✓ Foothold bordered on the West by a sea	✓ Foothold bordered on the East by an ocean
✓ Expansion to the East	✓ Expansion to the West
✓ Split by Civil War	✓ Nearly split by Civil War

✓ Northern Tribes seceded	✓ Southern States failed to secede
✓ Did not dominate subcontinent	✓ Dominated sub-continent
✓ Capital in the South	✓ Capital in the North Stay Outta Our Neighborhood!

STAY OUTTA OUR NEIGHBORHOOD!

As America began to grow and flex its muscles, it decided that the time had come to let Europe know that it was no longer welcome in the Western Hemisphere. Up until that point in time the political structure of the entire Western Hemisphere was the result of European colonization, settlement and manipulation. England, France, Spain, Portugal and Holland had all taken turns trying to establish a foothold with varying degrees of success. Spanish influence had been strongest of all early on, particularly in Central and South America and on the West Coast of North America. But as Spain's power in Europe began to wane, her influence in the west began to wane as well. The French removed themselves from the running through the incompetence of their ruler and the Dutch really only had one small foothold to begin with, where the current New York City stands today. By process of elimination, that left the English. The War of 1812 gave Britain its second straight licking at the hands of those upstart colonists and established our dominance over North America. But there was still quite a bit of meddling going on, and we decided to step up and let everybody know, in a strange combination of chauvinism and courage, that the Western Hemisphere was **our** turf now and that nobody had better come around messing with us!

We didn't word it quite that way, but that's what we actually meant. It is fascinating to read the wording of the Monroe Doctrine, written in 1823. Here is the text of the message:

> *"In the discussions to which this interest has given rise and in the arrangements by which they may terminate the occasion has been judged proper for asserting, as a principle in which the rights and interests of the United States are involved, **that the American continents**, by the free and independent condition which they have assumed and maintain, **are henceforth not to be considered as subjects for future colonization by any European powers**... Of events in that quarter of the globe, with which we have so much intercourse and from which we derive our origin, we have always been **anxious and interested spectators**. The citizens of the United States cherish sentiments the most friendly in favor of the liberty and happiness of their fellow-men on that side of the Atlantic. In the wars of the European powers in matters relating to themselves **we have never taken any part**, nor does it comport with our policy to do so. **It is only when our rights are invaded or seriously menaced that we resent injuries or make preparation for our defense.***

> **With the movements in this hemisphere we are
> of necessity more immediately connected**, *and by
> causes which must be obvious to all enlightened and
> impartial observers.*"

Whew! Now, let's strip away all the legalese and see what we actually said.

1. North America and South America are no longer to be considered targets for colonization by the various European nations.
2. We are keeping an eye on you guys, watching what you are doing.
3. We will try real hard to keep our nose out of your business.
4. We will only get involved if you start messing in our business.
5. Don't mess with us and we won't mess with you!

This declaration effectively established America as the **Alpha Female** of the **Western Hemisphere.** The fact that this political declaration went basically unchallenged by the European powers was simple proof in and of itself that America was strong enough to hold sway over its own neck of the woods.

STEPPING UP TO THE NEXT LEVEL

The new status quo established by the Monroe Doctrine stayed pretty much unchanged until World War I was thrust upon us. America did not want to become involved in that war and viewed itself as isolationist until events transpired against our own ships that made it impossible for us not to become involved. We were, after all, just trying to maintain the conditions which we had established ourselves in the Monroe Doctrine by staying out of European affairs. By the way, it was at this point that the **First Seal of the Scroll of Revelation** was opened. That seal is represented by the **White Horse of War**, with the rider going forth **conquering and to conquer**, wearing a **crown** and carrying a **bow**. Only nations conquer other nations. Crowns indicate the leadership of those nations and a bow might be used for hunting sometimes but in this context it can only represent a **weapon of war.** In comparing a parallel text in Zechariah Chapter Six, we also discover that this action will occur in the **Northern Hemisphere**. By joining the two passages together, we find that the First Seal represents **war between nations in the Northern Hemisphere.** How interesting it is that both world wars have been fought between protagonists exclusively in the Northern Hemisphere.

Let's take a brief look at the Central Powers as they were aligned in the First World War.

It should become immediately obvious that **Germany**, **Austria-Hungary**, **Bulgaria** and **the Ottoman Empire** were the nations that started World War I. It is amazing that these very nations are named by their tribal, ancestral names in Ezekiel 38. Ezekiel names **Gog Magog** (or Gog of the Land of Magog), **Meshech**, **Tubal**, **Gomer** and **Togarmah** as some of the principal tribal groups who will come against Israel during the end of days. Magog refers to the Germanic tribes who settled in Germany and Austria. Meshech and Tubal refer to those Germanic tribes that settled in the western part of Russia. Gomer refers to the Eastern European area, and includes Bulgaria. Togarmah clearly refers to Turkey, which at that time was referred to as the Ottoman Empire. Even in this first conflict, the protagonists were beginning to line up for the final conflict. To be truthful, this so-called *"World War"* was not truly global in scope. It was, however, successful in embroiling the United States in the conflict, thereby involving at least three continents in the battle. By the end of the First World War the scope and influence of the United States had increased considerably. Up until that time our focus and concern had been limited to our hemisphere per our own statements found in the Monroe Doctrine. Now those artificial barriers had been broken by the actions of others. We would never retreat from our expanded role in the world. We now became the Alpha Female for three continents; North America, South America and Europe.

DO WE HAVE TO DO THIS AGAIN?

You would think that Germany, having received such a beating in the First World War, would not be eager for a rematch. But the Triple Entente, the group of nations that opposed them in the First World War, wanted to make sure that Germany was punished severely financially for their role in starting the war. America was not in favor of this but other nations in Europe where the damage had been most severe would not be deterred. England and France demanded annual financial reparations of such magnitude that it forced the German Mark, their equivalent of our dollar, off of the gold standard. As soon as that happened, hyperinflation took control in Germany, effectively destroying the German economy. As a result, German anger and resentment smoldered during the years between the wars and finally erupted when the economies of Europe in general and Germany in particular collapsed due in part to the hyperinflation which we had successfully and inadvertently aided and abetted by our Great Depression. World War II was basically a rematch of the opponents of World War I but with a few new members of the supporting cast included in. Let's take a look at the Axis Powers of World War II and examine the differences.

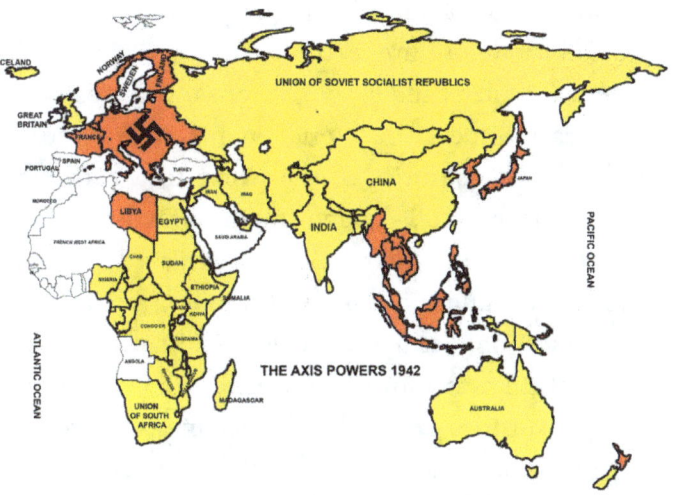

The map above doesn't do true justice to the actual nations involved in starting the war. It shows the extent of the Axis occupation at the peak of the war. This time, Turkey was not a major player on either side. Instead **Italy** took their place led by *Il Duce*, Benito Mussolini. But Italy was not the real problem. Just as in the First World War, **Germany** and **Austria** were the key instigators in this second global conflict. This second war could more accurately be described as a truly world war. This time the African continent would be the scene of many great battles, particularly involving Field General Rommel and his Panzer divisions. The Japanese would spread the fight into the Far East and involve China and most of the nations of the region in the fight. Epic battles would be fought in the Pacific and the war would spread all the way to peaceful Hawaii. Much more than the First World War, this was truly a World War, involving all of the First World, also called the Old World or Europe, the Second World, including America, Canada and untold espionage all across South America and the Third World, entangling many of the undeveloped countries of the world in a battle they wanted no part of. Again America was reluctant to enter the war, but a German U-boat attacked our supply ships flying under a flag of neutrality, forcing us to declare war on Germany. We were still not involved in the Pacific Theater until the treachery of Pearl Harbor, when a surprise attack by the Japanese destroyed a huge percentage of our Pacific fleet, an action which took us several years to recover from. At the end of the Second World War, Germany had been bombed into rubble and two major Japanese cities lay smoldering as radioactive wastelands. Never before in the history of the world had the two initiators of a war been so soundly defeated. Never had a nation so displayed its overwhelming military superiority. Never had a nation risen so rapidly to global prominence. America had been thrust into the position of being the Alpha Female for a huge percentage of the world. We had not gone out of our way to seek the position. It had been thrust upon us by the ungodly actions of others. By the end of World War II the following nations had now become dependent upon us as *"Big Momma"* in the world, setting the political and economic tone for them and their economies:

England	Denmark	Italy	Formosa
France	Finland	Greece	Indonesia
Spain	Sweden	Turkey	Malaysia
Belgium	Norway	Japan	the Philippines
Portugal	Netherlands	Korea	Australia

Doubtless I have missed several nations. That part doesn't really matter. What really matters is that all of this now goes back directly to the **Dormitory Effect** that we discussed at the beginning of this chapter. Yes, America was the Alpha Female now for **all** of these nations. But the monthly cycles of the women within the study took three to four months to synchronize. Let's take a look at the ratios involved for a second. It took **three to four months to synchronize a cycle that is one month in duration.** Does anybody out there see the light? Catch the drift? Understand the clues? **Once again, the pattern of threes has asserted itself.** How many cycles involving a **three** have we already discussed in this book? There is a pattern here that we must pay **very** close attention to. Please notice that it took **three times the length of the cycle to standardize the cycle for all parties concerned.** Say that to yourself a couple of times over until you have locked the principle firmly in your mind. **It takes three times the length of a cycle to establish a new cycle.** Once everyone is on the same page **then and only then can the new cycle proceed in full force again.** Now think about that fourth K-Wave that seemed to launch itself between World War I and World War II. Can anybody see where this is going? At the end of World War I America had a number of new women enter the *"dorm"* of our economic influence. All of those Western European economies coming into the economic house of our own K-Wave disrupted the K-Wave and threw it out of sync. Then, just as we had experienced our own major crash, the demands of the Second World War threw us out of sync **again**. And at the end of World War II a **huge** number of new economic cycles came into the house, disrupting the cycle **again. Each time the cycle was disrupted, it had to restart, this time with an even larger number of players involved in it.** It's kind of like a little snowball that starts at the top of the mountain and just starts rolling downhill. The further it goes, the bigger it gets. Person after person gets swept up in the snowball as it goes farther downhill. Each new impact slows the snowball down slightly but when it picks up speed again it is going faster than ever. Heaven help the house that it hits when it finally gets to the bottom of the hill!

OH, NO! NOT AGAIN!

Just when our own poor K-Wave thought it was safe to come out of the closet, yet another economic crisis shook the world, sending dozens of nations scurrying to our house for safekeeping. What am I referring to? **The economic collapse of the USSR in 1991.** First it had been Western Europe at the end of World War I. Then it had been the Far East at the end of World War II. Finally it was the entire Communist Block and all the nations in Eastern Europe in 1991. Add to that the ladies already living in the house, including all of North and South America, and by the time you add all the ladies up, the only ones **not** in the house are mainland China, which has been largely agrarian until the last few decades and has, up until recently, been unattached to any economic loop other than her own, and Africa, which may end up being a non-factor by the end of the century given the current rate at which deadly diseases and ethnic and religious genocide are spreading. It is not without significance that massive revivals are taking place there right now. This kind of thing happened in the United States just before the Civil War broke out. It happened in Cambodia just before Pol Pot and the Khmer Rouge butchered several million people in the Killing Fields of their own nation. Every time a major bloodbath is about to occur, God quickly harvests as many souls out of that nation as possible so as to maintain the Revelation 7:9 balance in the Bride so that She is truly from every nation, kindred, tribe and tongue. A little too grim for you? Check out the history books for yourself. The evidence is all there, staring us in the face. We just don't want to look at it closely enough to acknowledge the obvious truth.

Now can you begin to understand why our mysterious Fourth K-Wave has not crashed yet? Every time a major influx of new nations came into our own economic loop, it **reset the loop** at least partially, and threw the entire cycle off. This has happened at least **three** times since our last crash. That is why it has built into a **super-cycle of at least one hundred years in duration, fifty years up and fifty years down!** And given that it takes the equivalent of **three cycles to**

establish a new cycle, we may not even be done yet! Technically, this could build into a **mega-cycle of one hundred and fifty years or even a hyper-cycle of two hundred years before it comes crashing down.** But when it finally tips over, oh brother!

WHAT THEN SHALL WE DO?

As we can now clearly see, this super- or mega- or even hyper-cycle is building with all the force of a natural tsunami. It has been driven to an artificial height of unprecedented scale. It has been forced into a time frame two, three or even four times the normal length and height of a K-Wave. This will cause all of the characteristics we outlined earlier in this chapter to be stretched out to an abnormal length, height and depth, making them gigantic in proportion to a conventional K-Wave. **Every aspect of this Fourth K-Wave is now two, three times or more the duration of a conventional wave.** And because we are riding in the midst of the wave, it has made it almost totally undetectable by conventional economists. Everything is so gigantically out of proportion that the individual characteristics of this wave are difficult to see, much like an ant on your arm would have a great deal of difficulty trying to describe the monster on which it was now riding. All it would know would be the details of your arm. It would have no way of seeing the rest of enormous you. It might take pride in knowing about the dozen or so giant stalks (hair!) around it and the lumpy, uneven surface with pot holes (pores!) that it was carefully avoiding, but not much else.

Courtesy of our new understanding of K-Waves, we, on the other hand, can now see this enormous beast on which we are riding and we can clearly tell that we have gone over the top of the mountain and are starting to come back down on the other side. What should have been a seven-to-ten year period of plateau activity may now have been stretched to fourteen to twenty years or even twenty-one to thirty years. **But when the crash portion of the cycle comes, it will stretch into a period of terror, poverty and despair unprecedented in the history of all mankind.**

Is there still time left to prepare for the inevitable crash? And if so, exactly what is it that we can do to prepare ourselves for what is to come? That is the subject of our next chapter, in which we will study the plans that one great man of faith made to protect an entire nation from the side effects of its own economic crash. Now it is time to look at **Chapter 5 -- The Days of Joseph.**

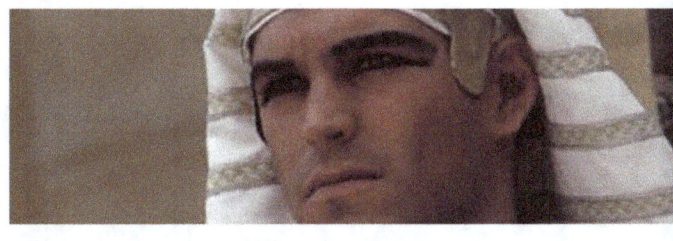

CHAPTER 5

The Days of Joseph

WHERE DO WE GO FROM HERE?

In our previous chapter, things got a little scary. We had a chance to stare into the jaws of the dragon and that will always be unnerving. I hate to do that to people but most people simply won't listen unless they are confronted brutally with the hard cold facts. The problem still remains, however. Exactly what is it that we are supposed to do to prepare ourselves for this coming mega-crash?

In order to find our answers, we must go to the best Answer Book in the whole world. For virtually every problem in the world, the **New Testament** holds the **principle** of how to solve the problem and the **Old Testament** holds the **example**. You're going to say to me, *"C'mon, Pastor Ray! There are no examples of an economic crash in the Bible!"* Ah, dear friend, yes there are. Remember what I told you the symptoms of a crash are? Think back to 1929. After the economic crash of the banking industry and the stock market, what **associated condition** also occurred? Think carefully, now. That's right. **The rain stopped falling. A drought occurred. The Dust Bowl era engulfed America's farmers.** God hit America with a banking crash left hook and a Dust Bowl right cross and we went down for the count.

Now that we know what to look for we can scan the Old Testament and the New Testament for examples of famines. Since the vast majority of the people in those times were farmers any significant crash would have to strike the farming community to begin with. Everything begins and ends with the soil, even today. Now that we know what we are looking for, it doesn't take long for us to find a major drought in the Bible. All we have to do is turn to the Book of Genesis and the story of Joseph. We won't recount the entire story but we will touch on the high points. Joseph was the highly favored son of Jacob's favorite wife, Rachel. His father had given him a coat of many colors which immediately triggered jealousy and cries of favoritism among his brothers. They weren't wrong, either. Jacob is a classic example of a father who had difficulty loving all his children equally and impartially. With twelve sons all clamoring for their father's approval it was probably a full-time job. Joseph didn't help, either. He was also a classic example of the Favorite Son Syndrome: a young man of seventeen, highly anointed of the Lord and capable of having supernatural dreams and revelation from God, yet so full of himself, arrogant and proud, like most seventeen-year-olds in this world today. So sure of himself. So absolutely convinced that he knew it all. This combination of circumstances didn't play well with the brothers so they conspired among themselves first to kill him and then, softened by their brother Judah's pleas, simply decided to sell him into slavery in Egypt. From the slaver's chains into the house of Potiphar, we now see a young man who has had the wind taken out of his sails. No longer was he his daddy's darling little boy. Now he was just a slave and he had to learn to **survive and thrive in a negative environment**. Slowly but surely his character began to develop. He became the dominant person in the household. Disaster quickly followed as his boss's wife decided he looked just a bit too delicious in that toga for her to leave him alone. Once again he was plunged from the position of most highly favored to the bottom of the trash heap. Again he faithfully rebuilt his life. Then two men entered his life who would change it forever. One would be brought out of prison to be impaled on a pole. The other would be brought out of prison to be restored to his former position as cupbearer to the king. But a promise made under the duress of prison was quickly forgotten as soon as he was restored to his former glory. But even though man fails, God does not. Joseph had languished in slavery for thirteen years. During that time, he had slowly changed from being the arrogant seventeen-year-old favored son of a tribal chieftain to a thirty-year-old man capable of quality leadership under the most difficult of circumstances. Finally, his big break came…

*⁹¹ Then it came to pass, **at the end of two full years**, that **Pharaoh had a dream**; and behold, he stood by the river. ² Suddenly there came up out of the river **seven cows, fine looking and fat**; and they fed in the meadow. ³ Then behold, **seven other cows** came up after them out of the river, **ugly and gaunt**, and stood by the other cows on the bank of the river. ⁴ And **the ugly and gaunt cows ate up the seven fine looking and fat cows**. So Pharaoh awoke. ⁵ He slept and **dreamed a second time**; and suddenly **seven***

*heads of grain came up on one stalk, plump and good. * [6] *Then behold, **seven thin heads**, blighted by the east wind, sprang up after them. * [7] *And the **seven thin heads devoured the seven plump and full heads**. So Pharaoh awoke, and indeed, it was a dream."*

— GENESIS *41:1-7*

Pharaoh awoke that morning with a start. No pizza dream, this! It was very clear that the gods (you and I know better now, but he didn't back then) were speaking to him. The only problem was that Pharaoh, who was supposed to be a god himself, had **absolutely no clue** what he was being told! He had seen seven skinny cows eat seven fat cows. He had seen seven skinny heads of grain eat seven fat heads of grain. None of it made any sense at all. It was at that precise moment in time that the Holy Spirit struck the chief cup bearer with unbearable conviction.

" [8] *Now it came to pass in the morning that his spirit was troubled, and he sent and called for all the magicians of Egypt and all its wise men. And Pharaoh told them his dreams, but **there was no one who could interpret them for Pharaoh**. * [9] *Then the chief butler spoke to Pharaoh, saying: 'I remember my faults this day. * [10] *When Pharaoh was angry with his servants, and put me in custody in the house of the captain of the guard, both me and the chief baker, * [11] **we each had a dream in one**

night, he and I. *Each of us dreamed according to the interpretation of his own dream.'"*

— GENESIS 41:8-11

Now Pharaoh was listening intently. The cup bearer had a dream. The baker had a dream. He also had a dream. They finally shared something in common. God knows how to connect the dots and He was doing so at that very moment.

> "¹² *Now there was a young Hebrew man with us there, a servant of the captain of the guard. And we told him, and* **he interpreted our dreams for us***; to each man he interpreted according to his own dream.* ¹³ **And it came to pass, just as he interpreted for us, so it happened.** *He* **restored me** *to my office, and he* **hanged him.***"*

— GENESIS 41:12-13

Now Pharaoh was leaning forward, listening intently. Having dreams was no big deal. **Interpreting them accurately was another.** And it appeared that he had finally found **someone** who could accurately interpret his dreams. Not only that, but this man of the hour was sitting in jail just down the street from the palace! Quickly word was sent from the throne room to the jailhouse. Find that Hebrew boy, get him cleaned up, shaved, properly clothed and get him over here, pronto! Hastily, Joseph was scrubbed down, dressed up and hauled over to the palace. His head must have been reeling with this turn of events. It had been two years since he had accurately interpreted the two men's dreams. At first he thought he had been abandoned and forgotten. Now it appeared that the Lord had remembered him after all. Hastily he was ushered through scenes of unimaginable pomp and beauty until he was facing the most powerful man in the world, someone who made former President Donald Trump look like a used car salesman.

> " *15 And Pharaoh said to Joseph, 'I have had a dream, and there is no one who can interpret it. But **I have heard it said of you that you can understand a dream, to interpret it.'** 16 So Joseph answered Pharaoh, saying, '**It is not in me; God will give Pharaoh an answer of peace.'**"*

> – GENESIS 41:15-16

Joseph had finally learned his lesson. The Bible says that we have this transcendent power in earthenware vessels to show that the power belongs to God and not to us. When he was seventeen it was all about him. Now that he was thirty and much sadder and wiser, he had learned that it is **all about God**. He quickly shifted both the credit and responsibility to God. Pharaoh was so used to individuals coming to him eager to toot their own horns that this came as a shock to him. Here was someone standing before him for the first and perhaps the only time. He was a slave. He could have used this opportunity to plead for his freedom. He could have used it to accuse Potiphar's wife of illegally placing him in jail. Instead, this unknown Hebrew slave was conducting himself with a dignity and selflessness that put his own palace advisers to shame. Pharaoh knew a good man when he saw one. Now he waited to see what this man would give as an interpretation. The personality of the man was made up of the right stuff. Did he also know what he was talking about? Pharaoh related his two dreams. Joseph stood there for just a second, with a faraway look in his eyes, almost as if he were listening to some Still Small Voice inside his head. Then he spoke.

> "25 *Then Joseph said to Pharaoh,* **'The dreams of Pharaoh are one; God has shown Pharaoh what He is about to do***:* 26 *The* **seven good cows** *are* **seven years***, and the* **seven good heads** *are* **seven years; the dreams are one.** 27 *And* **the seven thin and ugly cows** *which came up after them are* **seven years***, and the seven empty heads blighted by*

*the east wind are **seven years of famine**. [28] This is
the thing which I have spoken to Pharaoh. **God has
shown Pharaoh what He is about to do.**"*

– GENESIS 41:25-28

Pharaoh sat there stunned. In just a few sentences
this total unknown had tied everything in the two
dreams into a single, logical conclusion, one with telling
genuineness. Everything this Hebrew slave had said so
far rang true. But he was not done speaking just yet so
Pharaoh leaded forward again and listened intently.

" [29] *Indeed **seven years of great plenty** will
come throughout all the land of Egypt;* [30] *but after
them **seven years of famine will arise**, and **all the
plenty will be forgotten in the land of Egypt; and
the famine will deplete the land**.* [31] *So the plenty
will not be known in the land because of the famine
following, for it will be very severe.* [32] *And **the dream
was repeated to Pharaoh twice** because **the thing
is established by God**, and **God will shortly bring
it to pass.**"*

– GENESIS 41:29-32

The king was intrigued. Seven years of extraordinary
prosperity. That sounded good. But those seven years
of terrible famine, those didn't sound good at all.
This man certainly didn't lack confidence. He had
told His Imperial Majesty that the matter was firmly
established by God. Not even Pharaoh could keep it

from happening. And it would shortly come to pass. There was little time left. Starting today, the clock would begin ticking. They had seven years to prepare, and they needed to start **now**. The tone in Joseph's voice arrested Pharaoh. People didn't tell him what to do. He told them what to do. Under ordinary circumstances he would have had this impudent slave killed where he stood but he couldn't shake the feeling that he was being talked to by the very gods themselves. He listened on to see what else this remarkable man would say.

> " ³³ *Now therefore, let Pharaoh select a* **discerning and wise man,** *and* **set him over the land of Egypt**. ³⁴ *Let Pharaoh do this, and let him appoint officers over the land, to collect* **one-fifth of the produce** *of the land of Egypt in the* **seven plentiful years**. ³⁵ *And let them gather all the food of those good years that are coming, and* **store up grain** *under the authority of Pharaoh, and let them keep food in the cities.* ³⁶ *Then that food shall be* **as a reserve** *for the land for the seven years of famine which shall be in the land of Egypt,* **that the land may not perish** *during the famine.* "

> – GENESIS 41:33-36

The king's jaw dropped to the ground. He had no lack of men who could tell him what was wrong in any given situation. What he was always short of were men who could tell him how to **solve** the problem. Now, literally out of nowhere, here stood a man who had correctly identified the greatest problem his administration would ever face and in the very next breath also identified how to solve the problem. Here, placed before him, was a logical, professional solution to the problem. For the first time in his life the man who was proclaimed to be a god of Egypt was completely blown away.

> "³⁷ *So the advice was good in the eyes of Pharaoh and in the eyes of all his servants.* ³⁸ *And Pharaoh said to his servants, 'Can we find such a one as this,* **a man in whom is the Spirit of God?'** ³⁹ *Then Pharaoh said to Joseph,* **'Inasmuch as God has shown you all this, there is no one as discerning and wise as you.** ⁴⁰ ***You*** *shall be over my house, and all my people shall be ruled according to* **your** *word; only in regard to the throne will I be greater than you.'* ⁴¹ *And Pharaoh said to Joseph, 'See,* **I have set you over all the land of Egypt.**'"

> *— GENESIS 41:37-41*

Suddenly, everything that Joseph had endured was swept away in one glorious moment of time. He had been catapulted from prison to palace in the space of a few sentences. He was now the Shell Answer Man for the most powerful nation in the world. Pharaoh was smart enough to know that you don't let a good man go by without hiring him. He was also smart enough to know the hand of God when he saw it. Joseph's brilliant analysis of the two dreams and his insightful solution to the problem clearly marked him as the man to put the plan into action. The rest, of course, is history. Or is it? We have concentrated on the **man** to the exclusion of his **solution**. Let's follow the timeline just a little further and look at the answer which Joseph proposed, also under the inspiration of the Holy Spirit.

> " *46 Joseph was thirty years old when he stood before Pharaoh, king of Egypt. And Joseph went out from the presence of Pharaoh, and went throughout all the land of Egypt. 47 Now **in the seven plentiful years the ground brought forth abundantly**. 48 So he gathered up all the food of the seven years which were in the land of Egypt, and laid up the food in the cities; he laid up in every city the food of the fields which surrounded them. 49 Joseph gathered very much grain, as the sand of the sea, **until he stopped counting, for it was immeasurable**.* "

> – GENESIS *41:46-49*

So far, so good. Seven abundant years had brought significant resources into the land of Egypt. And Joseph had faithfully carried out the plan given to him by God. Every year, he had laid aside **20% of the nation's income in the form of grain and placed it in storehouses.**

> " *53 Then the seven years of plenty which were in the land of Egypt ended, 54 and the seven years of famine began to come,* ***as Joseph had said****. The famine was in all lands,* ***but in all the land of Egypt there was bread****. 55 So when all the land of Egypt was famished,* ***the people cried to Pharaoh for bread****. Then Pharaoh said to all the Egyptians, 'Go to Joseph;* ***whatever he says to you, do.****' 56 The famine was over all the face of the earth, and* ***Joseph opened all the storehouses and sold to the Egyptians****. And the famine became severe in the land of Egypt. 57 So all countries came to Joseph in Egypt to buy grain, because* ***the famine was severe in all lands.*** "
>
> *– Genesis 41:53-57*

Seven good years had passed. Now we would see if Joseph had really heard from the Lord. Please notice the kind of timetables that He uses. Very few things happen quickly. Many things happen slowly, over a long period of time. He is in no rush, even though we are. And sometimes we have to wait a long time for Him to fulfill His promises. Peter even addressed this when he said that God is not slow as some men count slowness. **Joseph had to stand on faith on the Word of Knowledge that he had received for not seven, but**

eight years. For it would only be in the **eighth year** that all would know if he had been correct or not. Suddenly in the eighth year the rains stopped falling. The Nile River did not overflow its banks as before. And Egypt experienced its first year of crop failure and famine.

I want to stop for just a second in this timeline and jump to another timeline, this one found in the Revelation of Jesus Christ. In the Third Seal there is a time of crop failure of wheat and barley in the Northern Hemisphere. If Joseph's famine lasted seven years, what makes us think that the same kind of event in Revelation will be of any less duration? Again, we have grossly underestimated the timetable of the final book of the Bible. From a Biblical and historical perspective it is probable that the events of Revelation, beginning with the opening of the First Seal all the way the pouring out of the Seventh Bowl might take as much as **one hundred and fifty to two hundred years** to take place. Don't believe me? Just wait, like Joseph did. And see.

What happened during the ensuing seven years is even more instructional to us today than what occurred during the first seven years of prosperity. For it is in examining this timeline that we will discover what will happen to us during the first few years of the crash. What we find will be very disturbing indeed.

> " ¹³ *Now there was* **no bread in all the land***;*
> *for the famine was very severe, so that the land of*
> *Egypt and the land of Canaan languished because*
> *of the famine.* ¹⁴ *And* **Joseph gathered up all the**

money *that was found in the land of Egypt and in the land of Canaan, for the grain which they bought; and Joseph brought the money into Pharaoh's house.* ¹⁵ *So when the money failed in the land of Egypt and in the land of Canaan, all the Egyptians came to Joseph and said, 'Give us bread, for why should we die in your presence?* **For the money has failed.**'"

— GENESIS 47:13-15

Remember this phrase: **"For the money has failed"**. Remember it well. We will come back to it very shortly. Let's travel down the road just a little bit further.

" ¹⁶ *Then Joseph said,* **'Give your livestock**, *and I will give you bread for your livestock, if the money is gone.'* ¹⁷ *So they brought their livestock to Joseph, and Joseph gave them bread in exchange for the horses, the flocks, the cattle of the herds, and for the donkeys. Thus he* **fed them with bread in exchange for all their livestock that year**."

— GENESIS 47:16-17

Now remember this phrase also: ***"Give me your livestock"***. Write it down just under the phrase ***"For the money has failed"***. We are making a list. Soon all of this will make sense. We just need to travel a little bit more.

> " [18] *When that year had ended, they came to him the **next year** and said to him, 'We will not hide from my lord that **our money is gone**; my lord also has **our herds of livestock**. There is **nothing left** in the sight of my lord but **our bodies** and **our lands**.* [19] *Why should we die before your eyes, both we and our land? **Buy us and our land for bread**, and **we and our land will be servants of Pharaoh**; give us seed, that we may live and not die, that the land may not be desolate.' * [20] *Then Joseph bought **all the land of Egypt** for Pharaoh; for every man of the Egyptians sold his field, because the famine was severe upon them. So the land became Pharaoh's.* [21] *And **as for the people**, he moved them **into the cities**, from one end of the borders of Egypt to the other end."*

> – GENESIS 47:18-21

It is at the end of the third year that things begin to get grim. The **money** is gone. The **livestock** are gone. All that remains is the **land** and their **lives** and the land, devastated by the drought, is effectively worthless. But, being farmers and emotionally and economically tied to growing crops, it was impossible for the farmers to let go of their farms. They still believed, against all evidence to the contrary, that somehow the rain would start falling again and that **this** year, if they planted, they would reap. As a result, both the ownership of the land and their personal freedom became forfeit under the grinding burden of lack and want. First **finances**, then **freedom**. Let the reader beware. America is not exempt from any of these things. Egypt was the greatest nation in the world. In seven short years, the people of Egypt were reduced from being a nation of relatively well-off independent land owners to slaves without any personal freedom. In seven years. **Seven years!**

> " 23 *Then Joseph said to the people, 'Indeed I have bought you and your land this day for Pharaoh. Look, here is seed for you, and you shall sow the land.* 24 *And it shall come to pass* **in the harvest that you shall give one-fifth to Pharaoh.** *Four-fifths shall be your own, as seed for the field and for your food, for those of your households and as food for your little ones.'* 25 *So they said, 'You have saved our lives; let us find favor in the sight of my lord, and* **we will be Pharaoh's servants.**' 26 *And Joseph made it a law over the land of Egypt to this day, that Pharaoh should have one-fifth, except for the land of the priests only, which did not become Pharaoh's.*"
>
> – GENESIS *47:23-26*

To add insult to injury, Joseph now instituted a **permanent income tax of twenty percent** on all the farmers of Egypt. Just in case you don't know, our current income tax legislation in the United States was put into place in the early 1900's and was supposed to be a **temporary tax.** In addition, those who have studied that legislation now strongly suggest that the IRS may well have no legal right to levy this tax on us because the correct rendering of the legislation seems to indicate that these taxes shall be levied on **corporations,** not on **individuals**! Unfair, illegal taxation is always the sign of an unfair, oppressive regime. This now enabled the government of Egypt to take monies from their citizens which they were not entitled to. Always remember, **times of duress and difficulty give governments the excuse to enact legislation that would never be tolerated during normal times.** Again, I wrote these previous words back in 2006. Now, history has once again proven the revelation which the Lord has given me to be correct. I will explain what I am referring to in just a second. Just as with Joseph, I can take no credit. By myself, I would never have come to the understanding I have. He, not me, initiated this whole process and literally compelled me to write this book. In so doing, He has revealed marvelous things to me that I never knew, thus fulfilling Jeremiah 33:3, God's Phone Number, which says *"**Call to Me**, and I will answer you, and show you great and mighty things, which you do not know"*. The Economic Stimulus Package of 2009 was rushed through Congress **without even being read**. I understood the sense of urgency which President Obama had and perhaps rightly so. But the Republican members of the Congress were outraged that a **one thousand page document** would be blindly passed by the Democratic majorities of both the House and the Senate without even a moment's thought. Then, when the crisis had finally passed the oppressive legislation would remain, enduring long past the time when it was needed. Let me provide you with a true historical and highly relevant example right out of the pages of our own history books.

POSTMASTER: PLEASE POST IN A CONSPICUOUS PLACE.—JAMES A. FARLEY, Postmaster General

UNDER EXECUTIVE ORDER OF THE PRESIDENT

issued April 5, 1933

all persons are required to deliver

ON OR BEFORE MAY 1, 1933

all GOLD COIN, GOLD BULLION, AND GOLD CERTIFICATES now owned by them to a Federal Reserve Bank, branch or agency, or to any member bank of the Federal Reserve System.

Executive Order

FORBIDDING THE HOARDING OF GOLD COIN, GOLD BULLION
AND GOLD CERTIFICATES

In 1933 at the height of the Depression, President Roosevelt presented Congress with a radical and unprecedented piece of legislation, the **Emergency Banking Act** which Congress passed on March 9 **without having read it and after only the most trivial debate.** House Minority Leader Bertrand H. Snell (R-NY) generously conceded that it was *"entirely out of the ordinary"* to pass legislation that ***"is not even in print at the time it is offered."*** He urged his colleagues to pass it all the same: ***"The house is burning down, and the President of the United States says this is the way to put out the fire. And to me at this time there is only one answer to this question, and that is to <u>give the</u>***

President what he demands and says is necessary to meet the situation."

I hope you weren't chewing gum when you read that last sentence. Surely, if you had been, you would have swallowed it whole in utter astonishment at how closely the circumstances of that event parallel the events of January 2009 and subsequent legislation passed during the recent Covid shutdown.

Among other things, the act **retroactively approved the president's closing of private banks throughout the country for several days the previous week, an act for which he had not bothered to provide a legal justification.** It gave the secretary of the Treasury the power to require all individuals and corporations to **hand over all their gold coins, gold bullion or gold certificates** if in his judgment *"such action is necessary to protect the currency system of the United States."* The Emergency Banking Act reached back in time to amend the Trading with the Enemy Act of 1917, which had originally been intended to criminalize economic intercourse between American citizens and declared enemies of the United States. One provision of the act granted the President the power to regulate and even prohibit *"under such rules and regulations as he may prescribe... any transactions in foreign exchange, export or earmarkings of gold or silver coin or bullion or currency... by any person within the United States."* In 1918 the act was amended to extend its provisions two years beyond the conclusion of hostilities, and to allow the president to *"investigate, regulate, or prohibit"* even the *"hoarding"* of gold by an American. When the highly modified and distorted regulations were re-enacted in 1933 the reaction of the American public was one of astonishment and often anger. Many good citizens correctly assumed that the President had completely lost his mind and buried their gold coins in canisters and jars in the back yard or tucked them safely away in some rafter in the roof of the house. But many U.S. citizens willingly gave up their gold, in some cases in significant amounts because the government offered to do two things. The first thing was to issue **paper currency** supposedly of equal value to the gold in exchange for the precious metal that was being offered up. Unfortunately, President Roosevelt then embarked for the next six months on a crazy-quilt of policy changes regarding the fair market value of gold, often on a daily basis. Needless to say, by the time all the *"shucking and jiving"* had finished, the paper money supposedly equal to the gold turned in had been so badly devalued that it meant that the gold had effectively been stolen from the American public. The other thing which convinced many Americans to turn in their gold was the **promise by the Federal Government itself that as soon as the crisis had passed, their gold would be returned to them.** Apparently, even today that crisis has never passed, because **not one ounce of gold was ever returned to the citizens of our country.** In fact, subsequent legislation tacked on by the President made it **illegal** for any U.S. citizen to own or *"hoard"* any significant amount of gold beyond a few dollars worth.

The parallels between the Great Gold Robbery of 1933 and the 2009 *"Recovery Act"* are too numerous to miss. Particularly unnerving was the fact that in both cases **fundamentally illegal legislation was passed** by both Houses of Congress without even knowing what the legislation contained.

Beware, fellow countrymen and Brothers and Sisters in the Lord! There will come a time again when Americans will be asked to submit to some form of financial or moral insanity without our permission or review under the promise that *"things will get better soon"*. Although Paul tells us to be submissive to the governing authorities, he also tells us not to submit again to a yoke of slavery. While his original concern was primarily doctrinal for the Galatian church, it is wrong for someone set free through the shed blood of Jesus Christ to submit to any yoke of slavery, be it political, physical, financial or spiritual. As our personal freedom disintegrates under the enormous pressure of economic events, we will have to fight harder and harder just to maintain what little freedom we still possess today.

Let me provide you with a Joseph-style timeline for what has happened in the U.S. since the Great Depression. We already documented the Great Gold Robbery of 1933 and how and why it took place. I also issued a stern warning that **ANOTHER** similar situation would eventually arise, stealing yet more away from our precious freedoms and without even the slightest scrutiny by those that we elected to protect those freedoms. That initial warning was issued in 2006.

In 2009, **only three years later**, without warning, the Recovery Act was passed **before the legislation had even been printed out for Congress to read, study and scrutinize!** The same logic was given by our then-legislators as had been given back in 1933. The House was once again burning down, this time almost literally! Legislation was enacted that not only enforced **economic** mandates into place but which, **just like in 1933, took away personal rights and freedom!**

In my 2016 update of the book I issued another warning to my readers in the paragraph beginning with the words, *"Beware"*. Only five years later, the very thing I had warned about came to pass. In 2021 a series of economic crises, triggered by the Covid 19 weaponized virus accidentally released in China **but created in America by a Harvard professor**, triggered a massive series of legislative actions, **again by Democrats**, doling out huge amounts of money for public assistance but also intermingling with that **legislation restricting personal freedoms even more.** In his first year of office supposed-President Joe Biden and his Democrat cronies like Nancy Pelosi and Chuck Schumer effectively passed **the American Rescue Plan**, a sweeping piece of legislation that poured out **1.9 TRILLION dollars of financial aid to Americans.** That would be well and good if it hadn't poured even more gasoline on the economic fire of inflation that has been burning down the house of America for decades, pushing us further and further over the edge of the cliff and speeding up the descent of the giant snowball I described earlier in this book. I am frankly amazed at how far God is letting us go over the edge without the tree branch that we are desperately holding onto snapping and sending us plunging into the void. Remember what I said earlier about hyper- and mega-economic loops and the attendant massive size of the crash when it does come? Friends, it's getting bigger and bigger and bigger and bigger. I shudder to think of how this will end.

The American Rescue Plan would have been bad enough from an economic standpoint, but once politicians are given free reign by a deceived electorate eager for the public dole and spineless legislators who live for two reasons: (1) to get elected and (2) to stay in office, there is no limit to which they will go. It wasn't long after the passage of the American Rescue Plan that **additional** legislation was passed, this time with an even more ominous theme. During the Depression, President Franklin D. Roosevelt signed into law a staggering **3,721 Executive Orders**, laws which, despite the requirements of the U.S. Constitution, **were never validated or approved by Congress.** Coupled with the massive free giveaway of government money to the public have been a very large number of Executive Orders signed by Biden. Granted, his list doesn't begin to compare to Roosevelt's, but the **content** of his Orders, which also violates the Constitution, is just as bad. In September of that year, as part of a push to get more Americans vaccinated, Biden directed the Labor Department to **require** all businesses with 100 or more employees to ensure their workers are either vaccinated or tested once a week. He also signed **an executive order requiring all government employees to be vaccinated, with no option of regular testing to opt out**. And he **required** the 17 million health care workers at facilities receiving funds from Medicare and Medicaid to be fully vaccinated, expanding the mandate to hospitals, home care facilities and dialysis centers around the country. Suggest, yes. Even plead, appealing to people's *"better angels"*, certainly! But **require??? Demand???** Fortunately, the Supreme Court struck down part of the legislation but not all of it.

Not content with the American Rescue Plan, Biden and his Democrat cohorts then proposed the **Build Back Better Act.** It was a bill introduced in the 117th Congress to fulfill aspects of President Joe Biden's Build Back Better Plan. It was spun off from the American Jobs Plan, alongside the Infrastructure Investment and Jobs Act, as a mere **$3.5 trillion** Democratic so-called "reconciliation" package that included provisions related to climate change and social policy. Following negotiations, the price was lowered to a mere **$1.7 trillion**. The bill was passed 220–213 by the House of Representatives on November 19, 2021. Interestingly enough, the package, **proposed** at $3.5 trillion dollars and **scaled back** to a miniscule 1.7 trillion dollars had as one of its primary selling points the fact that it was supposed to *"curb inflation"*. Seriously? Are you kidding me???

Now, in keeping with other Executive Orders that remove personal freedom, just as Joseph did by forcing people to move to the cities so that it would be easier to feed them *(Patriots and fellow Believers!* **BEWARE!!!** *The Holy Spirit just came on me with great power as I wrote those words, confirming to me that during the Final Great Crash, the government will attempt to do the exact same thing again! Do not submit again to a yoke of slavery!!! The inner cities of America will burn with rioting and violence just as Minneapolis did a few years ago once the public dole is cut off and anyone who appears to have anything will be a target for rape, pillage and murder. Flee to the Cities of Refuge which I will discuss later on in this literary work.)*, the Democratic Party has proposed sweeping legislation since at least 2012 which would make it **illegal to promote or discuss facts that disagree with the official party line.** This, my friends, is nothing short of Communism at its very worst! Labeling it *"disinformation"* allows the then-ruling party in office to decide what **is** and what **is not** *"disinformation"*. Let me give you a very true, very accurate example of what I am talking about. In doing so, I am going to make a number of statements that will be widely disputed, even in Christian circles, but Jesus Himself said that it is the **TRUTH** that will make you free, so here, my friends, is the **TRUTH.**

There is great controversy regarding the results of the 2020 Presidential Election. Democrat sources have repeatedly stated that it was the fairest election ever held in the United States. You know, there is something that **is** true about *"The Big Lie"*. If you tell a lie often enough, to as many people as you can, folks will begin to think that the **lie that you are spreading is the truth and the real truth that it is trying to negate and *"cancel"* is actually a lie!** During the 2016 Presidential Election and even for quite some time before the election, the mantra coming repeatedly from Democrat sources and the hopelessly liberal media kept insisting that Presidential candidate Donald Trump was involved with collusion, *"shady business"*, with Russia. In keeping with their plan to implement the Big Lie, they even manufactured a dossier implying that Trump was involved in unpatriotic activities. Then, even when he won the election despite a broadside of **real** "disinformation", they kept up the attack, repeatedly trying to impeach him on those grounds, so-called mental instability and every other piece of dirt they could think of to try and throw on him. The individuals involved in heading up the investigation were far from unbiased, but even so, when all the smoke cleared, the so-called Russian dossier proved to be the **real** lie, manufactured within the bowels of the Democrat hierarchy. Oh, yes, there really **was** collusion all right, not just with Russia but also with China as well! Who was involved? The man who currently sits in the Oval Office and his darling son, Hunter! No investigation was possible as long as the Democrat Party controlled the House. Hopefully now, as I write these words in 2022, in our 118th Congress, a razor-thin Republican majority of 222 to 212 will see the matter through and expose officially to the public the horrifying and disgusting activities of the *"Man who would be King"!*

That Big Lie was almost sufficient for the 2016 election, but even so, the Democrats lost the Presidency. It galled them to think that despite all their efforts, a man was living in the White House who actually knew how to run a successful operation, be it a business, many businesses or a whole nation. Under President Trump's leadership, America suddenly stopped skidding toward the edge of the cliff, turned the car around and kicked down hard on the gas pedal. During the following 4 years, despite never-ending harassment and lies, our country began to recover its economic vitality, even when Covid 19 clouded the skies.

And so a huge plot was constructed, aimed at the 2020 election, perhaps the first truly national attempt to **steal** a Presidential election. Key swing states were targeted: Michigan, Pennsylvania, Georgia, Arizona, Nevada, California, Arizona, New Mexico and any other state that held Democrat inner city majorities, majorities that **controlled the voting polls and the Dominion machines that ran them.** Up until late evening of that fateful day, President Trump held **clear leads** in each of those key states, even supposedly hopelessly Democrat California. Southern California may have been trying to lead the state down the primrose path to destruction but Northern California, more conservative by far, was pushing back hard. And then, officially, the polls closed for tabulation and reporting. But as soon as they did, mysterious activities began to occur. Trucks full of ballots began to appear out of nowhere. Politically neutral observers assigned to make sure that no dirty tricks happened were suddenly blocked and banned from the polling locations, often forced to "observe" from the other side of the street, unable to even see into the building to actually observe what was going on. Dominion voting machines, supposedly the safest ever to be used in a national election, suddenly proved to be disgustingly easy to manipulate, both in the coding that ran the machines and in the totals that they were carrying. When all the smoke cleared, every single state that Trump **had been winning** late into the evening that night suddenly and inexplicably **turned in favor of Joe Biden and other local Democrat candidates.**

The next morning, instead of President Trump winning a clear second term, Joe Biden was declared the winner! I have viewed videos documenting trucks pulling into voting stations and men being seen unloading box after box of *something* and carrying them into the polling stations. I have read affidavits and multiple testimonies of poll workers from multiple locations who were, in many cases, **forcibly removed from their polling location when they objected to what they saw was happening, a clear and deliberate attempt to steal a Presidential Election for the first time in the history of our country.** Now, to cover up the **Great Election Robbery**, even worse by far than the Great Gold Robbery of 1933, the **TRUTH** of what actually happened and was documented in innumerable ways was mysteriously labeled as *"misinformation"*. Why, there were no problems at all! Everything ran smoothly! Greatest, most honest election ever! And on and on and on and on…

One lie after another was propagated from the newly occupied White House, labeling any attempt to disseminate the real truth as misinformation, complete with legal threats and proposed legislation to make it **illegal** and punishable by fine or imprisonment for anyone to make an effort to challenge the official party line coming from the powers that be. They would label every word I have written on this subject in this book as disinformation. Even many Christians, deceived by the world around them, would do the same. Just remember, my friends, in the Parable that Jesus told in Matthew Chapter 24 there were not only five **wise** virgins but five **foolish** ones as well. Which camp are you a part of, my friend? Take a good hard look at what you **say** you believe and what you **practice** in your personal life and political decisions. Wise…or foolish. Which will it be? Remember the fate of the foolish. Remember…

All of this involves a theft even greater than the 2020 Presidential Election, hard as that may be to imagine. The greatest theft proposed in the history of our country is the theft of the right of individual Americans and groups thereof **to express opinions or documented facts that are in variance and violation of the official party line originating from the White House.** I am old enough to remember a time in American politics where open discussion and often hot debate of election issues was a **cherished right** and eagerly practiced by both sides and tolerated as such for the sake of **morality and fairness.** Clearly, both have gone out the door. I have never been more angry at our leadership on both sides of the aisle, Democrats for the deliberate lies that they have fomented and pushed on the American public and Republicans for the total absence of a moral spine to stand up to this horrible robbery and strike it down into the dirt where it belongs. Without a mighty revival that sweeps this country and changes the moral values of many individuals, America will soon lose all vestiges of freedom and the values, rights and privileges outlined in our Constitution and the Bill of Rights will be dumped into a political shredder to be replaced by an autocratic, authoritarian dictatorship. This **cannot** be allowed to happen! Please, Saints of God, **pray without ceasing for**

revival and **fight what is happening with every resource at your disposal.** For those of you who advocate retreating into a cave somewhere and only praying and fasting, I ask you to look at every Old Testament prophet. They didn't just battle spiritual wickedness. They also spoke out strongly against political and public evils brought about by that spiritual wickedness. In the New Testament, John the Baptist, Jesus Himself and even Peter challenged the authorities when they knew that those in power were wrong.

Finally, my favorite example is **Nehemiah.** God entrusted him with the task of returning to Jerusalem to rebuild the walls so that those living inside the city would have a reasonable chance of defending themselves and surviving in the case  of attack from the surrounding peoples and, given the less than excellent relationship which the Jews had with everyone around them, attack would have certainly been guaranteed. When challenged by Sanballat and Tobiah to come to a place involving a certain trap, Nehemiah replied that he was too busy to mess with the likes of them! But if he had done **only** that, it wouldn't have been enough. Instead, Nehemiah did **two very important things** that we need to pay very close attention to and copy in our country today. First, he **prayed.** That action must **always** be first and foremost. Every great man of God down through history, including the Apostles, who said that they needed to devote themselves to prayer and the ministry of the Word, to John Wesley, who said that he had to spend several hours in prayer each day to get anything done, to men like Benny Hinn, all say that the Believer must always begin with prayer. And Nehemiah did just that, but he did one additional thing that secured and pretty much guaranteed the desired outcome. What did he do? Some great spiritual activity? Gather all of the people for a prayer meeting? No, dear friends. None of those things. What did he do? **He posted a watch on the wall, his men working with shovels and trowels in one hand and a sword in the other!!!** (Nehemiah 4:17-18) When his enemies saw that the men of Jerusalem were willing to **fight for what they believed in**, they suddenly began to back down. That's the way it is with bullies. They threaten to do many things. But when suddenly someone stands up to challenge them, their words are often stronger than their actions. American can still be saved, my friends! Grab your Bible, your trowel and, perhaps not your sword just yet, but certainly your voice to be like the little widow woman with the unrighteous judge, harassing your congressional representatives and giving them no rest until the actually stand up and **do something to stop this!**

Just remember, **taxation without representation** caused the **first** American Revolution. It will, in some slightly altered form, cause a **second** American Revolution sometime during the Seventh Seal, the

Wrath of God. I am now speaking prophetically and not predictively, just so you know. At a certain point in the Seventh Seal, after the Rapture of the Bride at the end of the Sixth Seal, America will find itself compromised and betrayed by its leadership into aligning with a new, burgeoning super-power comprised of an alliance between Germany, Austria and the Germanic peoples of Russia and the Ukraine. That coalition will be headed up by a charismatic political figure who will be promising world peace and a cessation of violence in the Middle East. America and the rest of the world will have been brought to this position by a series of limited nuclear engagements, resulting in the nuclear destruction of Seoul, South Korea by North Korea, an abortive attempt by Iran, Iraq, Syria and Saudi Arabia to attack Israel with nuclear weapons, the subsequent destruction of the capitols of all four nations by Israel using its own nuclear weapons (didn't know that they had them, did you???) and a series of *"suitcase"* nuclear bombs which will go off here in the United States. New York, Atlanta and a location somewhere in Minnesota will be severely damaged, along with several others. Some of the top officials of our government will be slain as a result. The individual who steps into that vacuum of power will quickly negotiate with this mysterious figure from the European coalition and surrender a significant amount of American freedom into his hands. That condition will persist for a period of time. But a second American revolution will break out and, at least temporarily, wrest control of this country out of the hands of the Anti-Christ. The American military will play a major role in this uprising, aided and abetted by guerrilla warfare throughout the country. And for one brief moment in time the **wings of a great eagle,** the thunderbird that the ancient Indians honored as the totem of our continent and the symbol of the United States since its inception, will rise one final time and rescue the woman of Revelation 12:14, clothed with the sun, the moon under her feet and a garland of 12 stars on her head, **the nation of Israel**, and will skylift the survivors of Jerusalem away from the rapidly approaching Gog/Magog army to safety in ancient Bozrah (*"Sheepfold"*) in Moab until Christ returns victoriously to bring them back home.

Yes, I know, I know. There have been several movies produced somewhat along these lines. It is not from Hollywood, however, that I get my inspiration and information. Everything I have just told you was given to me in an open vision years ago at 5:00 AM. I was shown a stretched-out map of the world, with red lines going from North Korea to South Korea, from Iran, Iraq, Syria and South Arabia to Israel and then back to their respective capitols again and terrible red dots appearing in the various places in our country that I mentioned. I was not asleep. I was wide awake. The Lord had awakened me that morning and told me, *"Get up, get your tablet and a pen and come into the living room!"* It is not often that I have heard that tone or kind of urgency in His voice so I obeyed immediately. As I sat in my recliner, the whole scenario unfolded before my astonished eyes.

And one more thing occurred which tied down the absolute validity of what I was seeing. I saw a strange red cord extending from North Korea all the way to Syria, indicating that somehow the North Koreans were in collusion with the Syrians regarding nuclear weapons. When I shared this revelation with some relatives a few days later, I was laughed to scorn. What on earth did Syria and North Korea have in common? I just gritted my teeth and waited on the Lord. By the way, that's another exercise you get good at doing if you are in a true prophetic ministry. You hear from God with a mandate to tell people. When you tell them, they make fun of you or ignore you. It comes to pass anyway. You never hear from them again...So I waited. But I didn't have to wait long. Only two days later I was in my office working and my wife Beverly was sitting in the living room watching CNN (The **C**ompletely **N**egative **N**ews **N**etwork) when suddenly she ran into my office yelling, *"Ray! Ray! Syria! North Korea! Israel! What you said just happened!"* I quickly turned from my desk and asked her what she was talking about. *"Come quickly!"* she said. *"They're still talking about it!"* We both rushed back into the living room and listened to what was being said. Early that morning, the announcer said, a group of Israeli fighter jets had flown a surgical strike into Syria all the way to Damascus. Had they bombed some weapons warehouse? No, they had not. Perhaps a house where a known terrorist was being harbored? Not that either. What the Israeli jets had done was to target **one North Korean freighter docked on the Damascus River,** which runs through the city. They had utterly destroyed that single freighter and sunk it to the bottom of the river, never to rise again. The incredible, unbelievable thing was that Israel wasn't saying a single word about it, almost as if it had never happened. And neither was Russia, the military ally of Syria, nor was the United States. And, incredibly, **neither was Syria itself!** It was almost like the incident had never happened! But as intelligence reports began to come in, information became available about the **contents** of that North Korean freighter. What was buried deep within the hold of the ship? **The equipment necessary for Syria to build a nuclear reactor of their own and thus provide them with their own version of the atomic bomb!** That is exactly what the Lord had shown me! When we shared this new information with our skeptical relatives, they hemmed and hawed and quickly changed the subject. Say, how was the local football team doing? Sigh…Such are the perils of being a prophet of the Lord!

No, dear friends, what I received, I received from Heaven itself, from the Lord of Hosts. What Hollywood does not know, nor will it ever know or understand is that this momentarily revived America will **skylift the shattered survivors of Israel out of their country to a safe haven near Bozrah in old Moab until Christ returns and leads them back into the promised land in victory.** After that, America will be viciously suppressed and shattered into four separate pieces, never to be united again until the return of Christ Himself. Over the last fifteen years God has been pouring all of this into me, line by line and precept by precept.

These words have literally poured out of my fingertips as I have been typing. Please take these words and hide them in your heart. They will be confirmed to you by multiple witnesses as time goes on. Perhaps for some of you, I am not the first witness who has said these things. All good and well. The important thing is that God never does **anything** without first revealing it to His servants the prophets. I am a follower of Jesus Christ. I am an educator. I am a businessman. I am a pastor. But, above all else, I am a teacher, a prophet, and, in the Third World, an apostle. My job is simply to listen carefully to His Voice and to speak the Words that He gives to me. It is **His** job to bring them to pass.

We have heard the entire story. We must now turn from the prophetic to the practical. Embedded in the story of Joseph is a timeline for disaster. In that timeline there is also a model for future disasters that can be applied to us today. What happened **then** will happen **again** very soon. And the **way** that it happened then is the way that it will happen again. As a result, we have been provided with two models. The first model tells us how to prepare for disaster. The second model tells us what will happen if we do **not** prepare. Let's look at the prevention model first.

HOW TO SURVIVE A CRASH

1. **Lay aside 20% of your gross income <u>each year</u> and put it into some form of tangible assets.** At this point most Americans, Christian and non-Christian

alike, will simply throw up their hands in alarm and walk away. Why, **nobody** can save that much money! The little woman and I both need to work **two jobs** just to make ends meet. If that is the case, dear friend, then you have your **ends stretched far beyond your means.** Remember, I am not **suggesting** this course of action to you. I am **telling** you that this is the only thing that will work. I am constantly appalled by the level of denial in America. We are incapable of imagining that untouchable, perfect America could ever bring the Wrath of God down on it. It is for this reason that I often become angry with the Charismatic Movement and the phenomenal level of denial found in it even though it was through it that I received the Baptism in the Holy Spirit. I spent over forty years in the pastoral ministry. Time and time again, I counseled individuals who came to me saying, *"Oh, Pastor! I am in terrible distress! Whatever should I do? Please tell me. I will do **anything** to get out of this mess!"* I would dutifully listen to their sad, generally self-inflicted wound of a story. I would then open up the Word of God and show them, in context, **exactly** what they needed to do to rescue themselves from disaster. They would sit in the chair for a few moments, thinking it over and then exclaim, *"Well, Pastor. I'm real sorry. **But I'm just can't do that!**"* Earlier in my ministry, I would beg and plead with them, knowing full well what that course of action would bring into their lives. But I don't do that anymore. I just smile sadly and say,

"I guess I'll be seeing you again in about six months." I then pray with them, shake their hands, and go on to the next item on my agenda. Six months later they again will sit in my office, saying *"Oh, Pastor. I am in terrible distress…"* I will tell them again what I told them before. They will reject the same good and godly counsel again. And in about six months…

2. **Make sure that what you save up is not in the form of standard deposits in a bank or S&L.** Joseph stored **wheat**, something that could be bought and sold in the marketplace, a **tangible asset.** However, I realize that storing wheat may not exactly be the cup of tea for nervous investors who are used to dealing exclusively in terms of money. Remember earlier in this book that I mentioned my dear friend Orville Martin? Let me tell you an amazing true story involving both of us. Orville was a Spirit-filled Christian who lived in Rockport, Indiana. From a professional standpoint, he was an insurance agent, well-respected, fairly prosperous and had lived and worked in Rockport for many years. From a ministry standpoint, he was what the Methodist Church calls a *"Lay Pastor"*. In the early days of Methodism as the Cane Ridge Revival swept across America an untold number of little country churches were established at various country crossroads. Most of them were not large enough to pay a pastor a full-time salary. In some cases, multiple churches would be grouped into what were called

"Circuits". The Methodist Circuit-rider on horseback was famous during the formative years of Methodism in America. In some cases, where there were no nearby churches to group together, a single church would be pastored by a layman who also had a call to ministry and some reasonable training. Orville was that kind of pastor, as was I for many years, performing the dual roles of businessman and pastor. Even though Orville was not full-time in the ministry he had learned down through the years how to listen to the still small voice of the Holy Spirit. In his role as a successful businessman he had amassed a ten thousand dollar nest egg over the years. After considerable prayer, he decided to invest that nest egg in the stock market. Times were good and the market was moving forward aggressively. Orville found a small company which had a tremendous track record and was increasing in value at a remarkable rate. He put his ten thousand dollars into stock in that company. It wasn't too long before that ten thousand dollar investment had generated an additional ten thousand dollars worth of profit and turned his total holdings into a remarkable twenty thousand dollars. But one Sunday, after he had preached in the little country church he was pastoring and was driving back to Rockport, the Lord spoke to him clearly and loudly. *"Orville"*, the Lord said, *"I want you to sell your stock in that company you have invested in the very first thing Monday morning."* What the Lord said took Orville

completely off guard. It didn't make sense from a rational, logical standpoint. The company was generating a great profit. Why on earth did he need to sell and what was the big deal about this urgency to sell the stock the very first thing Monday morning? But after a brief discussion with the Lord as he was driving down the road, Orville relented and agreed to obey Him. He had learned down through the years that obeying God is one of the prerequisites to hearing from God. If you harden your heart and disobey too often, God will stop talking to you or at least your heart will become so hard and your spiritual ears will become so deaf that you can't hear what He is saying to you anymore. So the very first thing that Monday morning Orville called his stock broker and gave him clear orders to sell the stock immediately. The stock broker was even more astonished than Orville had been when the Lord told him to sell while he was driving in his car. The broker brought all the logical arguments to the table. Hadn't the stock performed just as he had said it would? Hadn't it generated a remarkable profit for Orville? Didn't the financials for the company indicate that this profitability would continue for a very long period of time? He pleaded with Orville not to sell the stock. But Orville had heard from God and that ended the matter. He firmly but gently told the broker he had made up his mind. Sell the stock. Sell it right away. The broker reluctantly obeyed Orville's instructions and sold the stock.

Now, Orville was sitting on twenty thousand dollars in cash, his original ten thousand dollar investment and his ten thousand dollar matching profit. He went about his way, knowing that he had obeyed the Lord but having absolutely no idea why it had been necessary. Later on that afternoon the broker called Orville in a state of near-frenzy. *"How did you know???"*, the broker demanded. *"How did you know that there was a scandal brewing inside of the company???"* As Orville listened in astonishment, the broker relayed the entire sad story. It turned out that the little company that looked like such a hot prospect had in fact been *"cooking their books"*, falsifying their financial returns from the very moment they had gone public. Instead of generating a handsome profit the company had in fact been losing its shirt from the very beginning. The owners had desperately been rigging their financial statements to make it look like everything was just fine but the further the situation degenerated, the harder it was to hide the facts of the matter. Finally, early Monday afternoon, the lid had finally blown off and all of the deception had become public knowledge. As a result, the public value of the company's stock had plummeted to a near-zero value almost instantly. Had Orville not obeyed God on that Monday morning, he would have lost **twenty thousand dollars**; his original ten thousand dollar investment and the ten thousand dollars worth of profit which that investment had earned would have been gone forever. If he had waited until Monday afternoon it would have been **too late**. The company would have crashed, taking its stock value with it. It was at this point in time that the plot thickened considerably. At the same exact time that the Lord had spoken to Orville and told him to sell his stock and consequently rescued both his ten thousand dollar initial investment and his ten thousand dollar profit, I was involved in an economic crisis of my own in my own home town. If you will remember, I mentioned two of my friends earlier in this book who owned a Christian bookstore and who were experiencing severe financial distress. I had entered the bookstore one day and discovered that they had virtually no inventory on the shelves with the holiday season coming up. Most people don't know it, but the typical retailer makes almost all of their annual profit during the final three months of the year leading up to Christmas. Unless their shelves are properly stocked with inventory, they will probably experience a significant loss in revenue. The little Christian bookstore was hanging on by the skin of their teeth and would not have survived a bad fourth quarter. I was a minority shareholder in the bookstore at the time and in the process of talking with the wife who ran the bookstore, she shared with me that it would take ten thousand dollars to properly stock the shelves for the holiday season. Obviously, I didn't have ten thousand dollars and frankly didn't know of anyone who had a spare ten thousand dollars that they didn't know what to do with, but God did. As I prayed about the situation the Lord spoke to me and said, *"Call Orville Martin"*. I was very reluctant to do so at first because Orville had loaned me five thousand dollars when I started my business and I had never been able to pay it back. In a remarkable turn of events, Orville had been in attendance at a conference where I was ministering and spontaneously cancelled my debt when he overheard the financial counsel about tithing I gave to a young couple just entering the ministry. But the Lord persisted and so I reluctantly called Orville. I explained what was going on, that the dollar amount in question was not for me personally and asked if he knew of anyone who could help in any way. After a brief pause, he asked me, *"How quickly can you get down here?"* I immediately cancelled my plans for the afternoon and drove as fast as I could to Rockport, Indiana, about an hour's drive time away. When I arrived at Orville's office, he took me into a back room where there was a massive ancient safe. He slowly turned the tumblers and opened the safe with a near-deafening screeching sound. He then took a metal security box out of the safe and told me to sit down. After I did so, he began to count out the ten thousand dollars into my opened hands in the form of ten one thousand dollars bills. I didn't even know that bills in that monetary denomination even existed! I was crying in amazement and joy by the time that he finished. It turned out that after the Lord had rescued his initial investment and subsequent profit he had dedicated the ten thousand dollars worth of profit to the Kingdom of God and asked the Lord to show him how those funds were to be used. It was only minutes later that the Lord told me to call him. He clearly recognized this as the hand of God and was once again obedient. I took the money, thanked him profusely and traveled as fast as I could back home and the little Christian bookstore. I entered the storefront and told the wife that we needed to go to the back office immediately. I then had her sit down in a chair just as Orville had done with me and I began to count off and place into her hands the same ten one thousand dollar bills, one at a time. By the time I had finished, she was a complete, blubbering mess, crying uncontrollably with joy and amazement. It saved the little bookstore that year and allowed them to continue to minister to the body of Christ in the local area. I count the experience as one of the high points in my service to the Lord. But what if Orville had not listened to the Lord on that fateful Sunday afternoon or disobeyed the following Monday morning? His money would have been irretrievably lost and with it any hopes of survival that little Christian bookstore had.

3. If you have significant amounts of money tied up in ERAs, 401-Ks and the like, you need to begin to move **now** to relocate those funds into gold, silver, platinum, land and other **tangible,**

non-depreciable assets, things which are not subject to the destruction of their value in the event of a crash. This will be almost as difficult for some of you as attempting to save 20% back each year. **Do it anyway.** In addition, you will have to be very discreet about the matter, doing it quietly and behind the scenes. There will come a time when angry mobs of wicked men and women will roam the streets, ready to descend on anyone they suspect of having any form of wealth. This is currently the way it is in the ghetto. While I still lived in Evansville, Indiana and was going to college there, I visited the home of the grandmother of a black radical friend of mine. She lived only about a block away from the corner of Lincoln and Governor and the dreaded *Blue Note Lounge*, where most of the bad stuff in Evansville's small inner city took place. When we came to the front of her little *"shotgun"* house, it looked as shabby as all the other properties around it. (By the way, a *"shotgun"* house is so-called because of the way it is constructed. In most cases the property on which it is built has a narrow frontage but a relatively deep lot. Many of these parcels were laid out during the days of early exploration by such men as Lewis and Clark. The theory was that a small cabin would occupy the front of the property, with a large garden cultivated in the back, behind the house for protection. Later on, when larger homes were built, they had no choice but to build the house narrow and long to match the boundaries of the property. It was said somewhat jokingly that if you opened the front and the back doors you could fire a shotgun blast through the house without touching anything. Hence the term, *"shotgun house".*) The paint was peeling off and totally gone in most places. The clapboard siding was worn and warped. The roof was patched and ugly. The porch gave the clear impression that it might cave in at any moment. Such was the outward appearance of the home. But when he and I stepped inside the home it was like we had jumped from the ghetto to the finest upscale neighborhood in the city. On the inside the home was beautiful, immaculately cared for and beautifully outfitted. Being the dumb white boy that I was, I remarked on not only the interior beauty of the home but also the contrast between the inside and the outside. My friend's grandmother just smiled and said, *"Honey, if they knew what I had, they would take it all".* Years of living around ungodly and violent people had taught her to maintain a low profile. We will all need to learn how to do the same.

4. **Multiply the number of years you anticipate that the crash will last by that same 20% to let you know the full amount you must have in reserve to survive the crash.** In Joseph's case, it required **1.4 years of income/grain in reserve to last out the full seven years of famine.** I arrived at that figure by simply multiplying the annual twenty percent (.20)

amount withheld times the seven year span that the crops were good, yielding 1.4 years worth of grain. Although I now know that the down side of the crash will last far in excess of seven years, when all of this began the Lord told me that America would go through seven years of economic devastation to match the seven previous good years. Now I know better. That part has changed for reasons I am not aware of. On the other hand, He has mercifully extended the number of relatively good years a little longer. Does that mean that the backside will also be extended? Hmm…I simply don't know as of the writing of this chapter. Perhaps this is a question I need to bring to Him very soon for additional clarification. Even as I say that I know that the Holy Spirit is prompting me that we have not nearly hit bottom yet and when we do we will be staying there for a quite a while. Right now we are sliding, but we are not in free fall just yet.

5. **Make every effort to ensure that any land you own is 100% debt free.** Remember the story I told you about the two farmers in Dubois County? What happened then will happen again. If you do not own land, make every effort to obtain at least enough to live on. You don't need 40 acres and a mule. But you do need to be debt free. The location of that land is also a major issue. When our economy totally crashes, much of the inner city will either burn to the ground or become even more dangerous than it now is. Downtown Detroit, for

example, would be a **really** bad place to purchase property. If possible, you will even need to avoid suburban land ownership because, just like my friend's grandmother's house, anyone with any visible appearances of prosperity will be a target for mobs and gangs roaming outside of the inner city in search of resources and food. We have some 7th Day Adventist friends who own an underground home outside of French Lick, Indiana. You have to know that they live there in order to know that anyone lives there at all. From the road, the back of the home looks for all the world like a simple hill similar to the mountainous terrain found all over the area. Only when you drive up to and around the little hilltop do you realize that there is a door and windows on the other side, almost like the Hobbits of *The Lord of the Rings* Trilogy. On their land they have made ample provision to survive indefinitely. Hidden just over another rise is a beautiful, well-maintained orchard with a wide variety of fruit trees found in it. Gloria, the wife, is an expect canner and maker of preserves. She has jams, jellies, canned vegetables and even canned meat! I had no idea that you could can meat. What does it taste like? I have absolutely no idea but I am sure that if I was hungry enough, it would be delicious. Proverbs says that to the hungry soul every bitter thing tastes sweet. Not only have they been laying aside enough for several decades for their own needs, they have also been amassing a huge warehouse of all manner of necessary items far beyond their own personal needs. You see, the Lord has already told them that they are going to have to act as a small scale **City of Refuge**, a concept that I will talk about in detail in the next chapter. They know that they are going to have to provide not only for their own family but also for many other believers like them for an indefinite period of time. Quite frankly, places like Montana, Idaho and the Dakotas are looking more and more inviting as time goes on.

6. I have to pause in the narrative for just a moment and share the most remarkable thing that just happened to me. I have been editing the book for its release, making changes, adding current statistics, fixing syntax and spelling errors and the like. I often work late at night when Bev is asleep and there are no distractions, phone calls or crises to pull my focus away. In addition, the Lord and I have had a long-standing pact, if you will, regarding meeting together for prayer around 3:33 in the morning. As I mentioned earlier in the book, Jeremiah 33:3 is called God's Phone Number and says, *"Call to Me, and I will answer you, and show you great and mighty things, which you do not know"*. I had been editing the book earlier in the day but quit for the evening and eventually Bev and I went to bed. I often awake in the middle of the night, most of the time to make use of the bathroom, but sometimes when I check to see what time it is, I find that it is exactly or near to

3:33 AM. If it is, I know that the Lord has ordained it to be a time of meeting and prayer. Such was the case tonight. Without knowing what time it was, I quietly slipped into my office, closed the door and turned on the light. I began editing the book again and then happened to glance at the clock on my computer screen. Sure enough, it was almost exactly 3:33! I took my old, beat up, multiple-underlined Bible and began praying in the Spirit (Unknown Tongues). As I did, I said, in English, *"Speak, Lord, for your servant heareth"*. That's what Eli told little Samuel to say when the Lord came to talk to him. I began praying in the Spirit again and then waited on the Lord to speak to me in my mind. Only one time has He ever spoken to me audibly and then only four words that forever changed my life. Most of the time He speaks to me as a Still Small Voice in my heart/mind/soul/spirit. I waited for a moment and He began to talk with me. He told me that He was going to raise me up and help me to build a City of Refuge of my own, complete with multiple houses, a central great house for meetings and worship and surrounding gardens, fruit trees and the like. I was astonished! Frankly, if Bev and I survived that long, I anticipated that we would have to flee to someone else's City of Refuge, the location of which would be revealed to us at the appropriate time. The Lord told me that He would provide me with significant wealth (Through book sales? Speaking engagements? Who knows?) and that this wealth would in turn be used to purchase hidden property in a wooded, rural area hidden from view just as our friends in French Lick have. That property would then in turn be developed into a City of Refuge. I never expected this but as I prayed He directed my fingers over my closed Bible and told me to open one place and then another without really knowing what I would find in the passages there. What I found was one Scripture after another confirming exactly what He had told me in my spirit. He then told me to tell you. I'm not sure why. Perhaps so that **you** can seek God yourself and have Him raise you up as what is called a Kinsman-Redeemer. But that is the subject of our **next** chapter and I don't want to give all the details away just yet. God is no respecter of persons and what He has promised to do for me, He can certainly do for you! Amen and Amen!!! Now we will return to the current topic. Thanks for putting up with the interruption but I have learned to obey God when He speaks to me. Life is **much** easier that way!

7. Ironically, these parts of the American west which have often been viewed as inhospitable and uninviting may turn out to be the most valuable pieces of land in the continental United States. In April of 2008 the U.S. Geological Service issued a revised report on an area in that part of the country called the **Bakken**. It includes the western two-thirds of North Dakota, western South Dakota, the

extreme eastern part of Montana and portions of Canada. It turns out that the Bakken just happens to be the **largest domestic oil discovery since Alaska's Prudhoe Bay** and has the potential to eliminate **all American dependence on foreign oil!** Ironically, when I first mentioned these states back in 2006 I had no idea what God had placed beneath the ground there. When you walk in the prophetic even the seemingly most insignificant details turn out to be from the Lord. The Energy Information Administration estimated it at **503 billion barrels of oil.** Even if only ten percent of the oil was recoverable, priced at fifty dollars per barrel, we are looking at a natural resource worth more than **2.7 trillion dollars!** The find contains enough crude oil to fully fuel the American economy for forty-one straight years. It has eight times as much oil as Saudi Arabia, eighteen times as much oil as Iraq, twenty-one times as much oil as Kuwait, twenty-two times as much oil as Iran and five hundred times as much oil as Yemen. What is galling about all of this is that we have known about it for a number of years and yet have done nothing. Why on earth, you might ask, is America sitting on resources like this and yet letting the Arab world repeatedly kick us in the teeth and forcing us to pay monstrously exorbitant prices for their oil? Because the environmentalists, special interest group lobbyists and far-left liberals in Congress have blocked all efforts to help America gain her independence from foreign oil. When I first learned about the Bakken I forwarded information about this oil find to all of the individuals who are on our regular email list. Listen to the response I got back from our dear friends Glenna and Rich in Ohio:

"Pastor Ray, Rich and I found out about this just a couple of months ago in the course of investment research. Major corporations in the US have to file form 13F with the SEC that details how much they have invested and what investments they are currently holding. It is considered a public record so anybody can access it. ***We have accessed 13F forms filed by Berkshire Hathaway (owned by Warren Buffet) and others. They're investing in domestic oil. T. Boone Pickens, being an oil tycoon, surely knew about this and has invested heavily in domestic oil.*** *The price of oil is projected to rise 300% by mid-September. Unfortunately, as a nation we've become borrowers and consumers instead of producers and savers and it is because we are importing much more than we're exporting that our trade deficit is so high. Our economy will not turn around until our nation becomes less service-oriented and more industrial. Not only will exporting increase with industry, reducing the trade deficit, but good paying jobs will return (manufacturing jobs generally pay more than the service jobs do.) All those goods we import from China are transported here on ships that use massive amounts of foreign oil... and then when the goods arrive, we still truck them from*

*the west coast to the rest of the country, using still more foreign oil! Think about how much better off we would be to produce most of the goods that we consume instead of importing them from other countries! And if we transition to other fuel sources, which President Obama is really pushing for, we likely won't need that oil 30 or 40 years from now. If we started relying on our own oil now and began to export some of it too, not only would we **not** be slaves to foreign oil, but our economy should begin to recover a little faster."*

I felt certain back then under the Obama administration, which had placed a premium on energy independence, that things would go forward but political maneuvering and manipulation as usual stalled most efforts to exploit those resources. Fears of something called *"fracking"* have also slowed the rate of development. According to the on-line encyclopedia, *Wikipedia,* fracking is defined as follows: *"Hydraulic fracturing (also hydrofracturing, hydrofracking, fracking or fraccing) is a well-stimulation technique in which rock is fractured by a pressurized liquid. The process involves the high-pressure injection of 'fracking fluid' (primarily water, containing sand and other proppants suspended with the aid of thickening agents) into a wellbore to create cracks in the deep-rock formations through which natural gas, petroleum, and brine will flow more freely. When the hydraulic pressure is removed from the well, small grains of hydraulic fracturing proppants (either sand or aluminium oxide) hold the fractures open."*

In addition to the potentially negative environmental effects, such as the pollution of ground water, one of the greatest fears about fracking is the possibility it creates for destructive earthquakes, often in zones where no earthquake activity is anticipated. Let's face it: when you pump materials out of the substrata underground you place pressures on it that normally would not exist. Those pressures will in turn produce conditions of stress that require a shifting of the rock strata in order to relieve those pressures. And those adjustments are often sudden and violent, like the snapping of a rubber band that has been stretched too far and suddenly breaks. That sudden and often violent adjustment to relieve the pressure creates what we know as an earthquake, sometimes a minor tremor, but potentially massively destructive to individuals and above-ground structures. So it seems to be with every step we try to take in the right direction. There are always unanticipated consequences to our actions that have to be weighed out after the fact to see if they justify the actions we are taking. There is no doubt that America could free itself from its mindless dependence on foreign oil. Is it worth the risk we are engendering in the process? Only time will tell. **Make sure that no matter where you live that your home is adequately stocked for repeated crisis situations.** To help you understand what I mean, let me offer some practical examples:

a. **Make sure you purchase a decent sized electric generator.** Back in 2006 when I first began developing this book I would never have thought of this, but in the ensuing years since I first put ink to paper we have witnessed an increasing number of natural disasters. A little over ten years ago, it was a freak ice storm in April, when bees are supposed to be buzzing, birds singing and flowers blooming. It was bizarre to step outside into three inches of snow and rock hard ice and look at all the beautiful blossoms frozen solid. Later on that year, we had a hurricane, of all things, in the Ohio River Valley! Hurricane Ike came inland near Galveston, devastating the city as it passed overhead. But even though storms are supposed to lose their clout as they pass over land and grow stronger as they pass over oceans, Ike stayed strong and brutal. It took me a solid week to cut up and gather all the fallen branches, some of them huge and still quite alive. No sooner had we survived Ike than we moved from the Cincinnati area to the Louisville area and found ourselves cleaning up our new rental home just as we had cleaned up our old one. Yeah, we rent. At one time I owned a very nice suburban home when I lived elsewhere but bankruptcy and other unnatural disasters stripped me of the assets I had. One of my personal prayers is to own a home with at least four or five bedrooms, one for Bev and I, one for a guest bedroom, at least one or two for immediate family that might be in need and one for my office, where I do all my writing. By faith we believe that the Lord will grant us that request. After dealing with the results of Ike we suffered through another very severe ice storm, even worse than the one the previous year. In all three situations, our power went out. In the Great

Ice Storm of 2009, power was lost in the Louisville area in some places for as much as two weeks. Utility repair crews were brought in from all over the continental United States to help deal with the crisis. Fortunately for us, we never lost any of the food in our refrigerator or small freezer. In the case of Ike, we were fortunate enough to live near a fellow believer who owned not one, not two, but **three** large portable generators! It seemed that he was in charge of maintenance for a chain of motels around the Midwest and kept all of these items in reserve at all times in his garage. He lived across the street from us and when the crisis hit, he ran untold hundreds of feet of high durability orange power extension cords from his garage where he had one of the generators assigned to us all the way across the highway between us and through our house to our kitchen. Talk about the Good Samaritan and brotherly love! As we near the End of Days, the weather patterns of our planet are going to become increasingly more unstable and unpredictable. As a result, you are going to need to have a way to generate electricity but not just to keep the fridge running. In our current home we heat the house using natural gas. But natural gas does you no good unless you have electricity to run the thermostat which monitors the temperature of your house and also drives the igniter mechanism which causes the gas to burn and create warmth. Although the peak temperatures of summer can be very uncomfortable without air conditioning, strategic use of fans can help. But when the temperature is ten degrees Fahrenheit, discomfort is the least of your worries. As a result, your generator needs to be strong enough to support your house's heating and air conditioning system while still providing enough hookups for your refrigerator, freezer, several electric-operated independent heating units capable of heating up a room or two and a few assorted devices, particularly any land-based phone you might have in the house. This means that the correct time to buy a portable generator is **not** at the height of the winter storm! During the winter of 2009 we saw places like Home Depot *"nobly"* selling portable generators to the thousands of homeowners without heat at **four times the normal price!** Weren't they nice? Not only do you need to be wise about **when** you buy your generator, you also will have to pay a little extra to get one that can be linked **directly into your circuit box**, wherever it may be so that it can feed power into your electric wiring just like the public utility does during normal times. In addition, you will have to also pay a licensed electrician to hook up the connection that you will plug into. I have learned the hard way not to mess with lightning, natural or man-made. You would be wise to do the same. All in all, it will cost you a little bit, but it will also prevent you from being evicted from your home in the midst of violent, sustained cold weather patterns. In addition, you are going to need to keep an ample supply of gasoline or some other type of appropriate fuel handy to run the generator. Understand that even in the best of circumstances, you will have to run the generator for a while, then shut it off, then run it a while longer. There are a few other things that you can try to acquire to protect you, particularly in cold weather. I mentioned just a moment ago that you need to have a couple of free-standing electric heaters. I don't mean the little junky kind. I mean something that has some substance and can be plugged into a wall plug. Your generator will supply the electricity and the little heaters will do the rest. We actually have some relatives who, due to a devastating flood several years ago that filled their basement with water and the negligence of a former husband lost their conventional furnace system. They still have an old-fashioned manual furnace, once you can fuel using wood but even when they keep it stoked up it still gets pretty cold in their house. They have resorted to using those small, independent electrical heaters to heat up one or two rooms and then bundling up when they go to bed, just like it used to be in times gone by. In previous eras before Thomas Edison and his world-changing inventions, you had to heat using your fireplace. Once you went to bed, the fire would burn down until only embers remained. In the morning you had to jump out of bed, slip your shoes on and hustle to load more wood in and get the fireplace burning brightly again. Everyone and I mean everyone clustered around the fireplace. And mentioning fireplaces also helps me remind you that if you DO have one or more fireplaces, make very, very sure that they are fully functional in the event of a winter-based crisis. Most fireplaces today are only used for decorative purposes but their original intent hasn't gone away. If you're house shopping, including several fireplaces in must-have list of features isn't a bad idea.

b. **Make sure that if you don't have a pantry somewhere you build one.** It doesn't have to be fancy. Scrap lumber will do the trick. It just needs to be sturdy. Just as with the other assets we are recommending, your pantry should be a quietly held secret. Remember, you are probably no longer surrounded by wonderful, Christian souls. And even many of those who say they proclaim Christ may well not remain Christian in the face of persecution and death threats. Jesus specifically said that men would betray one another. What you have in your larder should remain your business and yours alone. How do you stock your shelves? Just like my mother did when I was a child. I shared earlier in this book how she would torment me by making me go shopping with her. Every time we went shopping, mom would pick up a few extra cans of this and a few extra cans of that. The steps going down into our basement looked like a church food pantry. But mom had lived through the Depression, and she knew what it was like to not have food to eat. Make sure that you stock your pantry with **non-perishable** goods. If the United States suffers a breakdown in transportation, as I suspect it will, fresh fruits and vegetables will return to being a rarity, just as they were before we built our vast network of superhighways in the 70's and 80's. Before that, I can remember that as part of our Christmas treat at the little country Methodist church that we attended that we would receive a box of assorted chocolate candies **and an orange.** Fresh fruit was not nearly as available year-round back then as it is today. Make sure that you have plenty of canned fruits and vegetables to keep your diet balanced. Also remember that there may come a time when potable, drinkable water may be hard to find. There are a number of events in Revelation that speak directly to the poisoning of fresh water supplies by what for all the world looks like a comet which explodes high in the atmosphere, raining significant amounts of deadly trace elements such as mercury, zinc and arsenic down on our lakes and streams. The Book of Revelation even calls this comet *Wormwood*, a substance which is extremely poisonous. As a result, you will need a decent supply of bottled water or some sort of filtration system to purify water. I'm afraid that I'm not much of an expert on water purification, so I can't speak knowledgeably on the subject. Do some research and make what is for you the best choice. I do know that there have been some remarkable breakthroughs in this area in recent years. Although these new inventions have been created with the Third World in mind because of their extreme lack of potable water, those same devices will work just as well in America when the crash comes and our infrastructure and supply chains fail on a major level.

c. **Maintain a stock of crisis-related supplies.** This includes a decent first aid kit, a well-stocked tool box, jumper cables, blankets, flashlights, candles and the like. Think creatively. Imagine what you would need to function if the power went off and stayed off for an extended period of time. Include in your list of supplies such things as towels, soap, toothpaste and other toiletries and sundries that you use on a regular basis. Try to stock up on such things as shaving cream, shampoo and other things which might go into short supply in the event of a crisis. Good places to shop for such things, if you are not already doing so, are the myriad *"dollar"* stores which specialize in overstocked items and off-brands. Frankly, we buy most of our items there already, since our income is often modest and we have to stretch every dollar.

d. **Buy directly from farmers when possible.** When you go to the grocery store, even if you buy the generic foodstuffs mentioned in the next point, you are still paying **retail. Never** buy retail if it is humanly possible to do so. In every supply chain, you have at least three separate price checkpoint levels. They are **supplier/ producer, wholesaler** and **retailer.** Most wholesalers sell in bulk quantities to retailers, but some will also sell reduced quantities directly to consumers for an obvious reason: they can get a better selling price selling to you rather than to some retail giant like Wal-Mart or Kroger. You get a price less, sometimes far less, than retail and they get a better profit margin. You'd be amazed at how many wholesalers will sell directly to consumers but it generally doesn't happen because **consumers don't ask them to.** As an example from real life, in a town where we used to live there was a small, privately owned meat packing plant. They were clearly classified as a wholesaler but gladly sold directly to the public as well. We bought on several occasions from them; hamburger, beef and the like and, as an added side benefit, since you are buying meat **fresh** from processing the taste is often far superior to something frozen hard as a rock at retail. Not able to purchase from a wholesaler in the minimum quantities they require? Then go to other members of your family or neighbors and put together a little buying consortium of your own. Yeah, I know. You may not be able to afford a whole side of beef, but if four family members all divvy it up, your portion will fit just fine in your freezer (which we will talk about in just a moment). The Bible specifically says that we have not because we ask not. Ask! What harm is there in doing so? If they say *"No!"* you still have an even better price break available to you. You can go **directly to the supplier/producer.** Right now our *"Prepper"* (Preparing for Apocalypse / Armageddon / Anything) daughter is buying directly from a local farmer. You can buy meat, eggs, vegetables and virtually anything produced directly or indirectly from the soil from farmers for the exact same reason that you want to buy from wholesalers – better prices! Farmer's Markets are an excellent place to start your buying for the three reasons listed above – freshness, taste and price but it also doesn't hurt to go online and Google for farmers in your local area. They will probably be delighted to help you, since most of them are honest, hardworking, conservative individuals who hate where our country is going with a passion. Plus, you never know when a farmer might just turn out to be a mini-City-of-Refuge, a concept we will expand on in just a little bit. Having a few farmers as friends might just save your life by providing a safe place to run when chaos comes.

e. **Buy a freezer.** Small freezers capable of being placed in your kitchen aren't a bad idea but, given the length of the crash that will come, the larger the freezer you can obtain, the better. Many years ago we actually bought a full six foot long freezer from a farmer who no longer needed it and was replacing it with a newer model. Sure, it took four strong men and some hydraulics to get it into our basement, but we used it and used it well. We jokingly called it our *"Mafia on Ice"* freezer because you could have actually stuffed a dead body inside and made it fit, adding a touch of reality to the term, *"Ice him, Guido!"* Sadly, we had to leave it behind when we moved to a new location some distance away.

f. **Buy generic foodstuffs whenever possible**. Trust me, most of the generic equivalents work or taste just as good as the brand name stuff. Once the patent on brand name products, particularly prescription drugs, expires anyone can duplicate the published formula for that drug and offer it much more cheaply than the parent company did. As an example, check out the various four dollar generic drugs that such companies as Wal-Mart, Kroger and Meijer offer. When the doctor prescribes an antibiotic that costs one hundred and twenty dollars for eight tablets ask him to prescribe an alternative that you have to take **two** of instead of just one. Believe me, at four dollars a prescription versus one hundred and twenty dollars, you can swallow twice. It's easier to swallow an extra tablet than it is to swallow the one hundred and sixteen dollar difference.

g. **Begin paying attention to coupons and specials**. We were slow getting into this way of cutting costs, but now we look carefully for every possible way to save a penny. Benjamin Franklin, writing in his *Poor Richard's Almanac*, said that a *"penny saved is a penny earned"*. He's actually quite right in a way that most people don't understand. If I am in business and I increase **sales** by one hundred dollars, I don't increase my **profit** by one hundred dollars. Why? Because of the **cost** of purchasing the item for resale or manufacturing it. My profit may be as little as four or five cents on the dollar, depending on the type of business I am in. However, if I **decrease costs by one hundred dollars**, I also automatically **increase profit by the same amount.** A penny saved (by decreasing costs) is a penny earned (in pure profit). We must learn how to be frugal and wise in all our buying decisions.

h. **Avoid the Rent-A-Whatever Trap.** One of the most deadly financial traps I have ever seen involves firms that will *"rent"* your *"stuff"* to you at a modest monthly rate. Before you rent anything from a place like that, just whip out your little calculator on your smartphone and multiply the monthly *"rental"* amount you will have to pay times the number of months before the *"stuff"* finally becomes yours to keep. Given the often shoddy quality of much of the merchandise sold, it is a guarantee that whatever you purchased will probably break down or wear out long before you are done paying for it. It is also a guarantee that you will end up paying two to three times more for the item if you *"rent"* it, no matter if it is a love seat, a big screen TV, a microwave or anything else that you want to have rather than by **saving up for the item and paying cash.** Rental centers make a killing off the fact that Americans have been advertised into overdrive when it comes to lusting after things and having absolutely no sense of **deferred gratification.** This *"I've gotta have it NOW!"* urge is the same reason that young people are having sex and babies long before they get married if they get married at all. Places such as this prey on the poor and the young in particular, who want to have the same kind of *"stuff"* as the upwardly mobile yuppies on the next economic level above them. What they don't realize is that those yuppies are making the exact same mistake as they are but using their credit cards to do it. Repeat this mantra after me: *"It doesn't have to be NEW. It just has to be NEW TO ME".* After repeating this phrase about a thousand times, you will have successfully deprogrammed yourself from the terrible *"New and Improved"* curse. Learn to check out places like eBay, Craigslist and other similar sites that sell things that are, in many cases, only slightly or gently used and are still as functional as they were when they were brand new. Also, don't be afraid to visit Goodwill, the Salvation Army and other thrift stores and flea market operations. When I find I need something, I simply start to pray and then when I feel a *"Go!"* from the Holy Spirit I start doing a little searching. Almost without fail I find what I am looking for at ten cents on the dollar or less. I often get compliments in both my casual dress and ministry apparel. People ask me what high-end fashion store

I bought the outfit I am wearing at. I just smile and often say nothing but *"Thanks!"* and don't reveal my sources. The simple truth is that pretty much 90% of all of my clothes have come from Goodwill. When I shop there I am constantly amazed at how many **brand new** items are hanging on the racks and sitting on the shelves. Because I worked selling men's clothing at several high-end retail stores when I was going to college, I know how to match slacks and sport coats in such a way as to have multiple outfits. The right choice of two pairs of pants and two matching but contrasting sport coats will yield not two, but **four** outfits! Add a few well-matched shirts and ties and now you may well have multiplied the number of outfits you have all the way to **sixteen!** Always remember, the right tie will *"tie together"* almost any two pieces of clothing like a shirt and pants. Do yourself a big favor. **Never buy retail unless you absolutely have no other choice.** As I edit this book, I am sitting in a chair that I bought **used** for **fifteen dollars** at the University of Cincinnati used equipment store. The huge, beautiful wooden desk which holds up my laptop PC, a huge separate monitor, my router, my landline phone and my nifty new HP LaserJet Pro 200 high speed full color printer cost me a big time **thirty-five dollars!** The 1994 Lincoln Town Car with less than 100,000 miles on it that I used to drive cost me only **three thousand dollars** when I bought it, even though the Blue Book value for it was at least twice that when I purchased it some years ago. Listen, dear friend, you don't necessarily need new stuff. You just need stuff that works. If it doesn't look good, you can **make** it look good with a little elbow grease, a little cleaner and some polish or polyurethane as a final step. We have a cute little motto in our ministry that I came up with many years ago: ***"We the faithful have done so much with so little for so long that we can now do anything with nothing!*** After all, isn't that exactly how God created the universe? He started with nothing and look what He accomplished! You are His child, right??? I would assume that you are **just like your Daddy**, right??? If **He** created **everything** out of **nothing**, then you should be able to at least create **much** out of **little.** The Lord has given us broken and used things all throughout our ministry. Our job was to figure out what was wrong with them and fix them. In our living room we have a credenza made of solid oak that would normally cost at least eight hundred dollars. Our cost? **Zero!** We used to live in a town that had a great many woodworking factories. We were given two identical credenzas that had both been broken and were not sellable but it just so happened that they were broken in two different places. All we did was to disassemble them both, discard the broken components along with the duplicated good pieces and reassembled one perfectly beautiful and completely functional one from the remains of the two broken ones. We also have two beautiful bookshelves which were both assembled out of scrap pieces of wood by a friend's father who was a skilled laborer in woodworking. Our cost for each? **Twenty dollars!** In our dining room we have a beautiful multi-tiered hutch which would normally have sold for at least five hundred dollars. Our price? **Twenty dollars!** It was purchased at a church rummage sale. There was no price on it and when the individual helping us asked what we could pay, the Lord whispered in my ear, *"Twenty dollars"*. I almost choked trying to get the amount out, but when I did, the individual paused for just a second, smiled and said, *"OK!"* In the same way, He has always given us broken and used (and abused!) people to minister to. We have also learned how to figure out what was wrong with them through the Holy Spirit and in many cases fix them as well. And speaking of fixing stuff…

i. **Learn how to fix stuff.** We live in a disposable era. When our manufacturing companies began to send their plants overseas, some good things and some bad things happened at the same time. The good thing, of course, was that the cost of manufacturing any product decreased rapidly because Third World labor is so inexpensive. My Haitian friend Octa once told me that a Haitian man would gladly work for eight dollars. *"An hour???"* I exclaimed. *"Oh no!"*, Octa replied, *"A week!"* It seemed that the typical Haitian husband and father could easily feed his wife and his ten children for an entire week on the kingly amount of eight dollars. The bad thing that happened was that it became easier to **replace** an object rather than **repair** it. Our culture rapidly developed a *"throwaway"* mentality. It was simpler and cheaper to pitch the thing in the trash and buy a new one. Out of that disposable mindset came attitudes similar to it toward children, wives and marriage which today permeate our carnal ways of thinking. In fact, a movie came out a few years ago that had the title of *Starter Wife*, implying that once you were done with this one, you would throw her away just like an old Sony Walkman and go get a newer model. We have begun to think of individuals as disposable pieces of gear. Believe me, I have become the master of the creative fix-up! I have taken apart things I didn't know could be taken apart, and repaired things that I didn't think could be repaired. Fixing stuff also gets the gray matter in your brain working. You start thinking creatively. How can you fix this item instead of replacing it? Now, some things, like light bulbs, for instance, are really not repairable. Once dead, permanently dead. Hold a *Requiem Mortis* for the poor bulb and move on…But other things, like lawnmowers, automobiles and marriages are. Learning to keep the things and people in your life in good repair creates exactly the kind of mindset that I alluded to in an earlier chapter.

I realize that many of these suggestions may seem banal or trivial, but the simple truth is that Christians in America and all over the world are going to have to start rearranging the way that they think about things. We are going to have to re-adopt frugality, creativity and durability as a way of life. And frankly, that's not such a bad thing regardless of the political or economic climate.

8. **Disengage yourself from as much debt as possible.** For many of you, this is in the form of

credit card debt and mortgages. We will discuss this topic in far greater detail in the next chapter.

9. **Tithe to the Lord.** Man, I **know** you didn't want me to tell you that right now! Just remember this: **Isaac sowed and reaped 100 fold in a year of famine.** God's economy is not subject to the rules of the world. He can bless you and prosper you despite the circumstances around you. And, believe me, you will need His blessing in order to survive in what is coming. Most people stop giving to God immediately when things tighten up. Our daughter recently received an emergency appeal from a very well-known Charismatic ministry in the mail. They have a long-standing reputation for excellence in ministry, integrity in financial matters, a spotless record regarding morality and a clear-cut track record of carrying the anointing of God for healing and deliverance throughout the world. But as soon as the economy tightened up a little last year, suddenly Christians stopped giving by the thousands or even millions. Now, mind you, they didn't give up going to the movies or eating out or denying themselves any of their creature comforts. They just decided to chintz God instead. This is always a bad idea. It will be an even worse idea in the years to come.

10. **Change the way you live.** Grow a garden. Can and preserve. Learn to cut coupons. Learn to share resources inside the church instead of duplicating them. In one African-American church I pastored

in the Cincinnati area, I preached a sermon entitled, *"Everything I Need Is In Somebody Else's Garage!"* Virtually all of us have duplicated, unused resources in our garages, attics and spare bedrooms. Following that sermon, I posted an *"I Needa / I Gotta"* board at the back of the church in the foyer. What, you ask, is an *"I Needa / I Gotta"* board? I learned a long time ago that if I preach a sermon and then don't give my congregation a practical way of applying it in their lives, it often falls on deaf ears. In one ear, out the other! So the following Sunday I referred back to my sermon the previous week and explained how the board worked. If you needed something in your life that you couldn't afford but really had to have, you placed your name, your phone number and the item you needed on the *"I Needa"* side of the board. That way, folks who wanted to bless someone could scan the *"I Needa"* side to see if someone in the local body of believers needed something that they had an extra one of sitting somewhere on their property. At the same time, folks with extra things to donate simply listed those items on the *"I Gotta"* side of the board. Other individuals could then scan that side and see if there was anything available that they could use, but hadn't thought about at all or didn't think was possible. The results were overwhelming. Every Sunday, people would stand and praise the Lord and give wonderful testimonies about how the Lord had met a need of theirs through another brother or sister in the Lord. It became literally epidemic, with so many people so excited and eager to give their testimonies that the testimony segment of the worship service often lasted up to an hour. In fact, the joy of giving got so powerful that **SIX CARS** were given away during that first year that we had the board in operation, all of them to people who either didn't have a car at all or who were driving one that was beyond meaningful repair, including my wife and I.

11. At the same time, cut back on trivial expenses whenever and wherever possible. Make some quality decisions about your wardrobe, particularly you girls and women. You don't need brand names. You don't even need knock-offs. You just need something to wear. I already mentioned this but I have many very beautiful casual and formal shirts, ties, pants, sport coats and suits and almost every single one of them was purchased at our local Goodwill for a mere four dollars a shirt or eight dollars a suit. I've preached all over America, India and Africa wearing those clothes and no one, and I mean no one, has ever said anything about my attire except how well I was dressed. My precious wife, who is only two years younger than me, is constantly mistaken for someone in their early to mid-40's and is complimented on her gorgeous outfits. Little do they know that Beverly buys at the same exclusive apparel retailers as I do! She has also mastered the knack of knowing which local churches have the

best clothing ministries and food ministries. We've used them time and time again to make it possible for us to survive when we were going through difficult financial times and also helping our family make ends meet. It's time to scale back on flash and trash, things and bling. It's time to look hard at your budget, and actually learn to live within it.

12. **Begin to step outside of the world economic system.** Given that there will come a time very soon where no one will be able to buy or sell without the Mark of the Beast, it stands to reason that an alternate economic system must be developed, probably relying on barter as a basis of economy. There is no doubt that the current economic system of banking and credit cards will eventually be in the complete control of the Anti-Christ. If you are one of the unfortunate fifty percent of the church left behind after the Rapture, you will have to find a different way to row the boat in a hurry. Don't believe me? Then turn to Matthew, Chapter 25, Verses 1 through 13 and read the parable of the Wise and the Foolish Virgins. Then, also begin to realize that what Jesus said in that passage wasn't just a cute parable. **IT WAS A PROPHECY** spanning almost two thousand years and describing what would happen to the Church in His absence. It also clearly outlined the fact that half of the Church would be ready when He returned and half wouldn't. Compare that passage with what He said about

two in a field and two in a bed and only one being taken and then take a good, hard look at the quality of your Christian life and whether or not you are walking in the Spirit or in the flesh. As one precious Black Sister in the Cincinnati area put it, *"If you'se got more Spirit than flesh, you'se goin' **UP**! If you'se got more flesh than Spirit, you'se stayin' **DOWN**!"* Now, that may not be good grammar, but it is certainly good doctrine! Even if you plan on being in the Sky-lift Segment, still begin thinking outside the box now because, despite everything you have been told, none of us are getting out of this mess without having to go through some serious tribulation. Many Christians, particularly in America, nearly have a heart attack when I imply that they might actually have to break a fingernail for Jesus. One woman who claimed to be deep with God became very agitated when I bluntly told her that unless she was as willing to die for Christ as she was willing to live for Him, she wasn't going to make it. Jesus **NEVER** said that we would escape tribulation or **THE** Tribulation. In fact, He specifically said that in this world it was a guaranteed fact that we **WOULD** have tribulation but to be of good cheer for He has overcome the world. What we **ARE** promised **IF** we are faithful and holy is that we will escape the Wrath that is to come. What is that Wrath? If you read the Revelation of Jesus Christ carefully, you will see that the 7th Seal, the worst one of all, is called **THE WRATH OF GOD**. What is the difference between the Tribulation and the Wrath? It's really pretty simple. **TRIBULATION** is what the Devil does to God's people through ungodly, unholy and unsaved individuals, often cleverly embedded inside of the existing Body of Christ. **WRATH** is what our Heaven Father does to those unholy, ungodly, unsaved individuals as punishment and retaliation against them for what they did to His Kids, namely us! What we go through to become part of the Kingdom of God is far less painful and far less permanent than what our Heavenly Father intends to mete out to those who have come against us. Listen to me, Saints. Your willingness to submit to the Gospel of Jesus Christ had better not be based on some sort of conditional relationship with God. An attitude of, *"Oh, Lord! Bless me and I will serve you!"* is not going to get you where you eventually want to go. I know that what I just said doesn't necessarily fit under the category of stepping outside of the world's economic system, but in a sense, it does. You see, you need to remember that we are **IN** this world but we are not **OF** it. If we are too wedded emotionally to the things of this world, it will be very difficult for us to divorce ourselves both physically and spiritually from them. As a result, we then become a primary target for assimilation into the Great Whore of Babylon, the false religious system that will arise because people will want something **SUPERNATURAL** but not necessarily **HOLY**. Unlike the Borg of Star Trek fame, your assimilation will not occur against your will. Instead, you will insert those Satanic tubules into your own necks by embracing the things of this world a little too tightly. Just remember, if the Devil doesn't have your pocketbook, he probably doesn't have you, either. Paul said it this way, *"I desire not what is yours, BUT* **YOU!**"

13. **Listen to Men of God who are telling you what you <u>need</u> to hear, not what you <u>want</u> to hear.** This is critical. In Jeremiah's day, there were many prophets supposedly speaking for the Lord about the Babylonian situation. The vast majority of them including a certain Hananiah all prophesied that the evil Babylonian soldiers would go away and that all the temple items would be restored. The only prophet telling the truth was Jeremiah. He waited on the Lord until the Lord spoke to him about the false prophet and then spoke what God said **about** Hananiah **to** Hananiah. Two months later, the false prophet was dead, just as Jeremiah had prophesied. When a prophet gives you nothing but good news, be wary of him. True prophets are required to deliver **four things, all beginning with the letter *"C"*: Confrontation, Correction, Consolation and Comfort, <u>in that order</u>!** Certain denominations which claim to be Full Gospel and Spirit-filled forbid any kind of prophecy in their services except exhortation and edification. In short, they cut off any kind of correction or confrontation

at all, thereby stripping the true prophet of God of his or her most important function. It is not surprising, then, that absolutely no true prophets or apostles have come out of those organizations in at least forty years. Equally without surprise is the fact that only about twenty-five percent of their members now speak in unknown tongues. Without the power of the Apostle to transfer the baptism of the Holy Spirit through the laying on of hands, people are not receiving the Holy Spirit, or are receiving a fake baptism consisting of a phrase or two, which they repeat constantly. *"Honda, Honda, Yamaha, Yamaha"* is not what God intends for His people. In addition, please consider the examples of prophecy in the Book of Acts itself. I have a teaching on that subject entitled *"Don't Bug Agabus!"* Agabus is considered to be the prototype New Testament prophet, along with Peter and Paul. In all three cases, these men prophesied confrontation and correction **first**, only to be followed by comfort and consolation if those who had been confronted and corrected actually repented. As a result, we have Ananias and Sapphira dead and pushing up posies. We also have Agabus accurately prophesying a famine over all the land. **Listen to those voices who are not afraid to correct you! They are the ones who are truly from God.**

14. This next point is going to be very controversial for some folks but I cannot leave it out. **Make**

necessary provisions to physically defend yourself and your family in the event of attack. Frankly, too many people have been raised on the images of *"Gentle Jesus, meek and mild"*. Yes, I agree, the first time He was here He was here as the Lamb, not the Lion. He was born in a manger, surrounded by barnyard animals. The only times He got angry were when He overturned the tables of the moneychangers in the Temple, when He cursed that poor, innocent fig tree and finally, the many times when He chewed out the Disciples for being so dense. Even on the cross, He said, *"Father, forgive them because they don't know what they are doing"*. Just remember that when He comes back, He won't be coming back as the Lamb. He'll be coming back as the Lion. If you want to truly understand what that implies, Read Ezekiel Chapters 38-39, Zephaniah Chapters 1-2 (Yeah. I know. You'll probably have to search to find him. Sorry!), Zechariah Chapter 14 and Revelation Chapters 8-19. Friends, it's gonna get ugly. **REALLY** ugly!!! The Bible says that Jesus is coming back and is going to **fight** against the nations that have aligned themselves against Him. In the same way, I personally believe that Christians are going to have to be prepared to defend themselves and their families against marauding bands of rioters and looters, particularly when the economic crash comes and the inner cities burn. Now I don't know kung fu and at the age of 74 I'm no real threat to anyone physically, but there are some things I can do to try and help defend my wife and I. First of all, I have already obtained a license to carry permit. It only cost me about $50 dollars and enables me to own, use and even carry a loaded weapon. Now I have no intention of walking around Tombstone dressed like Wyatt Earp, but I do intend to purchase some sort of handgun in the very near future, along with enough ammunition to last a few rounds. Hopefully, I'll also have the opportunity to take training in how to use the weapon if a crisis arises. I am not in favor of banning all weapons across the United States. The 2nd Amendment guarantees us the right to bear arms. It was necessary in colonial times and it will most likely be necessary again. The constant push from the liberal left to confiscate all weapons is as misguided and useless as it could possibly be. Now, should it be more difficult for any individual to obtain a weapon? Probably so. But the real problem is that gang members and mass murderers don't exactly line up in a registration line at the county seat to register their tactical assault weapons. They buy them out of the trunk of a black sedan or pick them out of a box shipped from somewhere inside Russia or some 3rd World country. Banning all weapons doesn't stop the likes of them. It never has and never will. Crime will always find a way to obtain what it needs by whatever means necessary. Banning all weapons only prevents law-abiding citizens from protecting themselves from those hoodlums and monsters. We don't have a weapon in the house yet, but I do have a pretty potent Taser that I've tested out a few times. Hopefully, if something does happen, I'll remember where I hid it and how to use it without tasing myself. I don't expect everyone to agree about this. Everyone has to make up their own minds about this subject and even in the case of the Cities of Refuge that I will be discussing very soon there will be a breach of opinion between those Cities that are willing to defend themselves at all costs and those who just hope that they won't be found and looted, pillaged and killed. I know. It's a tough choice. I simply think about David. Remember that he is called a man after God's own heart. Yet the cry of the crowds was, *"Saul has slain his thousands, but David his **tens of thousands!**"* David had to fight most of his whole life, often personally, to save himself and those he loved. I stand with David. You pray and decide where you stand and who you stand with and trust God to help you make the right decision for you.

15. **Last of all, begin to learn to lean on the Lord for all your needs.** He is able to provide exceedingly, abundantly above all that you can think or imagine. He just doesn't use conventional means to do so. For example, when we lived in the Cincinnati area we rented a beautiful home on

over an acre of ground. People who came into our home said without fail how beautifully decorated it was. We told them that it was decorated by one of the most famous French decorators in all the world. We would tell them that his name is Jacques de **St. Vincent DePaul**. I hope you recognize the thinly veiled reference to one of the most well-known thrift store networks in the US. What we have has come to us through the most amazing set of circumstances. We have a church organ in our home, complete with the foot pedal base. Our cost? One hundred dollars. How long ago? Over fifteen years ago. We have a solid, dependable riding lawn mower to mow our yard. How much did it cost us? Nothing. It was a gift, given to us by our neighbor next door, who had **three** riding mowers. Our gasoline driven weed eater was a gift. It's not new. It just works. Everything we have was given to us, or came to us in a state of disrepair, and we fixed it. **We take care of the things that God gives us.** If you want God to give you more, take care of what He brings into your life. I know of so many people who squander, waste or destroy the things that come into their lives. **Look to God. Take care of what He gives you.**

NOW, FOR THE BAD NEWS!

It breaks my heart to think of how many Christians are going to be caught in the crash and the events that follow it. I know much to my sorrow that most American Christians won't even pick this book up. They want to read books that are entitled ***"Everything You Ever Wanted Right Now Without Having To Do A Thing To Earn It!"*** This kind of book is rather dedicated to the clear-eyed few who know that something is desperately wrong and want to know what they need to do about it. For the rest of you who think that nothing will go wrong, please allow me give you your timetable for disaster.

1. **The Crops / The Banks / The Economy Fail.** In an agrarian society such as Egypt all that had to happen was for the rain to stop falling or the Nile to stop overflowing its banks for one year. In a more complex society like ours, it would take a combination of events such as occurred in 1929. Either way, the **sources of revenue dry up and stop.** People begin to lose their jobs. People are forced to take jobs below their educational and professional credentials. People at the bottom of the totem pole lose their jobs altogether. Slowly but surely, this creeps up the professional ladder, picking off one person after another.

2. **Available Money Fails.** Once the source of income is gone, all that is left to spend is the **cash on hand.** For some people, that could mean tomorrow, for others next week, for a very few, a few months from now and for the very, very rich, perhaps never, based on their investments. Over the last decade, I have watched

more and more Americans living at the waterline economically. Right now, there are a growing number of Americans living week to week either out of their cars or in a hotel or motel room. Once you fall out of the loop of home ownership or even being able to rent an apartment or lose a working automobile you quickly drop into the category of people who cannot maintain a job. It's a vicious cycle. In order to apply for a job you have to have a permanent address. Most companies will not accept a P.O. Box. You also have to have reliable transportation. Once one or both are lost, you suddenly find yourself without a stable source of income. Without a stable source of income you are unable to come up with the security deposit and one month's rent in advance necessary to rent most homes or apartments. Now you are forced to live week to week, out of a motel room, with rates so astronomical that you will **never** be able to afford conventional housing again unless **someone lends you a hand up, not a hand out.** Many years ago we worked hand-in-hand with a local homeless shelter and were able to not only refer people to them but also provide some of the supplies that they desperately needed to make it from day to day. Our local representative on the city council was constantly harping about how that homeless shelter was servicing *"Drunks, addicts and the toothless vagrants"* of our city. Finally the director of the shelter had heard enough of his mindless rhetoric and asked him to attend their annual Christmas party for the occupants, where food and gifts of necessities like socks, clothing, underwear and the occasional toy were handed out to those who had no way to purchase them. Reluctantly he agreed to attend and found out, much to his astonishment, that over 75% of the occupants of that homeless shelter were **single moms with children, often beaten or abandoned by their fathers and left with just one or two part-time, minimum wage jobs that didn't even come close to paying the rent, much less utilities, food and the like.** He was forever changed by that experience and, as far as I know, actually became an advocate for the shelter from that point on.

3. **Discretionary income fails.** Having run out of available cash, you are now forced to part with the niceties of life. The boat gets sold. The car sitting under the spare carport that you have been meaning to work on for 10 years gets sold for junk. Your health club membership has to be let go. The summer timeshare goes by the wayside. Your vacation to the Bahamas has to be scrapped. Suddenly you find yourself trimming all the *"frills"* out of your life. Everything that is **optional, not mandatory,** gets cut out of your life. Unfortunately, many people have already had to dispense with such niceties. In fact, this trim-down process has been going on for about twenty years in our culture. Not everyone is doing it, but it is slowly creeping up the economic scale.

4. **Home ownership fails.** At this point, things begin to get serious. Remember that we established that **debt-free ownership of land is the basis for all prosperity**. When ownership of land is lost you have lost your ability to regenerate income. Slowly but surely all equity is drained out of your life. Debt increases dramatically. Bankruptcy laws tighten up (wait a minute! Didn't that just happen all the way back in 2008? Hmm...) You have now become a **disenfranchised citizen.** Without economic resources, you have also effectively lost all legal recourse against anyone who wants to come and defraud you. I used to work for a county government as a Systems Administrator and got to know more lawyers in a few years than I had ever met previously in my entire lifetime. I got to see the seamy underside of America's court systems. True, there were some good employees and good judges. But the frightening truth is that most people who work for the government at any level do so because they cannot obtain a normal job in the workplace. Instead, they are employed because their cousin Harry got elected Dogcatcher and the Auditor owes him a political favor. Do I sound too cynical? Not only did I work **for** county government, I also acted a vendor **to** county government for many years in my company. We had developed several software packages for county government, so I dealt with many counties and many employees. In every case, the entire courthouse was held together by one or

two intelligent women employees. All the other employees, including the office holders, who were mostly men, depended on the wisdom and know-how of those few women. Regarding legal matters, just remember that if you can't afford counsel, counsel will be appointed to you to ensure you the right of a fair hearing. Right. Sure. I've been on the inside. I know that the average PD (Public Defender) has a caseload in the hundreds of individuals and has maybe 30 seconds to review your case as he or she is walking down the hall from the previous case to this case. Think you're going to get fair representation? Dream on! Even though many PD's are good and decent people, without time to review your case and prepare a defense they just have to wing it when they come in. The only saving grace is that the Fourth Assistant to the Prosecutor, who has also been assigned your case, hasn't had any more time than the PD to review what you stand accused of. Sadly, the phrase *"The best justice that money can buy"* is more truth than fiction. Don't believe me? Then consider the Menendez brothers or the case of O.J. Simpson. *"If it does not fit, you must acquit!"* Or, for those of you who are younger, consider the legal circus surrounding the death of Anna Nicole Smith. How much is that baby in the window? The one with the billion dollar inheritance?

5. **Individual freedom fails.** This is a tough one for Americans to swallow. When I tell folks that there will come a day when slavery will once again be

an accepted practice in America, they look at me with disbelief. Only this time it won't be based exclusively on race. It will be a combination of factors, anchored in one overwhelming factor, **total loss of financial resource.** Because of the economic and racial inequality in America, many Blacks will be forced back into what we will euphemistically call *"Indentured Servanthood".* Doubtless the *Spin Meisters* will come up with a much more attractive term than that. But slavery is what it will be. Frankly, there are many illegal aliens of Hispanic origin who are living in virtual slavery right now, not just in the Southwest but all over our country given the absolute non-defense of our southern border by the liberal left and spineless so-called moderate and conservative politicians. They have no rights. They cannot or will not learn the language of the land. They have no advocates to speak up for them. But the new class of slaves won't consist entirely of ethnic minorities. Many whites will find themselves in the same predicament. Slavery has been gone from our country for about one hundred and fifty years, so it seems hard for us to believe that it actually was an accepted practice here for well over one hundred years. Men and women were considered to be property, things to be bought and sold, not human beings with inalienable rights and privileges. Even in colonial times, there were indentured servants, often young men or women whose parents had fallen upon hard times and who had *"rented out"* their children on a long-term loan to their creditors in order to pay for their unpaid bills. According to the contract, when those children had worked off their parent's debt they were supposed to be freed. But there was a catch. The *"employer"* often made sure that the cost of the food and lodging they provided to the servant was so significant that the meager wage that the servant earned would never pay the bill off. This was also the practice for many years in Appalachia, when men would work the coal mines for a lifetime and never get out of debt. Why? *"You load sixteen tons, and what do you get? Another day older, and **deeper in debt**. Saint Peter, don't you call me, 'cause I can't go. **I owe my soul to the Company Store!**"* Greedy, manipulative mine owners made sure that their employees purchased all their needs from the Company Store, at prices so ridiculously marked up that it cost the employee more to live than they earned, effectively making them slaves in the truest sense of the meaning of the word. Look for many such situations to arise during the crash and the depression that follows it. When men are given the opportunity to oppress one another, politically or financially, they will do it without fail.

6. **Democracy is completely replaced by Socialism.** That, dear friends, is **already** happening and has been happening for at least several decades. The end result of this process is that when **individual property ownership is lost, individual liberties**

will be lost shortly thereafter. The two are inextricably intertwined together.

7. **Socialism is completely replaced by Totalitarianism.** Most people think I mean Communism when I say this. That is not the case. Actually, pure Communism is taken directly from the pages of the Book of Acts, where no one said that anything they owned was their own and the *"collective"*, or Early Church, had all things in common. The only mistake that Lenin made was trying to implement a revolutionary form of government without first having a revolution in people's hearts. Totalitarianism, on the other hand, is the brutal, oppressive rule of the majority by the minority. Dictatorship is another name for it. It is men like Hitler, Stalin and Saddam Hussein. The more desperate the times are, the more people clamor for a strong leader to deliver them from the adversity that they find themselves in. The more difficult the situation, the more willing people are to trade freedom for security. This has been proven historically again and again. And the more adverse the conditions, the less tolerant people are of differing opinions, particularly those regarding religion. It is precisely in this kind of environment that witch hunts arise, looking for a scapegoat to blame for everything that is wrong. The Cancel Culture of the far left is a classic example of this kind of thinking. A horrifying coalition of radical

left politicians, big business and the hopelessly liberal media have been systematically trying to eliminate conservatives in general and conservative Christians in particular because we are *"prejudiced"*. Yes, I admit it. I am, in their eyes, a *"Hater"*. Why? **Because I am told by the Bible to LOVE righteousness and HATE sin!** That doesn't fit into the current political and social tune being sung in our country. It is the perfect reason to persecute and eventually physically harm and even kill Christians and, of course, the eternal scapegoat, the Jewish people. The more adverse the times, the more irrational people become. Sweet reason flies out the door. Emotions become explosive and then violent. As the people become more irrational, strong military government becomes necessary to keep violence from erupting. It is ironic to note that the adverse economic conditions of the Middle East are at least partially responsible for the violent, irrational behavior of so many Muslims there, which in turn necessitates a brutal, oppressive regime. That brutal, oppressive regime creates adverse economic conditions by channeling so much money into military venues that the people are forced to go without. And around and around and around we go.

8. **The Anti-Christ takes advantage of this global penchant for a strong leader and gathers together a three-nation confederacy which then expands into a ten-nation coalition, from which he launches his conquest of the rest of the world.**

Don't think this could happen? Then you haven't read your history books. Let's look at the exact sequence of events in Egypt during the days of Joseph. When Joseph stood before Pharaoh, Egypt was a nation of small business owners and farmers, just as the United States was in the early 1900's. Most of Egypt was self-sustaining. A small tax base kept the government funded with all the money it needed. **Individual prosperity** funded **national prosperity**, just as it should be. The seven good years did nothing to discourage this. There is one thing I have always wondered about, though. It has always puzzled me why the critical information about the coming crash was not shared with the individual property owners and farmers. Had they been properly warned, they could have done exactly what the government of Egypt did, saving up enough cash reserves in the form of grain in silos to outlast the seven bad years. Perhaps the king was afraid of a national panic. Perhaps they were warned, but chose to ignore the warning, viewing Joseph as some crackpot foreign prophet. No matter what the reason, it was painfully clear in the first year of the famine that the individual property owners were not ready for what happened. Since farming is generally a year-to-year proposition, you can't count on last year's crop to feed you beyond this year. In the fall you bring in the crop. All things being equal, that crop will be enough for you to **eat** off of for the following year until the next crop comes in and we start the process all over again. In addition, the fall harvest must also provide **seed** to be planted in the spring. If you eat your seed you will have nothing to plant when it is time to do so. In a good situation, there is enough left over for you to plant a little more seed each year. That way your crop in the fall will also be exponentially greater as well. Given good weather over a series of years and good farming techniques, a diligent man could develop quite a farm over a period of time, assuming that enough farmland was available for planting. In the case of Egypt, no grain had been saved up individually during the previous seven years. That left the individual property owners vulnerable in the event of a bad year. What had the surplus been spent on? Probably the very things I just cautioned you would have to been sold early on in the process. The farmers probably tried to enhance their symbols of prosperity. Their wives probably had a little more *"bling"* on year after year. Whatever the case, the excess crop was not invested wisely. Only Pharaoh and his court were prepared for the inevitable disaster.

Because of this, at the end of the first year of crop failure there was no grain to eat. This placed the Egyptian farmers in the unenviable position of having to purchase the grain for the coming year from the government, who was amply prepared, and who was more than glad to take their money in exchange for the grain. This grain fed the farmers through the winter and provided enough left over for seed to plant the following spring. Being farmers, they assumed that this bad year was an exception to the rule and that conditions would return to normal. Unfortunately, they didn't. The government already knew they wouldn't. Now the farmers were forced to come to the government once again for a *"loan"*. Only there was no cash left to spend. It had been completely spent in covering the previous year's fiasco. And this government didn't make loans. The only way that grain could be purchased would be through a **barter system** in the absence of cash. The only thing that the farmers had left that would be sufficient to purchase a whole year's worth of grain would be their **livestock.**

By the end of the second year, the farmers had been stripped of their **liquid assets** and their **tangible assets.** Their **cash** had gone in the first year and their **livestock** in the second year. The third year would bring only more heartache. After two straight crop failures the only significant assets the farmers had left were their **croplands** and their **lives**. Remember that I told you that a loss of **economic freedom** will always be followed by a loss of **personal freedom?** Egypt is a textbook example of this. Let's review from Scripture exactly what happened in that third terrible year.

> "[18] *When that year had ended, they came to him the **next year** and said to him, 'We will not hide from my lord that **our money is gone**; my lord also has **our herds of livestock**. There is **nothing left** in the sight of my lord but **our bodies** and **our lands**.* [19] *Why should we die before your eyes, both we and our land? **Buy us and our land for bread**, and **we and our land will be servants of Pharaoh**; give us seed, that we may live and not die, that the land may not be desolate.'* [20] *Then Joseph bought **all the land of Egypt** for Pharaoh; for every man of the Egyptians sold his field, because the famine was severe upon them. So the land became Pharaoh's.* [21] *And **as for the people**, he moved them **into the cities**, from one end of the borders of Egypt to the other end.*"

> – GENESIS 47:18-21

What can I say to add to this terrible picture? In just **three years,** Egypt was reduced from a prosperous **nation of small business owners** to a **nation of slaves**, no longer in control of their own lives. Since they **no longer owned the land,** Joseph could do with them as he pleased and so he moved them into the cities so that it would be **easier to feed them.** That way, the food supplies would be in proximity to the people he needed to feed. But this also meant that farm after farm now lay in hideous ruin with only the encroaching sand left, covering everything that they had worked so hard for all their lives. In addition, they were now refugees, without funds, without assets, without a home and finally **without personal freedom.** Individual rights had now effectively disappeared from Egypt. Ironically, a Hebrew had been responsible for the loss of individual rights for the citizens of Egypt. Only a generation later, the Egyptians would be responsible for the loss of the individual rights of the Hebrews living in Goshen. Perhaps the *"New pharaoh who did not know Joseph"* also remembered that Hebrews had been responsible for the radical change in the nation's economic structure and wanted to even the score. Stranger things have happened! A trend that Joseph had unwittingly released in Egypt came back to haunt his people after his death.

Many years ago, there was a wonderful car commercial with a gruff garage mechanic chewing on a cigar. **"You can pay me now,"** he growled, **"or you can pay me later".** That is the situation we find ourselves in today. How much time is left before the trigger event that will cascade America and the world into the greatest economic cataclysm in the history of the world? I honestly don't know. But I do know this. **Unless you start preparing now, you will <u>never</u> be ready.**

ARE YOU SURE ABOUT THIS DROUGHT THING?

For quite some time now we have been living in total ignorance of the fact that the Western part of the United States has been in the deadly grip of a major drought. How bad is it? Well, the Rio Grande or *"Great River"* was so depleted of water that it stopped flowing several hundred yards shy of the Gulf of Mexico some time ago. Embarrassed, US officials decided to dredge out enough sand so that a small trickle of water could make its way through to the sea. The mighty Colorado River is also in danger of running dry because so many cities along the way are diverting water from it to meet their ever-growing needs. In some places in California the water table has dropped so far that the ground itself is dropping in elevation. According to an online Newsweek article dated December 6, 2022, a Lake Mead water level forecast has shown that the Lake, fed by the Colorado River and created by the Hoover Dam, is rapidly approaching a *"deadpool"* level. Deadpool is the level when the water in a reservoir drops so low that it can no longer flow downstream from a dam. That would mean that all water supplies drawn from the dam would cease, along with all hydroelectric power generated by the turbines through which the water passes. Lake Mead, which provides water to the states of Arizona, California, and Nevada as well as some of Mexico, providing sustenance to nearly 20 million people and large areas of farmland, is the biggest man-made reservoir in North America, and its water levels are rapidly evaporating. The lake, which lies across Nevada and Arizona, is drying up due to the ongoing **mega-drought** in the western United States.

I hope you caught the significance of the word I just outlined in bold. Yes, that's right. Not just a drought. Not even a major drought. Not even a severe drought. A **mega-drought**. I warned that this was happening almost 20 years ago.

When I first wrote this book back in 2003, the drought was already clearly documented by both the news media and the scientific experts. On February 13 of that year, Reuters News Agency reported that **one-fifth of the United States remained in a drought with some Plains and Western states facing the worst conditions in a century**, US government weather forecasters had said that week. The drought, **which began the previous year**, had already **withered grazing pastures**, **dried up water reservoirs** and **reduced crop yields**, according to the National Oceanic and Atmospheric Administration. *"From year to year, it is not unusual for some area of the country to be in drought at some point,"* Douglas LeComte, drought specialist with NOAA's climate -prediction center had said. *"However, the extent of last summer's serious drought conditions measured by the Palmer Drought Indices has not been seen since the mini-dust bowl drought of the mid-1950s. **Even now, over one-fifth of the nation is in severe drought.**"*

On November 5 of 2003, the Associated Press ran an article stating that a group of experts attending a national conference in Denver said that **more than seventy-five percent of the regions in the American West still were deep in a drought and that no one knew how long it would last**.

Now, those two articles were from 2003 and so someone might have argued, *"Well, I'm sure that things have gotten much better since then. I'm sure that was only a temporary condition".* To which I would have had to reply,

"Nope! In fact, it's gotten much worse!" Here is an article dated back on June 11, 2007. Read carefully what it had to say. I have highlighted all the *"good parts"* for you.

"The Wrath of 2007: America's great drought by Andrew Gumbel in Los Angeles, published: 11 June 2007.

America is facing its worst summer drought since the Dust Bowl years of the Great Depression. <u>Or perhaps worse still.</u> *From the mountains and desert of the West, now into an* **<u>eighth consecutive dry year</u>,** *to the wheat farms of Alabama, where crops are failing because of rainfall levels* **<u>12 inches lower than usual</u>,** *to the vast soupy expanse of Lake Okeechobee in southern Florida, which has become* **<u>so dry it actually caught fire</u>** *a couple of weeks ago, a continent is crying out for water.*

In the southeast, usually a lush, humid region, **<u>it is the driest few months since records began in 1895</u>.** *California and Nevada, where burgeoning population centers co-exist with an often harsh, barren landscape, have seen* **<u>less rain over the past year than at any time since 1924</u>.** *The Sierra Nevada range, which straddles the two states, received only* **<u>27 per cent of its usual snowfall</u>** *in winter, with immediate knock-on effects on water supplies for the populations of Las Vegas and Los Angeles.*

The human impact, for the moment, has been limited, certainly nothing compared to the great westward migration of Okies in the 1930 - the desperate march described by John Steinbeck in The Grapes of Wrath.

Big farmers are now well protected by government subsidies and emergency funds, and small farmers, some of whom are indeed struggling, have been slowly moving off the land for decades anyway. The most common inconvenience, for the moment, is the restriction on hosepipes and garden sprinklers in eastern cities.

*But the long-term implications are escaping nobody. Climatologists see a growing volatility in the southeast's weather - today's drought coming close on the heels of devastating hurricanes two to three years ago. In the West, meanwhile, a growing body of scientific evidence suggests a movement towards **a state of perpetual drought by the middle of this century**. 'The 1930s drought lasted less than a decade. **This is something that could remain for 100 years**', said Richard Seager, a climatologist at Columbia University and lead researcher of a report published recently by the government's National Oceanic and Atmospheric Administration (NOAA).*

While some dry weather is cyclical - California actually had an unusually wet year during 2008, so many of the state's farmers still had plenty of water for their crops at that time - some of it portended more permanent changes. In Arizona, the tall mountains in the southern Sonoran desert known as 'sky islands' because they have been welcome refuges from the desert heat for millennia, have already shown unmistakable signs of change.

Predatory insects have started ravaging trees already weakened by record temperatures and fires over the past few years. Animal species such as frogs and red squirrels have been forced to move ever higher up the mountains in search of cooler temperatures, and are in danger of dying out altogether. Mount Lemmon, which rises above the city of Tucson, boasts the southernmost ski resort in the US, but has barely attracted any snow these past few years.

*'A lot of people think climate change and the ecological repercussions are 50 years away,' Thomas Swetnam, an environmental scientist at the University of Arizona in Tucson, told The New York Times a few years ago. 'But it's happening now in the West. **The data is telling us that we are in the middle of one of the first big indicators of climate change impacts in the continental United States**.' Across the West, farmers and city water consumers are locked in a perennial battle over water rights - one that the cities are slowly winning. Down the line, though, there are serious questions about how to keep showers and lawn sprinklers going*

in the retirement communities of Nevada and Arizona. Lake Powell, the reservoir on the upper Colorado River that helps provide water across a vast expanse of the West, has been less than half full for years, with little prospect of filling up in the foreseeable future.

According to the NOAA's recent report, the West can expect 10-20 per cent less rainfall by mid-century, which will increase air pollution in the cities, kill off trees and water-retaining giant cactus plants and shrink the available water supply by as much as 25 per cent.

The most striking effect of the dry weather has been to expose large parts of the bed of Lake Okeechobee, *the vast circular expanse of water east of Palm Beach, Florida, which acts as a back-up water supply for five million Floridians. Archaeologists have had a field day - dredging the soil for human bone fragments, tools, bits of pottery and ceremonial jewelry thought to have belonged to the natives who lived near the lake before the Spanish arrived in the 16th century.*

Environmentalists are not entirely upset, because the lake is notoriously polluted with pesticides and other farm products that then poison nearby rivers. River fish stocks in the area are now booming.

Nothing, though, was so strange as the fires that broke out over about 12,000 acres on the northern edge of the lake at the end of May. They were eventually doused by Tropical Storm Barry last weekend. State water managers, however, say it will may take a whole summer of rainstorms, or longer, to restore the lake."

Two years later, in 2009, Don Wilhite, director of the National Drought Mitigation Center in Lincoln, Nebraska said, *"The truth is, none of us knows when this thing is going to break. This may go on for quite a while."* His comments came at a federal conference in Denver on how to develop better forecasting, conservation and monitoring tools to reduce future drought-triggered water disasters in the parched Western United States."

Now, bear in mind that I wrote and quoted those words from information gleaned in 2003, 2006 and 2009 respectively. Frankly, the issue of ongoing drought in the Far West and Midwest is no longer a debatable issue. Some years ago, there were proponents for and against the argument that we were headed into disaster. Now, with only a few dissidents, the overwhelming majority of forecasters are predicting long-term disaster headed for the Midwest, the West Coast and Southwest. To see how truly bad it is, go to the Drought Monitor website, https://droughtmonitor.unl.edu and take a good, hard look. It doesn't take long to see that **the entire United States**, with the exception of most of the East Coast and the southern part of Florida, are gripped with conditions varying anywhere from abnormally dry (yellow areas) to exceptional drought (brown areas). Even the Hawaiian Islands are drying up! As of December 15, 2022, this is what the Drought Monitor looked like:

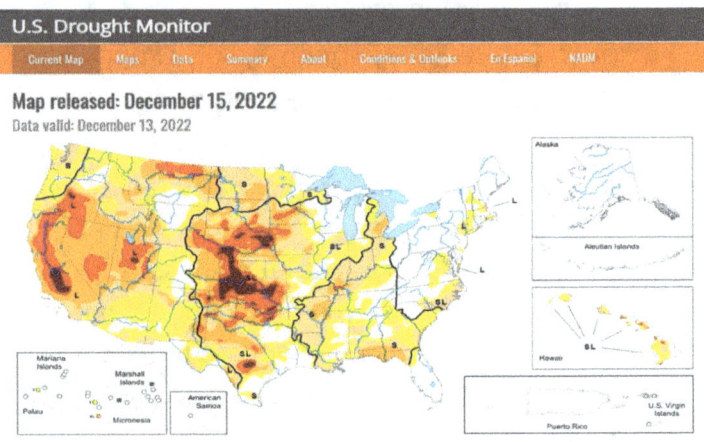

This is serious stuff, folks. The areas impacted include what we refer to as the *"Breadbasket of America"*, the place where we grow most of our wheat. Now, look at this map again and then, taking your Bible in hand, turn to the Book of Revelation, Chapter 6, Verses 5-6. In those verses, the rider on the Black Horse has a pair of scales in his hand. Those scales, to the people living in John's day, would not have meant justice, as they would to those of us today. Rather, the scales would refer directly to **commerce**, the buying and selling of goods. Can that be supported? You bet! In Verse 6, it describes how bad it will get. It tells us that a **quart of wheat** will sell for **a single day's wages** and **three quarts of barley will sell for the same.** When I first wrote this book, I asked a number of women who had a reputation of being pretty good cooks how many loaves of bread a quart of wheat would be able to produce. All of them agreed that a single quart of grain could produce perhaps **two loaves of bread.** Got that part? Now let's look at that *"day's wages"* (a denarius) thing. Let's say that you're making minimum wage, $15.00 an hour. Let's further assume that you worked an 8 hour day, so your **day's wages** would be 8 x $15.00 or **$120.00.** Since a single day's wages can only buy **two loaves of bread**, that means that you will be paying **$60.00 for a single loaf of bread!** Sound impossible? It happened in Germany between World War I and World War II and it was much, much worse than that. I have actual photos of men pushing wheelbarrows full of *MillionenMarken* notes. Please understand. I'm not saying that the men were pushing a wheelbarrow with a million dollars (German Marks) in it. I'm saying that the wheelbarrow was **full of German million dollar BILLS!** What could they get for that remarkable amount of money? **ONE LOAF OF BREAD!!!** I have outlined what happened then elsewhere in this book. Remember that **political stability** rests on **economic stability.** What do you think is going to happen in America when the price of bread skyrockets to a mere $60.00 a loaf??? Barley isn't much better. Three quarts of barley would produce six loaves of bread, so take heart, my friends! You will be able to buy barley bread for the exceptionally low price of a mere **$20.00 a loaf!!!** It's time to get scared. **Really scared.** And **really serious about your faith, your ability to trust in God TOTALLY for your every**

need and about your need to prepare for what is coming. By the way, for those who might argue, *"Well, Pastor Ray, I'm sure this drought will pass but the real drought will happen somewhere else in the world"*, let me give you another Scripture passage to chew on. It seems that the prophet Zechariah was given remarkable insight into the End Times. In fact, more passages in Revelation point directly back to passages in Zechariah than any other book in the Bible, **including Daniel.** In fact, Daniel doesn't even come in second on the list. Isaiah does. Remember that the 3rd Seal, the Black Horse of Crop Failure, occurs in Revelation, Chapter 6. Would it surprise you to learn that **those very self-same horses**, complete with their four colors, **also appear in Zechariah, Chapter 6?** The Four Horses appear, but this time, instead of talking about **what the rider will do**, the passage talks about **where the horses will go.** In Verses 2-6, Zechariah outlines where each will be headed. He states that the **White Horse of War** will be going to the **North.** He also then says that the **Black Horse of Crop Failure** will **also be going to the North.** What is the best way to understand what is going on here? It's actually pretty simple. When cartographers (map guys) discuss global mapping, they frequently refer to **three major divisions** of our planet, the **Northern Hemisphere**, the **Southern Hemisphere** and the **10/40 Window** (the tropical center of our planet). So when we say that both the **White Horse of War** and the **Black Horse of Crop Failure** are headed to the **North**, it almost certainly implies that both are headed to the **Northern Hemisphere.** Sure enough, both World Wars were fought almost exclusively in the Northern Hemisphere, indicating that the 1st Seal has been open since the early 1900s and we didn't even know it! It also implies that, since crop failure is the 3rd Seal and it is clearly opened right now that the 2nd Seal of Ethnic and Religious Genocide also opened quite some time ago. Folks frequently ask me, *"Brother Ray, when do you think we will enter into the 7 Seals?"* I just sigh, shake my head and begin this explanation, over and over and over again...

THE GREAT DUST BOWL DISASTER

To give you some historical perspective into what is happening right now, the Dust Bowl was the result of catastrophic dust storms which caused major ecological and agricultural damage to American prairies in the 1930s. The fertile soil of the Great Plains had been exposed by removal of grass during plowing over decades of ill-conceived farming techniques. The 1st World War and immense profits had driven farmers to push the land well beyond its natural limits. When drought hit the soil dried, became dust and blew eastwards, mostly in large black clouds. This caused an exodus from Texas, Arkansas, Oklahoma and the surrounding Great Plains, with more than a half a million Americans left homeless in the Great Depression.

There can be no doubt that America has once again come under a curse because of its rebellion against God. I'm sure when Elijah told Ahab that except at his word there would be neither rain or dew that Ahab just chuckled, shook his head and went on his way. But thirty days later he was starting to worry. Sixty days later he was starting to panic. Ninety days later he was organizing search parties to look for that blasted old man. At the end of the first year Elijah was probably on the Ten Most Wanted List in Israel and by the end of the second year every law enforcement agency in the land was totally devoted to trying to find him. The vice closes slowly but surely. It is the **accumulative** effect of drought that makes it so devastating. As you watch everything and everyone around you slowly dying for lack of water you begin to panic. Soon you are consumed by the need for water. I'm going to make a simple prediction: it's going to get much, much worse than this with a dramatic increase in both violent weather patterns such as tornados and hurricanes and a dramatic increase in violent weather swings. You don't have to believe me. Just follow the weather channel carefully and see what happens.

And, finally, a grim reminder from the Prophet Joel:

> " ¹⁰ *The field is wasted, the land mourns;* ***for the grain is ruined, the new wine is dried up, the oil fails.*** ¹¹ *Be ashamed, you farmers, wail, you vinedressers,* ***for the wheat and the barley; because the harvest of the field has perished.*** ¹²
> *The vine has dried up, and the fig tree has withered;*

> *the pomegranate tree, the palm tree also, and the*
> *apple tree -- all the trees of the field are withered;*
> *surely joy has withered away from the sons of men."*

> *– JOEL 1:10-12*

One final observation about that passage. Did you notice the references to **wheat, barley, oil and wine?** Do you know that this parallels the **Third Seal** of Revelation 6:5-6? Revelation is a giant computer **matrix**, weaving untold hundreds of passages in the Old and New Testament into the most densely coded book ever written. Nearly every sentence contains multiple references back in time, with phrases and symbols which can only be understood if you know where in the Old Testament the passage is pointing to. Perhaps sometime soon I can share detailed information about all of this with you. I am prepared to do so. Only time will tell...

IS THERE ANY HOPE, PASTOR RAY?

There still remains one unanswered question. What about the millions of Christians who will never hear this message or who will choose not to believe or receive it when they do hear it? Is there no hope for them? What about the untold millions of believers who live in the inner cities of America? How can they ever hope to come into a position of economic security and stability such I describe in this book? Thank God that there **is** hope in the form of a Biblical figure known as the **Kinsman-Redeemer.** We will meet him in the next chapter. He is the hope of all true believers. We know Him as Jesus, but there will be many *"miniature"* versions of Him during this final, terrible time who will act to rescue His people from destruction. Let's turn to Chapter 6 now, and see how the whole mechanism of the Kinsman-Redeemer works.

CHAPTER 6

The Kinsman-Redeemer

THE KINSMAN WHO?

At the end of Chapter 5 we left America, the world and most of the Church in a terrible predicament. All through this book I have been carefully outlining and documenting for you **what** was going to happen, **why** it was going to happen and perhaps, within reason, **when** it was going to happen. Having established that set of facts we then set out to find out **how** we could respond in order to circumvent the circumstances and escape the devastation that is now inevitable. However, in doing this the vast majority of Christians, either through ignorance, disobedience or lack of finances, will have excluded themselves from deliverance. Now we must find out if there is any hope for them.

Even though I have tried to be as positive as I could throughout this whole book, there are times when circumstances are inevitable and the consequences of these circumstances are unavoidable. Let me tell you a tragic but true story from Armenia. Many years ago, about the same time that the Holy Spirit fell in America at Azusa Street the same event occurred in Eastern Europe and Russia. Some of these Russian Pentecostals migrated south into Armenia during the time it was ruled by the Ottoman Turks. As a result, a great move of God also arose in Armenia. Out of that movement came a young man called the Boy Prophet. His name was Efim Gerasemovitch Klubniken and he lived in the village of Kara Kala. His family was Pentecostal and they had emigrated from Russia along with others when he was very young and settled in the region. He was unable to read or write but frequently had visions of God which proved to be true time and time again. Suddenly, without warning, the Boy Prophet isolated himself, praying and fasting and refusing to talk to or see anyone. At the end of a week or so, he finally ended his intense time with God and announced that the Lord had been showing him open visions during that entire time. For over a week he sat at the wooden table in his home and began to copy all of the letters, symbols, diagrams and a map he had seen onto parchment. Although the Boy Prophet had never been outside of his village in his whole life and knew nothing of world geography, he had drawn a perfect map of the Atlantic Ocean and the

United States. New York City was clearly identified, as was Los Angeles. The young man said that he merely traced all the symbols and lines he had seen in the Spirit, without having any understanding of what they meant. In addition, the Boy Prophet had been given a very specific and detailed prophecy.

God had warned the people of Armenia that they were to flee their country because a great and terrible destruction was going to come on them. Their instructions were to immigrate to the United States and settle in the city of New York. There they would abide for a season until another set of instructions would be given to them to move to a city on the far side of America, a city called Los Angeles. This extensive prophecy was greeted with a wide variety of reactions. Some members of the Christian community were deeply moved by this visitation. Others were skeptical and openly scoffed at the Boy Prophet and his prophecies. It was all nonsense, they said. No such thing was going to happen. Others didn't know what to believe and vacillated between faith and doubt.

As it turned out, the Boy Prophet was tragically correct about his prophecy but it took some time to come to pass. God is rarely in a hurry when it comes to prophecy. Some things do come quickly, but consider Father Abraham. 25 years passed from the time that God promised him a son until Isaac was born. 25 years! If you have heard from the Lord about something that will come to pass in your life and it hasn't happened yet, do not despair. God is not slow as some men count slowness, said Peter. Trust in the Lord and in His Word to you. And having done all, stand on what He has told you until it comes to pass.

Fifty years passed after the Boy Prophet issued his prophecy. He was now no longer a boy. And then suddenly he announced to the villagers that the prophecy was about to be fulfilled. He and those who believed in him and the prophecy that God had given to him quickly fled the area and headed for the United States and the city of New York. Those who remained scoffed at them and ridiculed them as they left but shortly thereafter the Turks began a systematic extinction of the Christians in Armenia in one of the worst examples of genocide the world has ever seen. With remorseless efficiency the Turks began the bloody business of driving two-thirds of the population out into the Mesopotamian desert. Over a million men, women and children died in these death marches, including every inhabitant of Kara Kala. Another half a million were massacred in their villages in a pogrom that was later to provide Hitler with his blueprint for the extermination of the Jews. *"The world did not intervene when Turkey wiped out the Armenians"*, he reminded his followers. *"It will not intervene now"*.

Only those individuals who heeded the prophecy were saved. Ironically, sometime ago the nation of Turkey withdrew its diplomats from Russia in protest because the Russian government had called it to task over the wholesale slaughter of the innocent Armenians so many years ago. The Turkish government preferred to refer to it as a *"tragic mistake"*. The Russian government, on the other hand, preferred to refer to it as what it actually was, one of the worst cases of methodical genocide in the recorded history of mankind. Obviously, there is still a great deal of bitterness and resentment lingering around the horrible event. Some of those people who did escape destruction eventually ended up moving to Los Angeles. One of those families, the Shakarian family, eventually had a young boy named Demos, who later in his life founded the Full Gospel Businessmen's Fellowship International, a force for righteousness and the Kingdom of God for many years all across America. Many businessmen were born again and received the Baptism of the Holy Spirit through their ministry. I myself was baptized in the Holy Spirit at an FGBMFI meeting in Evansville, Indiana. Special thanks and a tip of the hat go to Brother Joe Turnbloom, who was president of the chapter at that time. Joe eventually entered the ministry and the FGBMFI has faded from prominence but it served its Lord and Savior well during Demos's administration.

Why do I tell you this story? Because sometimes it is impossible to escape the consequences of your actions or evade the results of your decisions. For many Christians during this final terrible crash there will be no way out. But for some there may yet be hope through the Kinsman-Redeemer. Let's take a look at the two foundational Scriptures on which He is based.

" *23 The land shall **not be sold permanently**, for **the land is Mine**; for **you are strangers and sojourners with Me**. 24 And in all the land of your*

> possession **you shall grant redemption of the land.**
> ²⁵ *If one of your brethren becomes poor, and has sold some of his possession, and **if his redeeming relative comes to redeem it,** then **he may redeem what his brother sold.** ²⁶ Or if the man has no one to redeem it, but **he himself becomes able to redeem it,** ²⁷ then let him count the years since its sale, and restore the remainder to the man to whom he sold it, **that he may return to his possession.***"

> — LEVITICUS 25:23-27

God even extended this provision to include the redemption of an individual from slavery because financial freedom without personal freedom is meaningless.

> " ⁴⁷ *Now if a sojourner or stranger close to you becomes rich, and one of your brethren who dwells by him becomes poor, and sells himself to the stranger or sojourner close to you, or to a member of the stranger's family,* ⁴⁸ **after he is sold he may be redeemed again. One of his brothers may redeem him;** ⁴⁹ *or his uncle or his uncle's son may redeem him; or **anyone who is near of kin to him in his family may redeem him;** or **if he is able he may redeem himself.***"

> — LEVITICUS 25:47-49

Remember how in Chapter 2 we discussed the Perfect Economy and how, based on the principle of the Year of Jubilee, the ownership of the family farm was returned to the family every fifty years? Well it turns out if we had just gone a little further in our Scripture study we would have found that there was actually another supplemental clause which would allow the land to return to the family **before** the fifty years had transpired. It can be assumed that the reason the land was sold in the first place was because of economic hardship on the part of the landowner. But remember that in God's economy this isn't a Lone Ranger kind of thing. This is a **family affair.** And so, if there was another member of the family, a **kinsman**, who had the financial wherewithal to **purchase back the farm** and so **redeem it**, he could do so, at any time and with no penalty incurred (unlike most of our Gentile lending institutions!). In fact, should the man who originally sold the land experience a financial recovery, he could purchase back his own property or his own freedom as well. All that was required was that the land be purchased back at the fair market value as calculated by multiplying the annual net value of the land by the number of years remaining until the next Jubilee. We did several examples in Chapter 2 to illustrate to you how this kind of thing worked. This was a wonderful concept and provided deliverance from someone in your family if they or another family member were willing to redeem the situation.

The greatest example of this principle in action is found in the Book of Ruth. Ruth is a wonderful love story but it is also a story of economic redemption and that latter truth is our principal concern in this book. The story begins with the sale of family property to someone else due to economic hardship.

> " ¹ *Now it came to pass, in the days when the judges ruled, that there was a **famine in the land**. And a certain man of Bethlehem, Judah, went to dwell in the country of **Moab**, he and his wife and his two sons*"

> — *RUTH 1:1*

Just as in 1929, God's judgment was on the land in the form of a famine. He had warned Israel about this in the Book of Deuteronomy.

> " ²³ *And your heavens which are over your head shall be bronze, and the earth which is under you shall be iron.* ²⁴ ***The Lord will change the rain of your land to powder and dust**; from the heaven it shall come down on you until you are destroyed.*"

> — *DEUTERONOMY 28:23-24*

The time of the Judges was a time of great civil unrest and spiritual disobedience. In the final verse of that book it says, *"In those days there was no king in Israel; **everyone did what was right in his own eyes**".* How very much like America today, when rules and standards have been cast aside so that everyone lives by a subjective set of personal guidelines which change constantly to meet the circumstances. God cannot and will not abide such a lawless condition, particularly from people who say that they belong to Him. And so judgment falls precisely because the people will not heed the leadership and counsel of the judges themselves. When a nation refuses to listen to the men and women that the Lord sends to them to correct them there is only one recourse. God must discipline them Himself. And when He has to become personally involved, it is never pretty.

Compounding sin on sin, Elimelech never bothered to consult God about what he should do in that situation. Not only did he live in a lawless land but he himself was not submitted to God. Isaiah must have felt much the same thing when he said, *"I am a man of unclean lips, and I dwell in the midst of a people of unclean lips"*. But even without consultation he should have known better. Moab was a nation reserved for the descendants of one of the daughters of Lot, the result of an incestuous relationship between a drunken, incoherent, unaware Lot and one of his two ungodly daughters. Moab belonged to them. Israel had expressly been forbidden to attack them or enter into their land when they crossed over the Jordan to take control of their own promised land. What should Elimelech have done? **He should have stayed put and prayed.** He did neither.

What was the outcome of the matter? After his sons both married women of Moab he died. Then, one by one, each of his sons died, leaving three widows, one of them ageing and far beyond any prospects of remarriage. Now these

three women found themselves homeless, strangers in a strange land, with no source of income and no one to help them. Bitter and angry, Naomi decided to return to Bethlehem. She urged her two daughters-in-law to remain in Moab, for they were both young enough to remarry and rebuild their lives with someone else. Orpah (from whom Oprah Winfrey gets her name, somewhat misspelled by her parents) decided to return. But Ruth chose to stay by the side of her mother-in-law, recognizing that she was incapable of fending for herself. There was no Social Security Administration in those days. There was no Medicare. There was no Disability. Widows and orphans were most to be pitied because they had no one in their **family** to stand by them.

When the two women entered the city, Naomi was quickly recognized by her former neighbors and friends. But now she had no means of supporting herself and so she told them that she was no longer Naomi *("Pleasant")* but rather Mara *("Bitter")* because of what God had done to her. But was it God that had done this to her? No. Far from it. It was her husband's rebellion against the **known will of God** that brought about the chain of events that led to the death of the three Israelite men. Had Elimelech stayed put and not sold the family farm, things would eventually have turned around. That's why Naomi had finally come home. Word had reached her that the Lord had visited Israel and that the rains had started falling again. With the rains came the crops and this would prove to be the key to her deliverance. God's blessing is always the key.

If you need to be delivered, find out where the rain is falling and the harvest is being reaped. It is there that you will find your own needs met as well. The blessing of God blesses everyone who stands in its presence. **Find the rain, dear friend, find the rain.**

The rest of the story is well known. Ruth worked in the fields and just happened to impress an older, single, godly man known as Boaz (*"In Him is strength"*). Never was a man better named. He became the strength of his extended family and redeemed Naomi's property in accordance with Levirate Law regarding the reacquisition of property. But there was a bit of a hitch in the transaction. It seemed that another law was also involved in the transaction, and that had to do with Ruth, the widow of Mahlon and the fact that there was no male heir to the property. That wouldn't end up mattering in the long run. What did matter was her remarriage to Boaz. They both ended up in the threshing floor under the mantle of Boaz. But please remain calm, dear reader, for there was no hanky-panky under the sheets that fateful night. She had formally requested that he *"cover"* her in marriage by lying at his feet and uncovering them. Her symbolic gesture was that since his feet were uncovered and she was at his feet in submission to him that when he re-covered his feet, he would also be covering her, accepting her as his bride. Many people reading the Scriptures do not understand the symbolism and misread the text, assuming that compromise occurred before the marriage was finalized. Nothing could be further from the truth. Some people did have integrity even in that misguided, misbegotten age.

Boaz was delighted by her proposal but he had some legal matters to attend to first before the matter could be finalized. It seemed that there was a relative who was closer to Naomi than he was and, by law, that relative had first right to redemption. Before Boaz could intervene the other relative had to be consulted and given the opportunity to step up and do the right thing. Let's look at the narrative just to confirm the facts.

> *"⁷ And after Boaz had eaten and drunk, and his heart was cheerful, he went to lie down at the end of the heap of grain; and she came softly, **uncovered his feet**, and lay down. ⁸ Now it happened at midnight that the man was startled, and turned himself; and there, a woman was lying at his feet. ⁹ And he said, 'Who are you?' So she answered, 'I am Ruth, your maidservant. **Take your maidservant under your wing, for you are a close relative (Kinsman-Redeemer)**'. ¹⁰ Then he said, 'Blessed are you of the Lord, my daughter! For you have shown more kindness at the end than at the beginning, in that **you did not go after young men**, whether poor or rich. ¹¹ And now, my daughter, do not fear. **I will do for you all that you request, for all the people of my town know that you are a virtuous woman**. ¹² Now it is true that I am a close relative; however, **there is a relative closer than I**. ¹³ Stay this night, and in the morning it shall be that **if he will perform the duty of a close relative for you – good; let him do it. But if he does not want to perform the duty for***

**you, then I will perform the duty for you, as the
Lord lives!** *Lie down until morning.'"*

— Ruth 3:7-13

What a wonderful narrative! And what people of
sterling character! From the text, we can clearly tell that
although Ruth was still young and quite pretty, Boaz
clearly was not. He was deeply moved that a young,
beautiful woman of such character should come to
him. But even so, he was willing to step aside if the
nearer kinsman was willing to take care of business. But
our friend Boaz was not a successful businessman and
prosperous for no good reason. He had a card up his
sleeve and he would play it the very next day.

> " ¹ *Now Boaz went up to the gate and sat down
> there; and behold, the close relative of whom Boaz had
> spoken came by. So Boaz said,* **'Come aside, friend,
> sit down here.'** *So he came aside and sat down.* ² *And
> he took* **ten men of the elders of the city**, *and said,
> 'Sit down here.' So they sat down.* ³ *Then he said to
> the close relative,* **'Naomi**, *who has come back from
> the country of Moab,* **sold the piece of land which
> belonged to our brother Elimelech**. ⁴ *And I thought
> to inform you, saying "Buy it back in the presence of
> the inhabitants and the elders of my people.* **If you will
> redeem it, then tell me, that I may know; for there
> is no one but you to redeem it, and I am next after
> you** " ' And he said, **'I will redeem it.'** "*

— Ruth 4:1-4

So far, so good. Boaz was acting in strict adherence to Levirate Law as found in Leviticus Chapter 25. In fact the closer relative was financially well enough off to purchase the land back on behalf of Naomi, giving her a place to live for the rest of her life. But there was an unexpected catch to this deal and Boaz was about to play his trump card.

> " [5] *Then Boaz said, 'On the day you buy the field from the hand of Naomi, you must also buy it from Ruth the Moabitess,* **the wife of the dead, to perpetuate the name of the dead through his inheritance'**"
>
> – RUTH 4:5

Whoa! Wait a minute! Who said anything about getting married? I thought this was strictly a property deal! Well, yes and no. Yes, in that there was a piece of property that needed redeeming and restoring to the surviving owners, who would be Naomi and Ruth. It turns out that Ruth had as much legal right to the property as her mother-in-law because she was the widow of an Israelite man. But there was another law in place that kind of muddied the water. Boaz knew about it and knew this other relative well enough to know that bringing Ruth into **his** household would stir up a hornet's nest. What kind of law would do this? Let's take a look and see.

> " [5] *If brothers dwell together and one of them dies and has no son, the widow of the dead man shall not be married to a stranger outside the family;* **her husband's brother shall go in to her, take her as his wife, and perform the duty of a husband's brother to her.** [6] *And it shall be that* **the first-born son which she bears will succeed to the name of his dead brother, that his name many not be blotted out of Israel.** [7] *But if the man does not want to take his brother's wife, then let his brother's wife go up to the gate to the elders, and say, 'My husband's brother refuses to raise up a name to his brother in Israel; he will not perform the duty of my husband's brother.' "*

> – DEUTERONOMY 25:5-7

Hmmm... It seems that this law had mutated slightly over the years, extending beyond the immediate brother to the next available male in the family. So now the other relative not only had to redeem the property of Elimelech for Naomi, he would also have to **marry Ruth in order to raise up a male heir through her** who could inherit the family farm after both women had passed on! Things had gotten a little too tangled for this gentleman and so he asked to be excused from the responsibility in a most unusual manner.

> " [6] *And the close relative said, 'I cannot redeem it for myself,* **lest I ruin my own inheritance.** *You redeem my right of redemption for yourself, for I cannot redeem it.'* [7] *Now this was the custom in*

former times in Israel concerning redeeming and exchanging, to confirm anything; **one man took off his sandal and gave it to the other**, *and this was a confirmation in Israel.* [8] *Therefore the close relative said to Boaz, 'Buy it for yourself.'* **So he took off his sandal.**"

— RUTH 4:6-8

What an intriguing way of confirming a transaction! It actually had a much uglier origin and time had modified it to some extent. Let's go back to Deuteronomy for just a second to see how it all started.

"[8] *Then the elders of his city shall call him and speak to him. But if he stands firm and says, 'I do not want to take her',* [9] **then his brother's wife shall come to him in the presence of the elders, remove his sandal from his foot, spit in his face, and answer and say, 'So shall it be done to the man who will not build up his brother's house'.** [10] *And his name shall be called in Israel,* **'The house of him who had his sandal removed'.**"

-- DEUTERONOMY 25:8-10

Wow! That's pretty ugly, isn't it? Basically, what the sandal was saying was that the dead man's brother was **unwilling to walk in his shoes** and fulfill his obligation to his dead brother to create a male heir for his brother's property and to perpetuate his dead brother's name. Over the years the concept of walking in someone's shoes had become a general concept and had been softened somewhat by the teachers of the Law. In the days of Ruth and Boaz any time a business deal was transacted and **legal authority was being transferred from the person rightfully assigned to the situation to a proxy, a shoe was passed from the person stepping out of the responsibility to the person stepping into the responsibility.** It merely meant, *"Now I legally empower you to act on my behalf in this matter, walking in my shoes, fulfilling my obligation for me."*

Boaz knew that the other Kinsman-Redeemer had issues at home. Had he taken a second wife, particularly one from hated Moab, all you-know-what would have broken loose in his household. All Boaz had to do was to present the situation in the correct order and it would only be a matter of moments before the ball was right back in his court. As soon as he was legally empowered to act as Kinsman-Redeemer for both Naomi and Ruth, he swung into action without a moment's hesitation.

> " ⁹ *And Boaz said to the elders and all the people,* '*You are witnesses this day that* **I have bought all that was Elimelech's, and all that was Chilion's and Mahlon's from the hands of Naomi.** ¹⁰ *Moreover,* **Ruth the Moabitess, the widow of Mahlon, I have acquired as my wife, to perpetuate the name of the dead through his inheritance,** *that the name of the dead may not be cut off from among his brethren and from his position at the gate.* **You are witnesses this day.**' ¹¹ *And all the people who were at the gate, and the elders, said,*

> *'We are witnesses. The Lord make the woman who is coming to your house like Rachel and Leah, the two who built the house of Israel; and may you prosper in Ephrathah and be famous in Bethlehem.' "*

– RUTH 4:9-11

You know the rest of the story. It had a very happy ending. Naomi stopped calling herself Mara because now that she was back under the care of the Lord her bitter life had turned into a pleasant life again. God wasn't responsible for all that happened in the first place but He certainly did a good job of fixing it up, didn't He? It all turned out well for Ruth since she was no longer a widow but was now married to a kind, godly husband who had some financial resources. And she had a wonderful baby boy to show for it. All's well that ends well. But there is one point of curiosity left unresolved for us. Why in the world was Boaz, a good Jewish boy, willing to take a foreigner, a hated Moabitess no less, as a wife? Here's the fascinating truth behind that question. If we turn to the Gospel of Matthew, we can find the answer.

> " ¹ *The book of the genealogy of Jesus Christ, the Son of David, the Son of Abraham…* ⁵ ***Salmon begot Boaz by Rahab, Boaz begot Obed by Ruth,*** *Obed begot Jesse,* ⁶ *and Jesse begot David the king…* "

– MATTHEW 1:1, 5-6

Do you see the obvious? Rahab was **Rahab the Harlot** who hid the two Hebrew spies inside of Jericho until the search parties had left. She and her family were the only ones left alive after the walls came tumbling down. At some unrecorded point later on in the story a Hebrew soldier named Salmon fell in love with her. They were married, Rahab *"retired"* from her previous occupation, they had a little boy named Boaz and they all lived happily ever after. Boaz wasn't afraid to marry a foreigner because **his own mother was a foreigner and a former madam of a brothel of sorts at that!** The word *"innkeeper"* used in some translations does not adequately describe what kind of services that type of place provided to their customers. Remember, it was a very ungodly place and a very ungodly time. To show the incredible redemptive power of the Almighty, just consider the rest of the genealogy. The name of Boaz and Ruth's little boy was Obed. Obed had a little boy named Jesse and Jesse had a little boy named David, the man who is called a man after God's own heart elsewhere in Scripture. And, of course, from the lineage of David comes Jesus, the Messiah, the Savior of the world. By acting as a Kinsman-Redeemer for Naomi and Ruth, Boaz opened the door and set the precedence for the ultimate Kinsman-Redeemer to eventually come into the world for all of us!

NICE STORY, BUT WHAT DOES THAT MEAN FOR ME?

Agreed. There has to be a practical application to all of this. Let's take a look at this concept of the Kinsman-Redeemer as it applies to the Coming Crash.

We have already established that the vast majority of Christians are going to hit the wall hard when the crash comes. The economic devastation in America in general will be incomprehensible. The church's level of devastation will be only slightly less.

In this complete collapse of the existing economic system, a new, parallel system will have to arise, based on the concepts outlined in the Book of Acts as the operational model for the New Testament Church. Let's take a look at that model and see how it worked.

> " [44] *Now all who believed were together and had* **all things in common**, [45] *and* **sold their possessions and goods**, *and* **divided them among all**, **as anyone had need**. [46] *So continuing daily with one accord in the temple, and breaking bread from house to house, they ate their food with gladness and simplicity of heart,* [47] *praising God and having favor with all the people. And the Lord* **added to the church daily** *those who were being saved."*

> – ACTS 2:44-47

Pentecostals just love to quote Acts 2:38 but many of them forget that what happened in Verse 38 was not completely effective until it was implemented in the verses that followed. Verse 38 covers the spiritual aspects of that paradigm change. But Verses 44-47 had a profound, practical impact on the way that people lived their individual lives and their interactions with one another. I mentioned earlier in this book that I have a sermon I preach from time to time entitled *"Everything I Need Is In Someone Else's Garage!"* Truer words were never spoken. Right now, the church in the United States has everything it needs for the foreseeable future. In fact if the truth be known we probably have everything that the Third World needs as well. How can I say that? Just go look in your garage, attic, storage bin or wherever it is that you compulsively store all the things that you **just have to have but never use.** Remember that I told you that at one church I developed a simple one page **"I Needa - I Gotta"** sheet that folks filled out from time to time. Their job was to list on the *"I Needa"* side all the things that they needed but didn't have and then to list on the *"I Gotta"* side all the things that they had squirreled away for a *"rainy day"* but hadn't used in forever and would be willing to part with. The response was tremendous. Folks needed furniture. Folks had furniture. Folks needed refrigerators. Folks had refrigerators. Folks needed baby clothes. Folks had baby clothes. And so on and so on and so on...

It turns out that you didn't have to be a rich Boaz with multiple farms and a work crew to be able to be a

Kinsman-Redeemer to someone in your congregation. For that matter, why not expand that kind of network across your entire city, state or even region? Why not network the entire body of Christ across the US and even the world? The only thing holding us back is selfish competition between individuals and ministries. Everybody is busy feathering their own nests instead of taking care of God's business first. That's why we have a zillion little churches with congregations of twenty or less, all with their own little buildings. The devil knows what he is doing. Divide and conquer. Same old scam. Just new rubes to try it out on. Why not build church complexes using simple pole barn building techniques that have one large sanctuary, three or four mid-sized sanctuaries and another three or four small-size sanctuaries? Then add in a few classrooms, a common dining area, a common office with printer, copier, fax, internet and secretary and lo and behold, we have a **ministry clearing house** capable of supporting perhaps ten churches all at the same time. We have got to get beyond this *"us four and no more"* mindset. Unless we start acting as Kinsman-Redeemers for one another we are all going to go into the waste basket at the same time. I have talked previously in this book about the blessings that God has given us. I have also told you where some of them came from. In many cases we were blessed not with money to buy the thing we needed but with the actual thing itself! On other occasions we were able to provide something that we had into the lives of individuals or other ministries. Whatsoever you sow, you reap. We always preach that Scripture regarding money or doing bad things but the truth is that **whatever** you put into the lives of others will come back to you in an abundance far beyond your initial investment. Everything in our universe operates on that principle. Consider a single kernel of corn. If planted and carefully tended to, it will eventually sprout and grow into a tall stalk containing anywhere from five to seven ears of corn, with each ear containing roughly 700 brand new kernels of corn. How do I know that? Simple! I was preaching a sermon on that topic and decided to use an ear of corn in my message as a practical example. There was only one problem. I needed to know how many kernels of corn could be found on that particular ear. I tried several times to count them, only to lose my place and have to start over again. Finally, out of desperation, I got a Sharpie magic marker and used it to mark each individual kernel with a little black dot once I had counted it. The technique worked and I came up with my count. Now let's do the math. Let's say, for simplicity sake, that this particular sample corn stalk only contains 5 ears of corn and that each ear of corn contains 700 individual kernels. If you multiply 5 x 700 you end up with **three thousand five hundred kernels of corn**, all from the planting of a single kernel. Not only do you reap what you sow. You sow the **wind**, so the Bible passage says, but you reap the **whirlwind (tornado/twister).** That is clearly far out of proportion to the initial action, no matter if it be good or bad. Whatever you plant in the lives of others will eventually come back to you **in abundance.** The world says it in a slightly different way but it's still the same truth. **What goes round, comes round.**

Another nice side feature of the barter and free gift system is that God doesn't have to give any of His money to the sales tax collectors. It's very hard for any government to try and tax a barter system. **It's even harder to tax a system where nothing is being sold!** We need to start having **all things in common.** It's time to start saying and acting like what we have doesn't belong to us, it belongs to God! Do I sound like some Bolshevik revolutionary? I'm just quoting the Bible and not some obscure Scripture passage either. I'm telling you **that's how the early church operated and it worked just fine for them!** It's going to get a lot more radical than that. We will come to a point in time where we will have to be peaceful enough in our lives to share communal housing just like the Amish and the Mennonites. Instead of Grandma and Grandpa living in one place, the three kids living in three separate places with their families and the grandkids living elsewhere we are going to see a time when extended families are going to have to come back together and live together in harmony! In fact, there was actually a utopian community in Indiana like that called New Harmony, founded by the Rappites, a millennial community of the 1800's. That experiment failed primarily because the men slept in one building and the women slept in another and fraternization of any kind between the two groups was expressly forbidden. Needless to say, they died out in one generation. Surprise,

surprise! We're not talking about anything like that. And we're not talking about anything kinky either, with some weirdo religious leader ruling over a mentally enslaved population and enjoying the benefits of an extended harem or simply having sexual access to all the women in the commune. What we are talking about is a radically transformed group of Christians who have sufficiently developed the personality of Jesus Christ by cultivating the fruits of the Spirit in their lives to such a point that they can really and truly get along with one another, just like the First Century A.D. It worked back then. It will work again. Necessity is the Mother of Invention and Desperation is its Father!

Those with excess resources will have to willingly sell those resources and make the cash from those sales available to the Apostles in charge so that group needs can be met. But it will be a two-way street. The Bible clearly says that if a man will not work he shall not eat. There will be no loafers or slackers in such a community. Those individuals who are *"Black Holes"*, absorbing resources continually without ever showing any improvement will be banished from the community. Those who refuse to walk in a Godly fashion will also be put out. These communities will shine like the sun in a culture which will be absorbed in lying, cheating, stealing and murdering to obtain things that they want. Christianity always shines best when it is subjected to adversity. It drives out the chaff and polishes the wheat until the true Christians simply glow. The days of the selfish, all-about-me Charismatic will be over. Immature

Christians and immature Christianity will not survive this crash. Mature, rational, prayerful, godly individuals will survive and will actually thrive, just like Isaac, who sowed and reaped one-hundred-fold during a time of famine. No one in these Christian communities will be hungry while all around them people will be starving. None of these true Christians will be homeless when all around them people will be sleeping in dumpsters, trash cans and cardboard boxes. No one will be abused or molested in these godly fellowships while all around them rape, carnage and pillage will dominate the landscape.

CAN YOU GIVE ME ANY PRACTICAL EXAMPLES OF A KINSMAN-REDEEMER?

Sure can! Let me introduce you to the late Bishop C. Vernie Russell, Jr. Russell was the pastor of Mount Carmel Baptist Church, located in Norfolk, Virginia. When I first wrote about him, he was alive and well, doing a great work for the Lord in Virginia. Tragically, he passed away about six years ago but while he was healthy and in the pulpit about once a month

C. Vernie Russell Jr.

his church would hold a *"debt liquidation revival"*, a **foot-stomping, hand-clapping outpouring of music**

and financial generosity aimed at **lifting members out of credit-card debt**. How generous? Well, as an example, Carl and Janice Beaver went to church one night owing **$10,500** on a slew of credit cards. When they walked out two hours later they were **debt-free**. The Beavers were at that time the **56th family** to have been *"delivered"* from debt since the revivals began when this book was first published. In that single night in May, church members not only raised the money to pay off the Beavers' $10,500 debt but also generated an additional $5,400 to liquidate the debt of another couple and had $500 left over for next "revival". Up to that point in time the congregation had wiped out a total of **$318,000 of debt**. Their feat was all the more striking because Mount Carmel isn't some suburban megachurch catering to the country-club set. It is in a vaguely seedy section of downtown Norfolk and volunteer security guards watch parked cars during services. The church's predominantly African-American members are **mostly under fifty** and are **drawn from across the economic spectrum**. Many are from military families posted at the huge naval base here, home port of the Atlantic Fleet. *"The credit-card companies don't like me too well"*, said Bishop Russell, who was an imposing figure with a graying, Santa Claus beard who accounted for all repaid debts in a pocket-sized, green notebook. But, he insisted, ***"You can't serve your Master and MasterCard at the same time."*** To an **overextended generation** accustomed to **instant plastic gratification**, Bishop Russell preached the **evils**

of **near-thirty percent interest rates** and the **virtues of saving money and paying cash**. At his urging, **one thousand church members had cut up their credit cards** and the shards were kept in a glass urn on the pulpit. People whose debt had been liquidated were asked to donate at least three hundred dollars at subsequent revival meetings to help other families.

This self-help refinancing project had a beneficial effect on church coffers as well. **As credit card balances declined, disposable incomes -- and church donations -- rose**. The amount tithed, for example, was **up twenty-five percent in that year**, according to Bishop Russell. In addition to money collected at debt revivals, Mount Carmel took in more than **two million dollars annually** to fund operations and community-outreach missions such as feeding and clothing the homeless. **The goal was to have the 3,000-member congregation debt-free, except for mortgages and car loans**. *"When you do something collectively, its better"*, Bishop Russell said. Losing Bishop Russell had to have been a real heartbreaking moment for his congregation. I do not know if the new pastor has continued his legacy.

Another example of a Kinsman-Redeemer is a person that I already introduced you to earlier in this book, my dear, late friend, Orville Martin. I first met Orville at a *"Faith Sharing"* conference that I was in charge of in the city where he lived, Rockport, Indiana. We soon became close friends because at that time we were both serving as Lay Pastors in the United Methodist Church, he in one district and I in another. When I made the decision to start my software design company, I felt led to approach him about a starter funds loan even though I knew nothing about his financial situation. It turned out that he indeed did have some discretionary funds and loaned me $5,000 to get my business started. My plan was to pay him off totally within the span of three years but my enthusiasm and projected profits did not match reality at the end of that span. Instead of paying him off fully, I had not been able to pay him back a single penny. I felt horrible about it, but Orville never asked me or pressured me about it, so I left well enough alone. About a year later, a remarkable, spontaneous ministry opportunity presented itself in the same county. I had been invited to attend a county-wide revival, but not as a speaker. In deference to my friends who had invited me I decided to attend the first meeting but then skip the remaining ones. I was seated in the *"honor"* section with other ministers, up front, because of the outstanding success that the Faith Sharing conference had achieved. A friend of mine was speaking and I was totally content to sit there and listen but the Holy Spirit had come on me in power and His presence was, as Jeremiah said, like a fire in my bones. I felt an enormous push from the Lord to get up and speak but I was determined not to try and take over something that wasn't really mine to begin with. The pressure kept building and building until finally I said to the Lord (in my mind and not out loud), *"Lord, I know You're pushing on me to do this but it just isn't right! If You REALLY want me to speak, have Brenda (my friend who was speaking at the podium at the time) turn and literally say to me, 'Pastor Ray, God has spoken to me and told me that YOU are supposed to be the speaker tonight!'"* No sooner had I said that to the Lord in my mind than Brenda abruptly stopped speaking, turned wild-eyed toward me and said, *"Pastor Ray, the Lord has just spoke to me and told me that YOU are supposed to be our speaker tonight!"* I was absolutely flabbergasted. Nothing like that had ever happened to me. I slowly got up and walked to the podium, hugged Brenda and quietly asked her if she was really sure she was supposed to do this, hemmed and hawed for a few minutes and then began speaking on what the Lord had put on my heart, an issue that was burning a hole in my soul. As I began to speak, the power of God began to fall on the audience and untold lives were touched and any number of people were baptized in the Holy Spirit and/or healed as well that night. At the end of the night, unbeknownst to me, the leaders who had organized the revival met privately and unanimously agreed that I should be the keynote speaker for every meeting left in the entire revival! When they told me about their decision I was stunned and almost said no but they urged me to accept the offer because the Holy Spirit had spoken to each one of them and told them to do so. I finally said yes. As the meetings went on, the power of God got stronger and stronger. Finally we held the last scheduled meeting. The revival had been a massive success, not because Ray Young was the speaker, but because the Holy Spirit was given the freedom to conduct business as He saw fit, not merely according to the ways and means of mere men. Near the close of the meeting, I was still praying with, prophesying to and counseling various couples and individuals. A young couple approached me and presented me with a thorny question. It seemed that they had been faithful members of a local congregation and, in the process of doing so, had made a financial pledge regarding a new roof project at the church. Since that time, however, the Lord had called them into full-time ministry and, although they might occasionally attend their old church, they would be on the road most of the time. The question that they posed to me was that given the fact that they would no longer be at their old church, were they then absolved of their financial commitment regarding the new roof? I got my Bible out and opened to the passage in the Gospels where Jesus said to let your *"Yes"* be *"Yes"* and your *"No"* be *"No"*! (Matthew 5:37) Christians have an obligation, if humanly or sometimes superhumanly possible, to honor the words that come out of their mouths. The Old Testament says that God is not a man that He should lie nor the son of man that He should change His mind (Numbers 23:19). We, after all, say that we are His children. Shouldn't the children follow after the Father in their conduct? That was the counsel I gave to them. They nodded somberly and agreed that they had been trying to shirk their financial responsibility. Then suddenly a voice behind me rang out, saying, *"Now I know why the Lord INSISTED that I come to this meeting! I hereby cancel the debt that you owe to me!*

You don't owe me a single penny anymore!" Startled, I quickly turned around and there, standing right behind me and beaming brightly was my dear friend Orville. *"I don't understand"*, I stuttered. *"You were told to come tonight? And you're cancelling my $5,000 business loan debt???"* *"Yes, Ray"*, Orville replied. *"Even though you haven't been able to repay me thus far, your HEART is in the right place and I'm going to honor that intent as if it were an actual action!"* Now both I AND the young couple were astonished. It was an awesome ending to a totally unanticipated but highly anointed opportunity.

Orville not only forgave me the $5,000 he loaned me. He also, as I documented earlier in this work, provided $10,000 to bail out the Christian bookstore in our home town and our dear friends. He also loaned $10,000 to the new owners when the old owners eventually decided to sell, but somehow that last deal turned sour and the new owners went back on their word. Orville forgave them and kept right on giving and sharing and loving people in need all around him until the day he died. Not all Kinsman-Redeemers are millionaires. Some are like Orville, successful on a limited scale. But others, like the members of my African-American congregation near Cincinnati, were almost **ALL** Kinsman-Redeemers. Some were redeemers of a vacuum cleaner. Some were redeemers of an ironing board or some cans of vegetables or children's clothes for a brand new baby born into a family that loved the Lord but didn't have much in the way of the world's goods and finances. Any time any individual gave something to someone that the person in question didn't have, they were acting as a Kinsman-Redeemer. The truth is that **every single one of us can act as a Kinsman-Redeemer**. It doesn't mean that you have to be the giver all the time. Sometimes you are the receiver, just like in the Book of Acts. Jesus is, of course, the Ultimate Kinsman-Redeemer and He is our Older Brother. Our Heavenly Father is also the Ultimate Kinsman-Redeemer, so we can say that we are simply expressing our family heritage when we give to others out of the goodness of our hearts, just like old Boaz, who never dreamt that helping a young widowed foreigner would result in God filling the empty place in his heart with a woman who loved him and a baby boy to delight in. Hannah, who had an empty womb, never imagined that in giving one child, Samuel, to the Lord, that it would trigger Him giving her **five more children of her own to keep.** Remember that Scripture says that *"whatsoever a man soweth, **that also shall he reap"*** (Galatians 6:7). When we give to God or to others around us out of the goodness of our hearts, we are truly being like our Heavenly Father and our Big Brother in the most important way. After all, doesn't John 3:16 say, *"For God so love the world that He **gave**…"*???

IS OUR DEBT SITUATION REALLY THAT BAD?

You already know about the amount of Federal Debt our nation carries. Let me give you some just-as-scary statistics about **personal debt in the US.**

I promised you I would do this earlier in this book. When I first wrote this book in 2006, I merely included some summary information. But as I did my research in 2009, I discovered an incredible and frightening web site that was called the ***Grandfather Economic Reports*** created by an amazing and diligent gentleman named Michael Hodges. What I am going to present to you is only some summary information and charts that I borrowed from that site, which for internet security reasons is hard to get to and, in a way, kind of risky. The statistics I will show you and the supporting graphs and charts will first make your blood run cold at the incredible mess that we have gotten ourselves into and then cause it to boil when you realize how badly we have been duped by our own government and how careless, reckless and irresponsible we ourselves have been. We have literally dug our own financial grave and then jumped in and begun to pull dirt down on our heads in an irrational attempt to bury ourselves. In the 1960's Nikita Khrushchev of the Soviet Union pounded his shoe on the podium of the United Nations and said that they would bury us. He was not referring to military might when he said that. He was referring to the fact that the former USSR was convinced that they could bury us **economically.** Fortunately for us the Union of Soviet Socialist Republics imploded under its own economic weight long before they could accomplish such a task. Unfortunately for us, we didn't need them to bury us. We were already in the process of burying ourselves. Here, then are the frightening facts about our collective indebtedness and outright stupidity as they existed all the way back in 2009. Once we have dealt with those statistics we will move forward in time to 2022 to look at the changes that have occurred. The rate of debt increase will make your blood run cold. Let's get at it!

Way back in 2009, here were some statistics regarding our total indebtedness:

- ✓ America's **National Debt** had topped **9 Trillion Dollars**
- ✓ America's **Consumer Debt** had topped **2 Trillion Dollars**
- ✓ **Personal Bankruptcies** in 2003 totaled **1.63 Million**
- ✓ Average Household credit card debt was **$9,200.00**
- ✓ Each year **9 Million** people sought help from debt counseling services
- ✓ The average NFCC client had **$15,700.00** in **Credit Card Debt** and only **$30,000.00** in **Gross Income**

By 2007, Consumer Debt had risen to **2.39 trillion dollars**. Granted, personal debt was not as bad as our Federal Government's debt, but that's kind of like comparing a fifty-foot-deep hole to a twelve-foot-deep hole. Without help you're not going to get out of either one. One is difficult, the other nearly impossible.

What I show you below are numbers compiled through the end of 2007. Bear in mind that when you look at these graphs and read these statistics, **they do**

not include the utterly traumatic events of 2008 and the enormously foolish financial decisions reached by our spendthrift government ever since then. We will document what has happened since then in a little while.

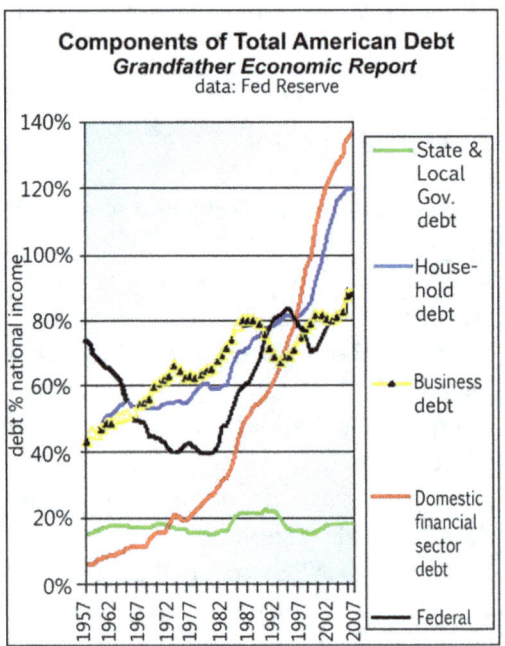

Let's begin with the ugliest news. This chart compares several trends since 1957. They are:

1. **State and Local Government Debt** as illustrated by the **green** line.
2. **Household Debt** as illustrated by the **blue** line.
3. **Business Debt** as illustrated by the **yellow** line.
4. **Domestic / Financial Sector Debt** as illustrated by the **red** line.
5. **Federal Debt** as illustrated by the **black** line.

Again, bear in mind that what you are looking at **does not reflect the disastrous events of 2008**, when the housing and sub-prime lending markets collapsed nor **does it reflect the over eight hundred billion dollar stimulus package** put into place in January of 2009. Nonetheless this graph clearly illustrates the insane policies and decisions made by both the U.S. populace and our legislators over the last fifty years. In the Old Testament, the Children of Israel spent **forty** years wandering around in the desert trying to **get** to the Promised Land. Today in America we have spent the last **sixty** years trying to **leave** the Promised Land so that we could put ourselves back in the desert.

As you can tell, **State and Local Government Debt** through 2009 had historically been fairly constant. That makes perfect sense. The further away from Washington you go and the closer to Main Street U.S.A. you get the more rational control has been exerted by the citizenry over what could and could not be spent. In the real world you can't spend money you don't have unless, of course, you put it on your credit card. But for State and Local Governments there was no credit card available and so they have always had to make do with what they had available to them through taxes and government programs. I am very proud of the fact that I live in the state of Indiana. Our state has maintained a **balanced budget** for quite some time now. In fact, this year my wife and I received a check from our state government which represented our share of the **surplus** that Indiana had left once it had paid all its bills! As I was researching all of this, I came across a number of stunning and eloquent graphs and charts that portray everything I've been talking about far better than I could. Truly a single picture is still worth (at least) a thousand words!

Let's take a look at how the individual states manage their own financial affairs. I was really proud of Indiana until I took a look at **ALL** of the states. What I discovered both shocked me and yet actually **affirmed** what I had been saying about Main Street, U.S.A.'s ability to control itself on a state level as opposed to the fantasy land that our federal legislators live in. Let's take a look at the entire United States as of 2021 to see if **individual state governments** were living within their means:

Total Reserves Vary Widely by State
Days each state could run on total balances, FY 2021

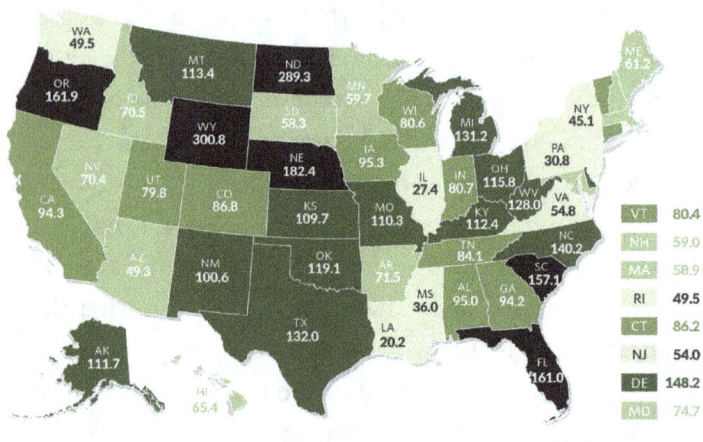

VT	80.4
NH	59.0
MA	58.9
RI	49.5
CT	86.2
NJ	54.0
DE	148.2
MD	74.7

20 to 54.9 days   55 to 74.9 days   75 to 99.9 days
100 to 149.9 days   150 days or more

85.1 50-state median

Source: Pew analysis of data from the National Association of State Budget Officers
© 2022 The Pew Charitable Trusts

Now, exactly what are we looking at? Well, each state is shown as of 2022, along with **the numbers of days that they could keep their legislative and administrative doors open for business if all income suddenly dried up.** My own state of Indiana could run for 80.7 days without shutting down. That's how much money they have stored in their state coffers. That's not bad, all things considered. But there are also states that are much worse off and much better off. Wyoming and North Dakota (Go, North Dakota State Bison!) could run for a long time, along with Nebraska, Oregon, South Carolina and Florida. Hats off to the state senators and representatives of those states! Bravo! But on the poor and mismanaged side we find Louisiana at the bottom, with only a little over 20 days of operating capital available in their checking accounts. Not far behind are Illinois, Pennsylvania, Mississippi, New York, New Jersey and Virginia. I'll let you draw your own conclusions about why those particular states are so badly managed. But even so, **every single state was running with a SURPLUS, not a DEFICIT.** Remember earlier in this chapter I said that the states were forced by their very nature to have to run **within a budget** and to be **fiscally responsible.** Even California, Virginia, New York and New Jersey, which draw staggering amounts of funding from the federal government in the form of public welfare, still somehow manage to keep a little stashed away for a rainy day.

Household Debt on the other hand **did** have those dreaded credit cards available to it. Let's look at that 1957-2007 chart again for a moment. Notice the steady increase in household debt until about **2000.** Then, suddenly, it takes off like a rocket headed straight out of the stratosphere. What on earth was going on? Do you remember that I

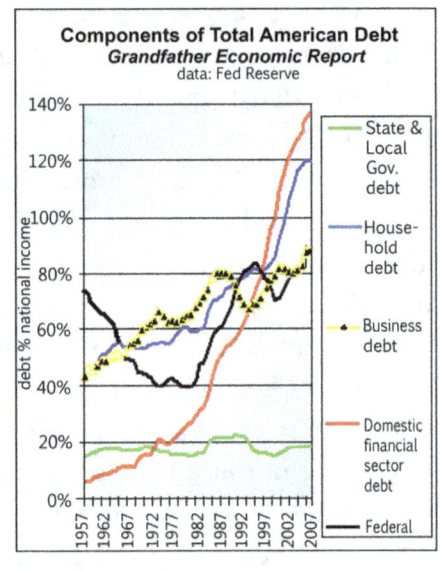

Components of Total American Debt
Grandfather Economic Report
data: Fed Reserve

State & Local Gov. debt

Household debt

Business debt

Domestic financial sector debt

Federal

told you that the **tipping point** in the possible one-hundred-year Mega-K-Wave was probably around 2000? From that point on things would logically begin to flow downhill in a negative fashion rather than uphill in a positive fashion. If, on the other hand, we're looking at a 150-year K-Wave **hyper-**cycle it could mean that this dramatic increase will only accelerate from this point on. Frankly, I'm not sure which it is or if it is some combination of the two. Other statistics that I have discovered point to a significant attempt in recent years by the American public to curb back on their credit card and mortgage debt at least to some extent. But as far back as the early 1980s a dramatic increase in credit card spending occurred because families suddenly found it much more difficult to sustain their lifestyle with the resources available to them and began to severely overload their cards in order to maintain the appearance of affluence. Many years ago there was a terrific commercial showing a smiling man riding on his expensive riding lawnmower, mowing the grass of his beautiful, two story, Cape Cod home in an upscale suburban neighborhood. Everything seemed to be just perfect. He had everything you could imagine. But as he rode on his mower, He was saying, *"Somebody please help me! I'm so deep in debt I don't know what to do!"* He was clearly not alone in his secret little crisis. Household debt was **13.8 trillion dollars** in 2007, up **one trillion dollars** over the prior year. Of that 13.8 trillion dollars, **10.5 trillion** was for **mortgages** and the remaining **3.3 trillion** for **credit card purchases**.

That latter figure was a dramatic increase over the **2 trillion** dollars of 2003 and the **2.39** trillion dollars reported earlier in 2007. But dollar figures alone don't reveal the entire story. In the 1960's and 1970's the household debt ration held steady at about **53 percent of the national income**, not good, but not terrible either. It meant that household debt was not growing faster than the growth of the total economy. By the end of 2007, that figure had exploded to **123 percent of our national income**, a debt increase of **100 percent since 2000!**

In addition, I found some excellent graphs showing the increase in household debt over an extended period of time. Let's look at them now to see the rest of the story. The chart I'm going to show you next tracks total household debt from 2003 through 2021.

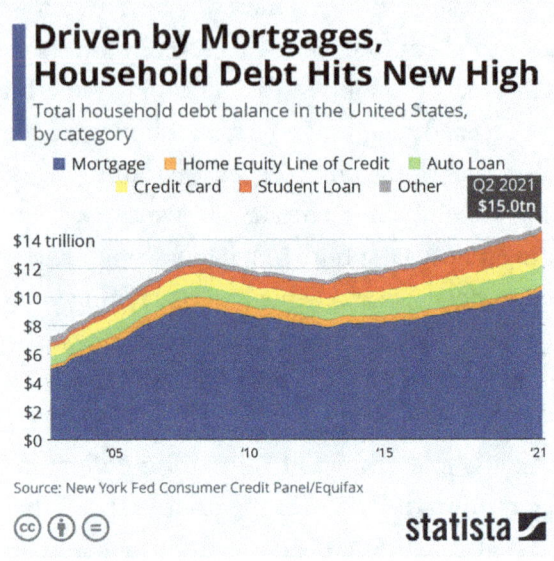

Driven by Mortgages, Household Debt Hits New High

Total household debt balance in the United States, by category

- Mortgage
- Home Equity Line of Credit
- Auto Loan
- Credit Card
- Student Loan
- Other

Q2 2021
$15.0tn

$14 trillion
$12
$10
$8
$6
$4
$2
$0

'05   '10   '15   '21

Source: New York Fed Consumer Credit Panel/Equifax

statista

This graph dramatically illustrates the steady increase of total household debt. It also clearly portrays how much of America's household debt is really debt on the house itself. As you can tell by the chart (this is one of the **many** reasons I insisted that this book be printed in full color rather than drab and unclear black and white!), the blue area of mortgage debt absolutely dominates the overall debt situation for individual Americans. Remember that much earlier in this book I outlined for you the dreaded **Rule of 78s** and how banks manage to bleed consumers dry by using that *"Seven Year Itch"* **Syndrome** I talked about, where homeowners swap their existing home out for a new one every seven years on an average, thus resetting the entire unequal interest process all over again…and again…and again. Guess who sits back and, like Pac-Man, gobbles up all the blue? Yup! Lending institutions, made fat and prosperous on the backs of hard-working individuals who just want a place that they can call their own, except it isn't really theirs, is it? That home that they work so hard to maintain is almost totally owned by the lending institution that holds their paper. How sad!

Student loans and auto loans come in a distant second and third in the race to acquire debt. Ironically, credit card debt, which I have soundly denounced, is actually only a small part of a much larger, much more disturbing picture.

Despite recent declines, U.S. household debt is still very high relative to disposable income

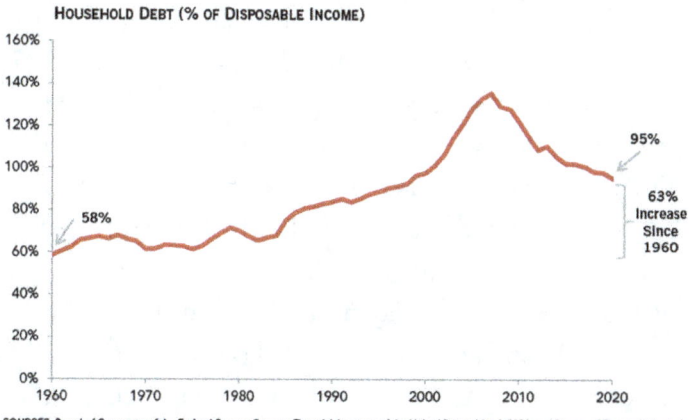

HOUSEHOLD DEBT (% OF DISPOSABLE INCOME)

95%

63% Increase Since 1960

58%

SOURCES: Board of Governors of the Federal Reserve System, *Financial Accounts of the United States*, March 2021; and Bureau of Economic Analysis, *National Income and Product Accounts Tables*, March 2021.
© 2021 Peter G. Peterson Foundation   PGPF.ORG

There is, however, a small ray of hope. At least some consumers have come to the painfully obvious conclusion that they can't keep on acquiring long-term debt the way that they have. In a fascinating twist of fate, American consumers went from spending over 120% of their disposable income in 2008 to under 100 percent. (Notice how this parallels the housing and lending market's crash at the same time?) While Washington continued to believe in a never-ending Fantasyland where poverty and depression never come, Main Street was starting to take a hard look at how much they were spending and what they were spending it for. By 2020 that more than 120% of disposable income had shrunk to 95%. Not awesome, but at least something to speak well of. Still, even with that decrease, Americans had increased their spending by 63% from 1950 to 2020.

I have another chart that I would like to show you, unfortunately. But I want to tell you yet another personal story before I do. I'm 74 now and with a fair number of things wrong with my body. I get around, but I am clearly not able to run and not get weary or walk and not get faint. But once upon a time, long, long ago in the Kingdom of Eastern Pennsylvania there lived a young Youngling named Raymond. He had always been a large child but nonetheless had some physical skills. He eventually ended up playing high school football and doing quite well at it. He controlled his weight and went to college on a partial football scholarship weighing in at 195 pounds, almost all of it solid muscle, running an average of five miles a day. I can barely imagine myself doing it now, but it is nonetheless true. After his freshman year he grew tired of being hammered in the head daily by an All-Conference offensive tackle who had steel plates secretly hidden in his forearm pads and decided that working part time in retail clothing was more profitable and far less painful a way to generate tuition funds. But even though he had stopped playing football and was no longer burning all of those calories, he continued to eat as though he were. In one year, little Raymond ballooned from 195 pounds to 230 pounds and had to purchase a whole new wardrobe. From that point on, *"Weight Inflation"* set up shop in the little town of Raymondville. Slowly but surely he got heavier and heavier and bigger and bigger until he was weighing in at 255 pounds. But he didn't stop there. By the time that he accepted a pastoral position near Cincinnati, Ohio, his weight had ballooned all the way to 304 pounds! It hadn't happened all at once. Instead, it was the result of a **consistent unwillingness and inability to control himself when it came to food.** Shortly thereafter, his whole world would come tumbling down on him as he battled for his life against cancer. The disease and even more than that the chemotherapy and radiation treatment for the disease caused him to throw up as many as five times a day. Unable to hold anything down, his weight plummeted from 304 to 235 in only five months. Convinced that he was going to die, the church he was pastoring met behind his back while he lay in the hospital and fired him, giving the job to the young man who had received a vision from the Lord and was told by the Almighty to come and help him. They say in the Bible that Judas hung himself. Sometimes I think that Judas never really died. At least the Enemy who inhabited him didn't. And the young man who was supposed to come and help him? Well, it was really prophetic, because that young man's name was **"Steels"**. Insert an *"a"*, delete an *"e"* and you have what that young man did. Did he get away with it? Nope! When you sow the wind, you reap the whirlwind (tornado!). Four years later, one of the four teenage girls he was having sex with on the side got mad at him, put a tape recorder under her bed and recorded the whole event. His beautiful and totally faithful wife walked out on him, he was fired and as far as I know, never recovered. Somehow, through sickness and betrayal by even close friends, Raymond survived and eventually started to recover. As he recovered, his weight started to go up, here a little, there a little, for the same reason as before, until he was back at 255 pounds. He stayed that way for a long time until another bout with illness dropped him to 227 pounds. He now hovers around 225-230, having **finally** learned his lesson about self-control.

A strange story. Maybe, or maybe not. I would be willing to bet, if I were a gambling man, that I am speaking not just about me, but about many of my readers. So much good food. So little time… And it is as a **person** goes that a **group** also goes and as a group goes, so goes a **state** and as a state goes, so goes a **nation.** Without the calorie-checking of budget restraints, America has been just like little Raymond, not giving in to wild gorging at buffets, but nibbling and nibbling and nibbling, even when our hunger was satisfied, running more on taste than good common sense. The graph I'm going to show you now should blow your mind and make your blood run cold. You are going to see a nation totally out of control, unable and unwilling to deal with its addiction to affluence and having tossed caution to the wind but first, I have a personal confession to make.

As I looked at that historical perspective, I began to see my own story as a microcosm paralleling our country. If I'm going to preach, I can't leave the pulpit and its occupant out, now can I? As a result of telling my own story, I have come under serious conviction about the remaining 35 pounds on my frame and so I promise you this, dear reader: I am going to **FINALLY** put my weight problems to rest and pray, fast and exercise until I am back at the 195 pounds that I weighed when I went out for freshman football in college back when I was 17. I have been noticing more and more frequently that additional, unnecessary weight becomes an increasing burden as you get older. Most of the older folks I know who are in good health are also slim and trim. My goal is to get back as much of the strength and stamina that I used to have as possible. How much is that? Well, I'll never know unless I try, unless I push myself and **refuse** to simply sit in a Lazy Boy recliner and watch the world collapse around me. Inasmuch as it is possible, I am going to, by the grace of God, make more of a difference during the remaining years of my life than I ever have before. My grandfather lived to be 85 and would have lived longer had our neighbor's German shepherd not attacked him and caused a stroke. My father lived to be 87 and was in good health until his last year or so. And my Grandma Young, bless her heart, lived to be **93** years old, put out a flower garden every spring until she was 83, and was clear as a bell mentally until near the very end. A friend of ours who moves powerfully in the prophetic had a dream about Bev and I some time ago. In that dream, Bev was 91 and still in good health. I'm two years older than her and I was also present in the dream. That would mean that at that time I was **93** years old! That would match my Gram Young! When the Final Great Awakening finally arrives, I want to be spiritually and physically ready to run the race set before me, just like Caleb the son of Jephunneh in Joshua 14:10-12, who told his *"Running Buddy"* Joshua that he was just as strong for battle and going out and coming back at the age of 85 as he had been many years prior to that when the 10 unbelieving scouts brought a bad report and caused Israel to have to wander in the wilderness for another 40 years. Caleb, buddy, here I come!!!

Household Debt in Historical Context

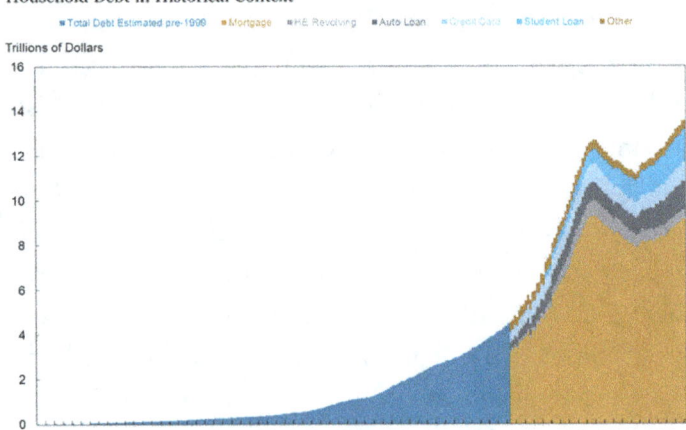

Source: New York Fed Consumer Credit Panel / Equifax; Federal Reserve Board.

Note: For comparability, we applied the pre-1999 quarterly growth rate from the Flow of Funds to splice the two series in 1999

You've heard the story of little Raymond. Now, finally, here is the sad, sad story of the little boy called *"America"*. We're going to pick up his story around 1945, near the end of World War II. He was in great shape back then. He had traveled to Europe and the Far East to fight tyranny and had won. In the process of battle he had grown strong and he was healthy and happy and wanted nothing more than to find a wife, have a couple of kids and relax and enjoy life for a while. For a while, things were good. But then came the Korean Conflict, then Vietnam, Power to the People, Woodstock, Drugs and, predictably, a loosening of the moral restraints inside the heart of America. And so conduct became more outrageous, more unrestrained and more expensive. Cocaine, LSD and other drugs didn't come cheap. Inflation began to rise and, with it, public debt. By the 1980s things were starting to get out of hand but the increase had been so gradual that no one felt alarmed except for a few economists who could see the writing on the wall. By the year 2000 the gates had been broken open and the stampede begun. Household debt has spiraled out of control, just like our Federal National debt. There was a brief moment of sanity around 2013. I still puzzle about what might have caused that. I will keep on researching to find the answer but it may not matter too much longer, because household debt has once again resumed its irrational race off the edge of the cliff, waiting for its feet to hit thin air and the precipitous drop to begin.

I know that showing you all of these charts must seem like beating a dead horse, but I have two charts left that you need to see. Both reveal disturbing and troublesome

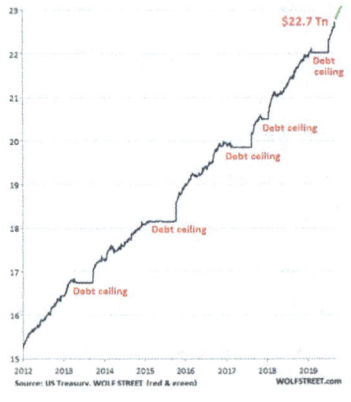

insights into America's plunge into moral and financial darkness. The first one has to deal with the Federal Debt and the Debt Ceiling that Congress is supposed to abide by. Notice that I used the phrase *"supposed to"*...

The debt ceiling was first enacted in 1917 during World War I through the Second Liberty Bond Act and was set at $11.5 billion to simplify the process and enhance borrowing flexibility. In 1939, Congress created the first aggregate debt limit covering nearly all government debt and set it at $45 billion, about 10 percent above total debt at the time. That alone should have sounded a warning bell, but no one was listening. Consider these facts: (1) only **22** years had passed since the creation of the debt ceiling, yet Congress had incrementally pushed the supposedly non-negotiable limit from a *"mere"* **11.5 billion dollars** to **45 billion dollars**, an increase of **33.5 billion dollars!** Once Congress became addicted to irresponsible, no-real-absolute stopping point spending there was no turning back. Since the end of World War II, Congress and the President have modified the debt ceiling **roughly**

100 times. During the 1980s, the debt ceiling was increased from **less than $1 trillion** to **nearly $3 trillion**. Over the course of the 1990s, it was doubled to **nearly $6 trillion**, and in the 2000s it was again doubled to **over $12 trillion**. The Budget Control Act of 2011 **automatically raised the debt ceiling by $900 billion** and gave the President authority to increase the limit by **an additional $1.2 trillion (for a total of $2.1 trillion) to $16.39 trillion**! Lawmakers have suspended the debt limit, rather than raising it by a specific dollar amount, seven times since February 2013. The debt limit was increased – not suspended – twice in 2021 in a December 2021 bill that formally increased the limit to **$31.381 trillion**! Even though I have researched this matter thoroughly and should be used to this madness by now, I cannot help but to shake my head in disbelief when I see what our legislators and leaders have done to us. The inroads to our nation's financial well-being occurred in step with the decay of moral standards and in the same manner – hold the line for a little while to make yourself look good and then *"compromise"* with the opposition by letting them get a little more of what they want time and time again. The Republican Senate Leader Mitch McConnell has made a career of this kind of compromising, always appearing to be a concerned moderate when in reality he is a career politician who is only concerned with looking good to his constituents and is willing to do whatever it takes to stay in office. Should we have term limits on our legislators? What do **you** think???

Look again at the graph. Since 2012 it tracks **five separate attempts** to *"Hold the Line"* on the budget, only to be overridden and abandoned in a pursuit to create more and more debt. I am not a conspiracy fanatic but as I look at all of these trends, I can't help but feel that evil, sinister forces beyond our imagining have been controlling people in power in our government for a very long time. Small wonder, then, that over 60% of the American public polled felt that government corruption was the most important issue that needed to be dealt with!

There is one final chart I would like to bring to your attention and this one has to deal with what is called **Public Debt per Capita.** In plain English, it represents **your personal share or responsibility for the staggering debt load acquired by this country of ours.** Here, then, is yet another mind-blowing set of statistics:

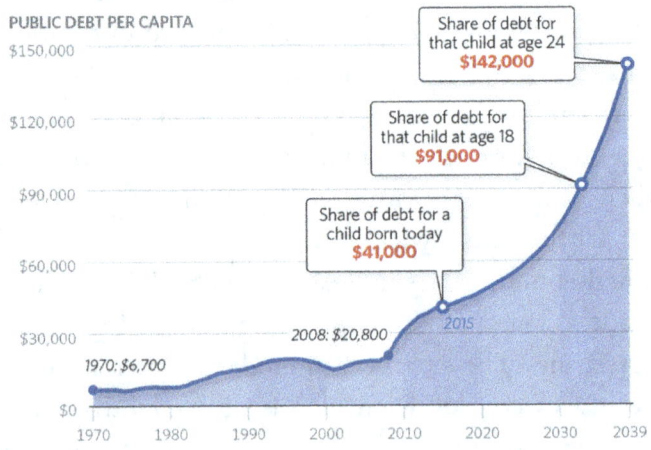

Let's take a look at what has happened gradually over a period of time to place an ever-increasing, unbearable load on the back of American taxpayers. Back in 1970, every person in the U.S. was technically responsible for **$6,700.00**. More debt than any of us would like to shoulder, but still within some reasonable boundary. By 2008, that burden had increased to **20,800.00 per person**. Ouch! My back hurts! But by 2015 that same burden had **more than doubled** to an astonishing **41,000.00 per person!** By 2035, only 12 years from the year that I am writing these words in, that burden will **more than double again** to an unbearable **$91,000.00** but even then the work will not be done because it is projected that in 2039 that individual debt burden will have ballooned all the way to **$142,000.00!!!**

What makes this even more terrible is that the overwhelming number of illegal aliens currently entering our country through our unguarded southern border will cause even those numbers to explode. We are about to cripple our country, perhaps permanently, if we don't take this undocumented, illegal alien problem to task. Many years ago we had a wonderful Hispanic lady as a friend who did a lot of ministry in her ethnic group. Because I had such a tremendous background on the End Times and the timing of the Rapture, she invited me to spend several weeks ministering to them through her translation skills. After one of those meetings she admitted to me that **at least 70% of those in attendance were in the U.S. illegally**. They held down jobs, had families, sported not-so-authentic Social Security and Medicare or Medicaid cards and even had, in many cases, doctored drivers licenses and insurance! And friends, that was a good ten years ago. Despite President Trump's attempt to stem the flow, the new Democratic administration which, in my personal opinion, was illegally enshrined in the White House, did everything that they could to completely unravel his wise decisions about the situation. Instead, they have literally opened the floodgates to border crossings and, as I write this, that volume is set to go to uncontrollable levels with the probable removal of Title 42 legislation. Title 42 is a public health order that allows Customs and Border Protection to expel migrants to Mexico or back to their home countries to prevent the spread of COVID-19 in holding facilities. The policy was created under the Trump administration and was issued by the CDC in March 2020, at the start of the pandemic. With border security guards under strict orders from Washington not to make any attempt to stop the overwhelming border violations that occur on a daily basis, Title 42 represented the only thin line of resistance. Now even it may be taken away. A massive influx of illegal aliens into our country will cause a complete collapse of the public welfare system. It would be like the Titanic, while in the process of sinking, inviting a whole new manifest of passengers on board as the water gurgled through the hallways and cabins. While staggering amounts of federal money are quietly and in many cases secretly being poured into providing for all of the needs of these interlopers, even to the point of paying for busloads and planeloads of illegal immigrants to be disbursed throughout the country (I have viewed videos clearly documenting these actions and also looked at documentation that verifies the same), legitimate citizens are often being denied basic assistance that they are legally entitled to. We have a granddaughter, a single mother with two children, who has had a running battle with federal programs that are supposed to be there to help her. She has often had to work two jobs to try and make ends meet because time after time, financial help owed to her has been denied or delayed indefinitely. For me, it brings the matter all too close to home.

It is finally time to add all the numbers up and see how really bad things are. In order to come up with these figures I had to draw from statistical information from both 2021 and 2022. Either way, I'm reasonable sure that I'm close to if not lower than the actual figure. Most of the debt in America falls into four categories: **Federal, Local Government, Corporate** and **Household**. Household debt is largely made up of housing mortgages, followed by credit cards, student loans and the like. At this point in time in 2023, the **Federal** debt burden is now sitting at a minimum of **28.3 trillion dollars.** Local government, as we have already established, isn't nearly as bad, coming in at slightly more than **2.8 trillion dollars.** Corporate debt runs right behind Federal debt at a troubling **22.5 trillion dollars.** Rounding out the total is Household debt, which is sitting at slightly more than **16.5 trillion dollars.** When all the smoke has cleared and the numbers are finally added up, total indebtedness in the United States now sits at **70.1 trillion**

dollars!!! I don't know about you, but my little pea brain is having some trouble wrapping itself around numbers like that. Do you see now why I insist that a crash and Mega-Depression is completely, one hundred percent unavoidable? We have pushed not only our country but also the entire world economic and political systems to the edge of the abyss and do not seem to be capable of letting up. Heaven help us all! The body of Christ will have to start helping one another whether we like it or not! Necessity is being laid upon us by the carelessness and recklessness of fifty years of American Christians and non-Christians alike. Shame on us! Don't you think it's time to stop and make a change???

Unfortunately, no one seems to be willing to make the changes necessary. Remember those Reverse Mortgages that we talked about earlier? Well, there's an interesting trend that has developed among lending institutions to allow their customers to take their credit card debt and roll it over into a refinanced mortgage. Stop and think about that and then remember what I showed you about the rule of 78s? Remember that when you refinance, your interest starts **all over again** and whatever principle you had is washed away. Who is the winner and who is the loser in a move like that?

Sure, Dick and Jane, we'll take your twenty thousand dollars in credit card debt and add it on to your mortgage. We'll just restart the mortgage all over again like it's day one. Sit down for a second and think about that first payment. How much was interest and how much was principle? Just keep repeating this mantra over and over again, *"The banker is my friend. The banker is my friend. The banker is my friend..."*

With the complete failure of sanity and credibility in the lending industry, churches must act as Kinsman-Redeemers for the Body of Christ either collectively or individually. But the pastor has to get the vision first and understand that if his people aren't paying three hundred dollars or more a month in interest they might be able to pay something on their tithe. I challenge you and your church, your Bible study or whatever Christian organization you are a part of to begin to think and act like Kinsman-Redeemers. We must start the process now. The more we can accomplish now before the Crash comes the less we will have staring us in the face after the Crash. In summary, it is high time for pastors, churches and denominations to start thinking **more about people** and **less about buildings,** more about **meeting the needs of their congregations** and less about **meeting their budgets.**

CITIES OF REFUGE

Another fascinating manifestation of this practical, Holy Spirit driven economy will emerge. When the crash occurs the cities of America will burn to the ground. There is no question about it. For many years I taught at an undergraduate level at a Junior College extension campus. Periodically I would ask my classes a question. It went something like this: In the Depression, a man could knock at the door of a farmhouse. He could admit that he had no money, no job and no idea where he was going or what he was going to do. But he could offer to chop up all that firewood by the barn and stack it neatly near the house. All he asked for in return was a good hot meal and perhaps the privilege of sleeping in the soft, warm hay in the barn. The good lady of the household in that day could usually agree to the proposition and not have to fear rape, robbery or any violence to her or to her household. The reason? Even though America had been living badly in the Roaring Twenties, She still had a conscience and some morality. Men still believed that they had a moral obligation to feed their families and to work a job. Then I would ask my question: **If America experienced another crash like the one in 1929, would that same housewife be able to trust that man who came to her door?** Almost universally, the classes would agree that it would be insane to trust someone today with access to the house, an axe, an idea when her husband would be home and a way out. America has lost its moral compass. She no longer has a sense of right and wrong. The situational ethics which have been taught systematically in our seminaries for the last forty years have finally infused themselves in our society to such a degree that there is no longer any such thing as absolute right or absolute wrong. Things are only right or wrong, according to their thinking, if they are right or wrong for me. If I am hungry and you have food and won't share it with me then it is all right for me to hurt you or even kill you for your food because it benefits me and is therefore right for me. Scary, isn't it? Even scarier is the fact that the last three generations of young people see nothing wrong with the previous statement. Homosexuality is OK. Lesbianism is OK. Everything is OK, as long as you don't hurt someone. Right. Sure. Is that what the Bible says? Oh, you don't know what the Bible says? Why is that? Is it because your parents never sat down with you and taught you the Word of God? Maybe it's because they never learned it themselves.

As the cities of America burn to the ground with murder, rape and looting wide-spread throughout every economically depressed area, people will pour out of the ghetto and head toward suburbia. It is then that we will find out just how truly racist America still is. Officially, slavery was abolished almost 150 years ago. Jackie Robinson broke the color barrier in baseball. We have black coaches in the NFL, MLB and other sports. Why, we even have black hockey players! But underneath that veneer of equality, there still smolders the coals of racism, just waiting for the fan of economic unrest to stir them up so that they can blaze into full flame again. Racism will explode across America and the world except in one unique case. Kinsman-Redeemers with undeveloped property in the rural areas of America will begin to build entire communities called **Cities of Refuge** where refugees from the war zones of the inner city will be able to come and live side by side with people from every ethnic background and with every color of skin and hair. Revelation 7:9, where the Bride is represented by every nation, kindred, tribe and tongue will be a reality on earth long before it also becomes a reality in the Rapture. Economic devastation will cause the true body of Christ to come together in a way that it hasn't come together since the First Century A.D. Necessity will make saints out of us, one way or another! These Cities of Refuge will be based on a modified Biblical principle found in Numbers Chapter 35.

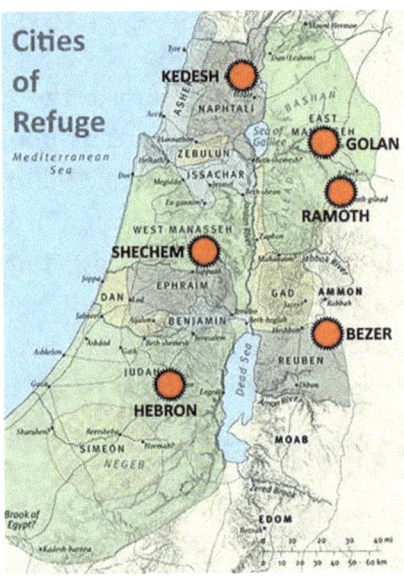

" *6 Now among the cities which you will give to the Levites, you shall appoint **six cities of refuge, to which a man slayer may flee**. And to these you shall add forty-two cities...*[11] *then you shall appoint cities to be cities of refuge for you, that the manslayer who kills any person **accidentally** may flee there.* [12] *They shall be cities of refuge for you from the avenger, that the manslayer may not die until he stands before the congregation in judgment.* [13] *And of the cities which you give, you shall have six cities of refuge.* [14] *You shall appoint three cities on this side of the Jordan, and three*

> *cities you shall appoint in the land of Canaan, which*
> *will be cities of refuge.* [15] *These six cities shall be for*
> *refuge for the children of Israel, for the stranger and for*
> *the sojourner among them,* **that anyone who kills a**
> **person accidentally may flee there.***"*

> – NUMBERS 35:6, 11-15

Originally, these six Cities of Refuge were intended as sanctuaries for individuals who accidentally killed someone, not as a premeditated act. This is where we get our legal distinction between murder and manslaughter. Murder is premeditated, a situation in which I intend to kill you and lay out a plan to do so. Manslaughter is when I had no intention of killing anyone but my car went out of control and six people died or the axe head slipped off the handle and struck my co-worker and killed him.

In the Final Great Crash the paradigm will be vastly different. God will have raised up Kinsmen-Redeemers all over America and the world, men and women who have amassed vast personal fortunes through successful business ventures. They will have been warned to convert their wealth into tangible assets and land purchases just before the ultimate crash of the stock market. Just like the Armenians under the Boy Prophet, these godly men and women will hear the Still Small Voice of the Holy Spirit and will withdraw all of their money quickly and quietly from the banks who currently service them. Land will be purchased secretly all over America, mostly in rural, undeveloped areas. Several years before the crash, there will be a mysterious surge of construction, but oddly enough, most of the workers will be Christians and most of the lumber will come from the land on which the buildings will be built. Whole Christian settlements will rise up, awaiting the burnt and scarred refugees from the cities. When the Crash comes, word will spread swiftly and silently throughout inner city congregations of these hidden Cities of Refuge. Families will begin to disappear all throughout the ghettos of America. Godly single moms with their children will no longer show up for their jobs. Pastors and whole congregations will simply vanish overnight, leaving startled bankers with their now-empty churches. Blacks will be there. Hispanics will be there. Asians will be there. Whites will be there. These communities will be established on absolute moral standards based on the Bible. There will be faith, hope and love throughout all the settlements. All of them will be interconnected in a loose network via the internet, although the ownership of the cities will be as wide and diverse as the individuals that they house. Unfortunately, there will be attacks on the cities. There will be times when the inhabitants of these cities will have to defend themselves. This will be a time of great controversy within the Body of Christ and the Church that remains alive will be split between those who advocate pacifism in all things and those who advocate necessary violence in order to protect the settlements against being destroyed by ungodly men just as the inner cities were. Unfortunately, what is left of the U.S. government will come down on the side of the rapists, murderers and plunderers. It will be a time of great polarization within the Body.

Despite all this, conversions will be constant and genuine. It will be during this dark and difficult time that unbelievers will see true Christian charity at work. Not only will the communities help each other, but they will reach out in true Christian love to those around them. Tales of Christian generosity will become legendary. Groups of missionaries will go out with food, clothing and furniture for those in need. The Bible says that we are to do good to all men, especially them that are of the household of faith. Charity will begin at the church, and once the needs of the body have been completely met, those resources left over, and there will be resources left over, will be extended to those who are not believers but who are struggling to live Godly lives of integrity and courage as their personal beliefs led them to act. Many conversions will occur as a result of these kinds of outreaches. But the church and the end-time communities will not spend one penny on those who are unwilling to try and live righteously. There will be no more funding of people whose lives are a constant affront to godliness. While the government will still attempt to support those who continually live in sin, the church will make no such efforts.

Paradoxically, while personal fortunes are being lost, there will be some Christians who will become phenomenally wealthy by buying assets for pennies on the dollar, sweeping up the discarded resources of the previously rich because they were wise enough to make sure that they had liquid cash assets and no liabilities going into the Crash. This will pattern itself after the

Crash of 1929 when as many millionaires were made as were destroyed. It will not be uncommon to purchase properties for two and three cents on the dollar as desperate, overextended businessmen grasp desperately for some way to forestall foreclosure. Cars, homes, gems, all manner of art and paintings, the wealth and culture of our nation, will be on sale for less than ten cents on the dollar. This will be true globally. There will be a major paradigm shift in who is considered wealthy in a matter of ten years. Most of the Fortune 500 will fall off the chart. Little known, obscure individuals who have been quietly living in the shadows will step forward and take control of America's economy.

At the same time, something terrible will happen to the former United States of America. A judgment from outside of our country, a judgment of nuclear import, will **shatter this country into four separate entities.** It will be a time of great distress for this country, and the flag of another nation will wave over us for a period of time, but at the end of days, **America will rouse itself as Sampson did, one last time, and will join itself together to strike one last blow for righteousness and for Israel at the end of days.** The fire that falls on Magog and on the nations of the sea will come from the **Eagle** who has watched over North America for five hundred years, long before the White Man came. **The Thunderbird** was assigned to watch over this continent for a reason, for by his wings will death and destruction fall on the enemies of God and on the enemies of Israel. America will watch over Israel against the Beast, the Anti-Christ, and will protect Her against all those who rise up against Her. And Her giant arrows of destruction, buried in their concrete quivers, will be launched against the land of Gog, Meshech, Tubal, Gomer, Togarmah and all those who stand against the Lord and against His Hosts.

WHOA, DR. YOUNG, WHAT WAS THAT?

I have occupied many positions in the body of Christ over the years. I began as, and still am, first and foremost, a teacher. I have been a pastor off and on over the last thirty-five years. I have led many to Christ as an evangelist. But I am also a **prophet and apostle**. And it was as a prophet and an apostle that I just said what I have said about the future. Some of the things that I have spoken earlier in the book are based on predictions of probability. Some things are based on empirical evidence, factual evidence based on hard, cold research. **But what I said in the last few pages flowed from the power of the Holy Spirit within me as prophecies from the Lord of Hosts.** Please take them and pray over them. The Bible says that every matter must be established in the mouths of two or three witnesses. Confirmation will come. Just wait and see. There are many more things that must be said about the end of the age, but not just yet. The time is not right. It will be soon. To the best of my knowledge and ability, I have presented to you what will happen, what you must do, and what God will provide in order for you to survive this coming time of hardship and difficulty. **Be like those Armenians who listened to the Boy Prophet and lived.** Do not be like those who scoffed, were skeptical and did not believe. **They perished in their sins.** Do not do the same. My earnest prayer is that your heart and mind will be open to these words of warning. Please take them to your heart and act upon them. Then share them with others so that they too can be prepared and can escape the Wrath to Come.

WHAT CAN I DO TO HELP?

A great deal. Here are some practical ideals of how you can alert the body of Christ and prepare them:

1. If you are a pastor, **you can sponsor a community-wide seminar using these materials.** I am totally committed to waking the body of Christ up before it is too late. **I will gladly come to you and conduct a seminar on these materials.** I have seven complete PowerPoint presentations to back these materials up. I can present the materials in a single session. I can present them in a two-session-a-day, three-day seminar. I can come in for a full week and do one presentation a night for six nights. In short, whatever format works for you works for me. I have learned to be all things to all men so that I might by all means save some. We would only request that transportation funds

be provided in advance, either via automobile or airplane, that we have a place to stay, preferably with a member of your congregation for the sake of fellowship and that a love offering be taken up each night that materials are presented. I would need to know in advance approximately how many workbooks I would need to bring. Each participant would be required to purchase their own copy for future reference. We will go anywhere in the world to present these materials. **All you have to do is be our** *"Man from Macedonia"* **and say,** *"Come over here and help us!"* We will gladly come.

2. If you are a pastor, catch the vision in your own church and **begin to have your own** *"Debt Cancellation Revivals"* **once a month**, just like Bishop Russell does. Talk to other pastors in your ministerial association. See if you can get other pastors to work with you in a community-wide effort.

3. If you are an individual, take these materials to your pastor and try to help them catch the vision. Or, simply begin to talk it up among your friends and associates. **Nothing would keep you from hosting your own seminar.** I don't know of anyone who doesn't want to get out of debt! We will also be bringing practical suggestions in the form of worksheets when we come to you.

4. If you are a businessman, **contact other businessmen** and share with them what is coming. No one wants to have their business destroyed and

businessmen in particular will be interested in the various aspects of K-Waves. That way they can keep an ear to the ground and monitor trends in the economy as they develop.

5. Some Christian businessmen will end up being the developers of the **Cities of Refuge** that we have mentioned. If you are such an individual, please contact us and let us know where you are and what you are doing, along with your progress toward creating a site fully capable of being put into use in a matter of hours. We will try to act as a national and perhaps even global clearing house and networking center for any and all efforts aimed at rescuing the Body of Christ from the perils that lie directly ahead. I already know of about three sites that are preparing to be converted into Cities of Refuge. We need to know about everyone who is willing to pull together in this rescue effort. Many Christian retreat centers located in rural areas will make excellent Cities of Refuge with only a minor amount of work. If you are reading this book and own such a place, please contact us.

6. No matter who you are, you can help us to spread this message by purchasing copies of the book and distributing them to people that you think are open to hearing what God has given us to say. Since the Global Revival Network is a 501(c)(3) corporation, your contributions are tax-deductible. Whatever you can do to help will allow us to put copies of this

book into the hands of decision makers across the nation. We need to impact leaders all across the United States to try and form a coalition of like-minded individuals who are willing to work together to start making provisions to ride out the storm when it comes. Direct contributions should be made out to **GRN** and mailed to the address shown below. Simply put, the more people read this book, the more people will be alerted to what is coming and the more people will be prepared when it comes. I know that not everyone that we present this message to will receive it but **some will.**

7. This seems too obvious to mention, but **pray without ceasing about this matter.** Let the Lord show you what you must do in order to secure your own family and protect them from disaster. And pray for us that the Lord would fund us and equip us to go all across the US and the world sharing this message. Although the crash will start in America, it will be global in impact.

8. We also have a tri-fold flyer and other materials presenting the core of this information in an attractive, eye-catching format. Please contact us to inquire about the availability of these flyers if you are interested.

Thank you again for purchasing and reading these materials. Our prayer for you is that you take these matters to heart and make the necessary changes in your life so that you are prepared when these events come to pass. Please feel free to write, email or call us if you have comments or questions. We would love to hear from you and we would love to pray for you and for your needs.

Don't forget to visit our ministry website for the Global Revival Network, www.grnu.org. In it, you will find materials on the Global Revival Network, the Global Revival Network Bible College, our books, my personal testimony, my professional and ministry resumes and a variety of other subjects.

I will close this final chapter with the same words I use in all of my correspondence to the Church. **May God richly bless you as you walk in faith and obedience to Him! Amen and Amen!!!**

MEET DR. YOUNG

Dr. Ray Young has been studying the **Revelation of Jesus Christ** for over twenty-five years. He has been in the ministry for over thirty-five years and is a **teacher, prophet** and **apostle** in the body of Christ. Dr. Young is also a professional educator and was a tenured faculty member heading up his own computer science department at a university level for eighteen years. He is the president and founder of Final Great Awakening Ministries and the Global Revival Network and is also a published author, having written the following books:

How to Survive the Coming Crash

Unrolling the Scroll Series:
> *Episode 1 – The Revelation of Jesus Christ*
> *Episode 3 – The Things That Shall Be*
> *Episode 4 – The Crucified Bride*
> *Episode 5 – The Time of the Beast*
> *Making Sense of the End Times*

He is currently working on completing the full **Unrolling the Scroll** series of seven devotional study guides to the Revelation of Jesus Christ, with three Episodes left to write. He is also working on a comprehensive book on Revival entitled ***Birthing True Revival.*** He can be reached at any of the phone numbers, email address or web site URL listed below.

Dr. Ray Young
Final Great Awakening Ministries
The Global Revival Network
42 Forest Drive
Jeffersonville, IN 47130

Home Phone: (812) 590-2395
Cell Phone: (513) 227-5416
URL: www.grnu.org
Email: pastorray@twc.com
Skype ID: pastorray48